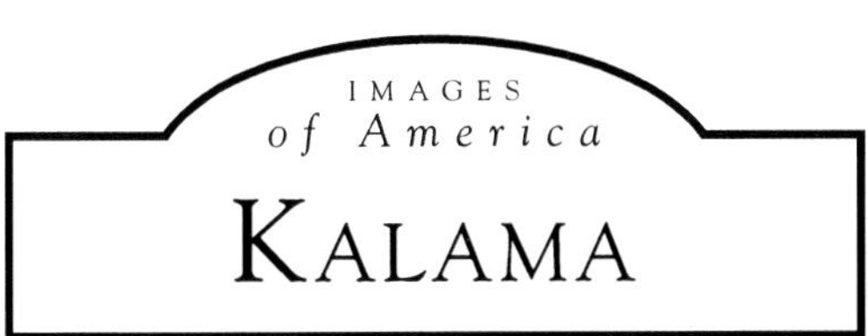
IMAGES
of America
KALAMA

ON THE COVER: Pictured is a group of men repairing a paddle wheeler docked at the bank of the Columbia River near Kalama. Lumber is stacked on the top of the deck, and more lumber is on the riverbank awaiting use. The Columbia River was a watery highway for early residents of the region. (Courtesy of Lee Bunn.)

IMAGES
of America

KALAMA

C. Louise Thomas

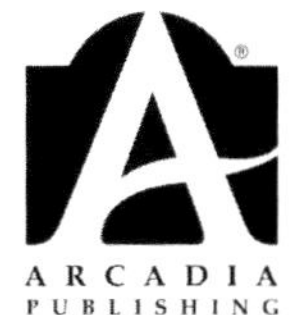

ISBN 978-1-4671-1623-7

Published by Arcadia Publishing
Charleston, South Carolina

Printed in the United States of America

Library of Congress Control Number: 2015952723

For all general information, please contact Arcadia Publishing:
Telephone 843-853-2070
Fax 843-853-0044
E-mail sales@arcadiapublishing.com
For customer service and orders:
Toll-Free 1-888-313-2665

Visit us on the Internet at www.arcadiapublishing.com

This book is dedicated to my sons Jason and Garth and my grandchildren Natalie, Tucker, and Ava.

Contents

ACKNOWLEDGMENTS

Many thanks go to those who helped create this book. They include the following: Amalak Women's Club and its president, Carole Day; Catherine Applegate; Joanna Boatman; Lee Bunn; the Cowlitz County Historical Museum, its director, David Freece, and employee Bill Watson; Art Godfrey; Elouise Hutton; Cleone Kockritz; Brian LaRoy; Jo Martin; John and Mary Norton; Mayor Pete Poulson and the City of Kalama; St. Joseph's Catholic Church and parishioner Pat Kennedy; Janice Whiteaker; and the staff of Arcadia Publishing. A special thank-you is owed to Sabrina Johnson for the computer help. Unless otherwise noted, all images come from the City of Kalama and are currently housed at the Kalama Library.

INTRODUCTION

It starts with the river and a bit of controversy. Where did the river get its name, Kalama? In 1847, John Kalama, a Native Hawaiian from the island of Maui, was employed by Cowlitz Farms. He worked at the mouth of a tributary of the Columbia River, repairing wooden barrels in which to pack salted salmon. The preserved salmon was shipped back to the Hawaiian Islands. Some believe the river was named after this early settler. However, in 1811 an Indian village was located at the mouth of this river. The river could have been named after the tribe, called Thlakalama (or Klkalama). It is also suggested that local Indians named the river Kalama, which supposedly means "pretty maiden" in the Chinookan language group. There is no question, however, of how the city got its name. In 1870, Gen. John W. Sprague, the director of the western division of the Northern Pacific Railroad, named the site of a proposed community along the Columbia River as Kalama.

Kalama was incorporated in 1890 but was already well established by then. There were no adequate roads yet, and the railroads had not been completed. Kalama was blessed with an area of wide flatland adjacent to the Columbia River. It had a port deep enough to handle the ships, steamboats, and paddle wheelers that operated on the river. The Columbia was a watery highway, and the ships and boats that traveled up and down the river provided the main source of easy transportation in the 1800s for people and products. The hills behind Kalama were heavily forested, and these forests provided timber that could be harvested to supply the boats on the river with cordwood to fire their boilers. Timber was also harvested to make railroad ties. Logging and sawmills became important industries in Kalama and provided a major source of employment.

In the late 1870s, the Northern Pacific Railroad chose Kalama as the site of a rail terminus from which it would build a railroad north to Puget Sound. Thousands of white and Chinese laborers came to this location to build the railway. The millions of salmon that returned to the river yearly to spawn were used to feed the workers. Fishing was also important commercially. Salmon were plentiful, and Kalama fishermen harvesting this bounty of the Columbia River needed canneries, which were used to process and then ship salmon around the world.

Kalama flourished, and its business district grew as settlers and entrepreneurs flocked to the area to provide services to those employed in various industries. In the 1800s, Kalama had hotels, sawmills, fish packing and timber companies, grocery stores, an opera house, and saloons. It was also a port for the *Tacoma*, a rail transport ferry operated by Northern Pacific Railroad.

The Washington side of the Columbia River did not have a rail line from Vancouver, Washington, so traveling north by rail was not an option. This challenge was met by the rail transfer ferry *Tacoma*. There was a rail line on the Oregon side of the Columbia River, which traveled from Portland, Oregon, to Goble, Oregon. Goble was located across the Columbia River from Kalama. Northern Pacific Railroad chose Kalama as the site for a dock for the ferry *Tacoma*. At Goble, the railcars and the locomotive would be loaded onto the ferry for a 20-minute crossing of the Columbia. At Kalama, the train was unloaded, reassembled, and then continued its journey north to Puget Sound. Also at this time, Kalama was the headquarters for the Northern Pacific Railroad Western Division as it built the rail line to Tacoma, Washington. The city grew in population with the addition of this enterprise.

It is estimated that by the 1880s the city of Kalama had 3,000 residents, and the city fathers used this density of population to gain the county seat. The county seat was previously located the small city of Freeport, located a few miles downriver. Kalama's population soon exceeded the population of Freeport, and since the citizens of the community with the greatest population could vote themselves as the county seat, Kalama residents used the power of the ballot box at the general election to wrest the county seat away. Being at the center of county government added to the growth of the city and its future prospects.

Kalama's future seemed assured, but then the city suffered a series of setbacks. Northern Pacific moved its headquarters to Tacoma, Washington, in 1873, and the completion of roads and rail lines eliminated the need for the rail transfer ferry *Tacoma*. North of Kalama, the citizens of Kelso, Washington, over a period of 20 years, tried in every general election to vote that the county seat be moved from Kalama to Kelso. After 20 years of losing elections, Kelso finally succeeded in getting the county seat in the 1922 vote when its population grew larger. Kalama then lost the revenue and jobs entailed in being the center of county government.

But the city had a flourishing agrarian base at this time. For many years, Kalama prospered with farms cultivating and processing strawberries. The city celebrated this bounty with an annual Strawberry Festival. Unfortunately, blight destroyed the strawberry crops, and the strawberry farms and packing plants closed.

Kalama survived floods, an earthquake, and a fire that destroyed the business district. The completion of Interstate 5 resulted in the loss of waterfront. The citizens of Kalama met these challenges by adapting and rebuilding. They brought new industries and businesses to the city. Today, Kalama has an active port and a thriving commercial district with businesses drawn to the area for the same reasons that the early pioneers came. With its location adjacent to the Columbia River, Kalama is beautiful. Two miles to the north, the Kalama River boasts some of the finest salmon fishing in the world. The city's location gives its inhabitants the ability to enjoy day trips to Mount St. Helens National Volcanic Monument, Mount Rainier National Park, the Pacific Ocean, and the metropolitan cities of Portland, Oregon, and Seattle, Washington. Kalama boasts several parks and a well-developed waterfront for recreation. Active community boosters present a wide variety of community activities through out the year. With its small-town charm, Kalama is seeing renewed growth as new businesses and residents settle where water, rail, and river meet.

One

Beginnings

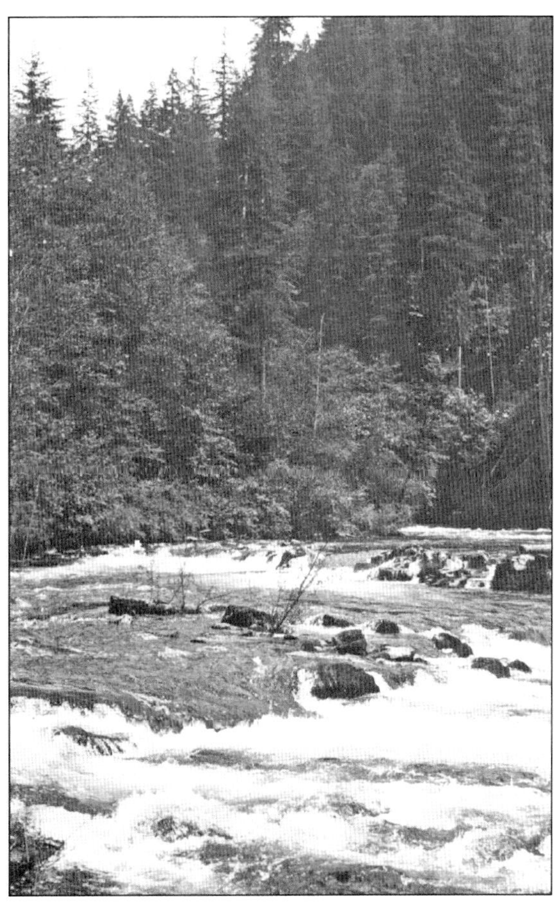

The Kalama River is located two miles north of the city that bears its name. The waterway originates in springs and is fed by small streams to become a river. Many residents live along the Kalama River, and it is a site for recreation for not only the citizens of Kalama but also the surrounding population of Cowlitz County. The river is also the source of the city's water. (Courtesy of Lee Bunn.)

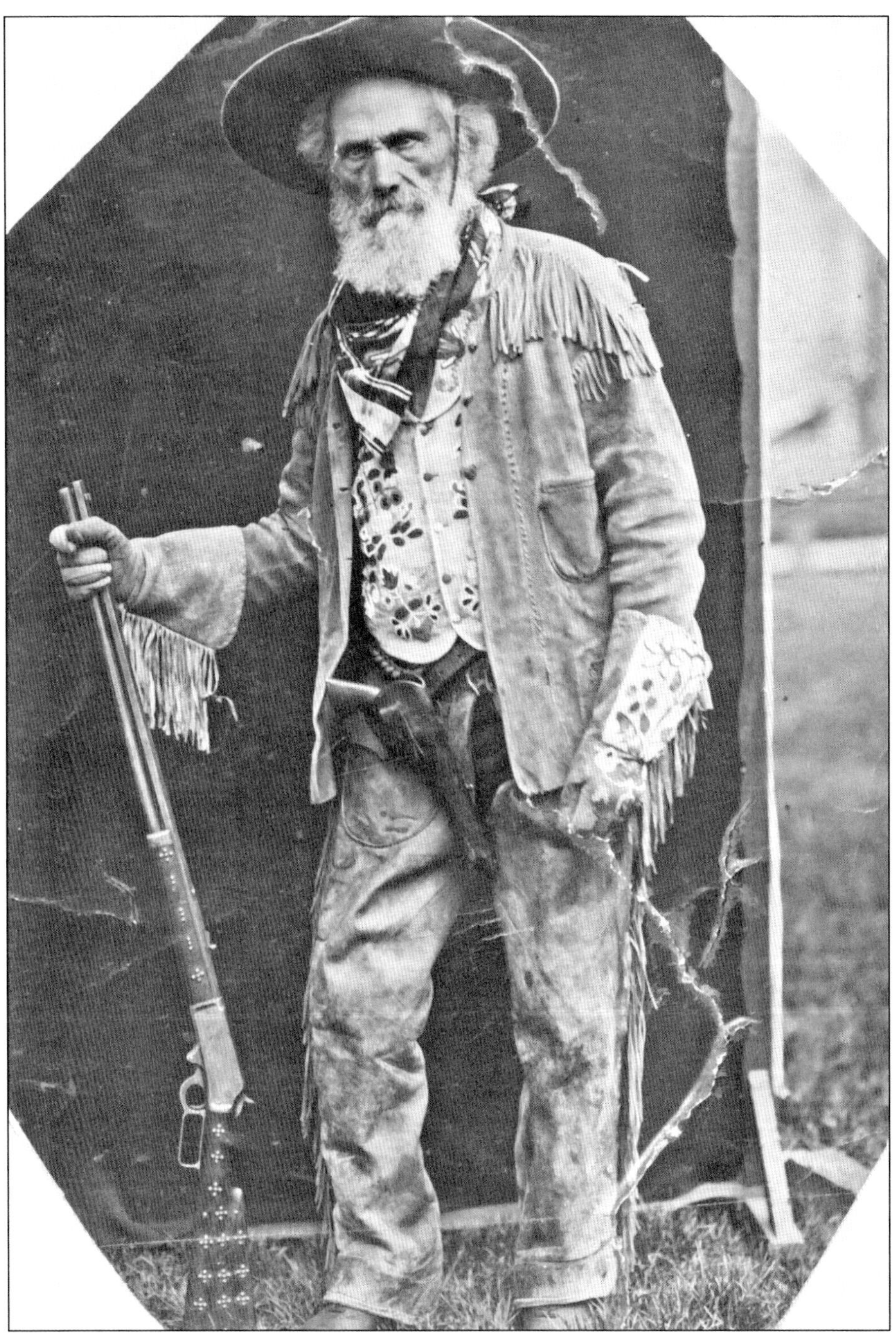

Ezra Meeker is a well-known pioneer of the Pacific Northwest. Meeker first settled in St. Helens, Oregon, where he ran a boardinghouse. When this business failed, he moved to Washington. On January 20, 1853, he filed a land claim in what is now Kalama, Washington. Ezra built a log cabin, and he and his brother logged timber from the surrounding hills. They floated the logs down the Columbia River to the Abernethy Mill at Oak Point and from there to Astoria, Oregon. With the money he received from the sale of the logs, Ezra moved his family to Puyallup, Washington. (Courtesy of Mary Norton.)

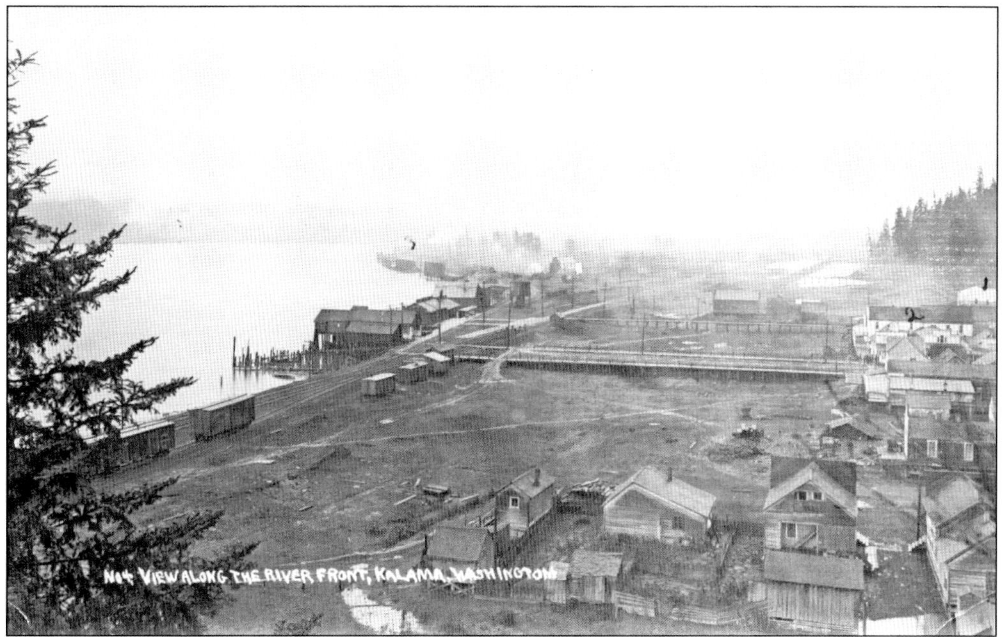

This photograph is a visual representation of why Kalama was chosen by the Northern Pacific Railroad as the point from which it would build a railroad north to Puget Sound. Kalama had a wide expanse of flatland for easy development, with good access to the Columbia River. The surrounding forested hills provided a ready source of timber to harvest and sell as cordwood to passing boats for fuel. (Courtesy of John Norton.)

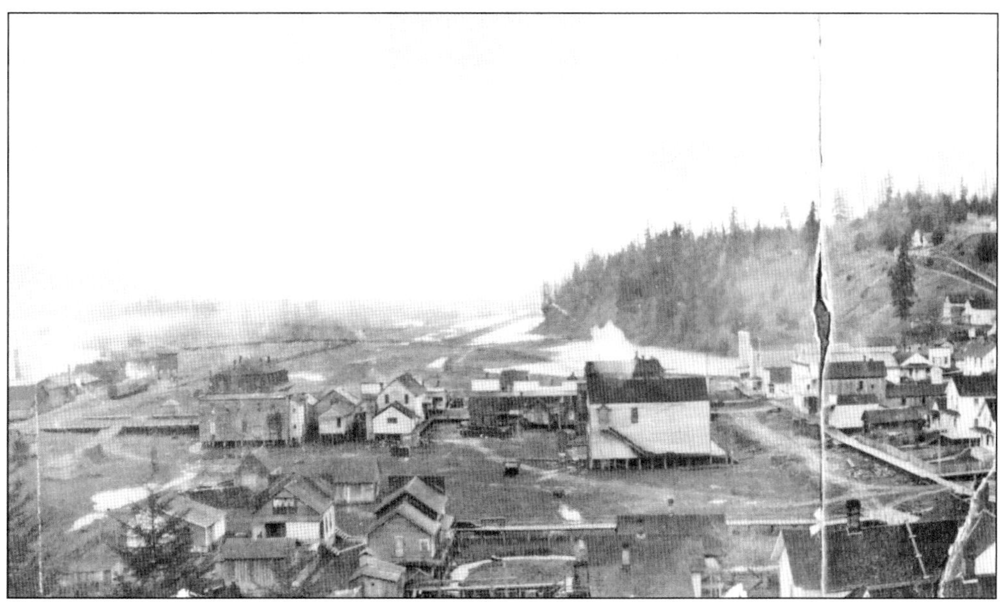

The city of Kalama in the 1870s was sparsely settled on lowland adjacent to the Columbia River and two miles south of the Kalama River. The houses were built on stilts to keep them above high water, and elevated boardwalks crisscrossed the city for the same reason. (Courtesy of Joanna Boatman.)

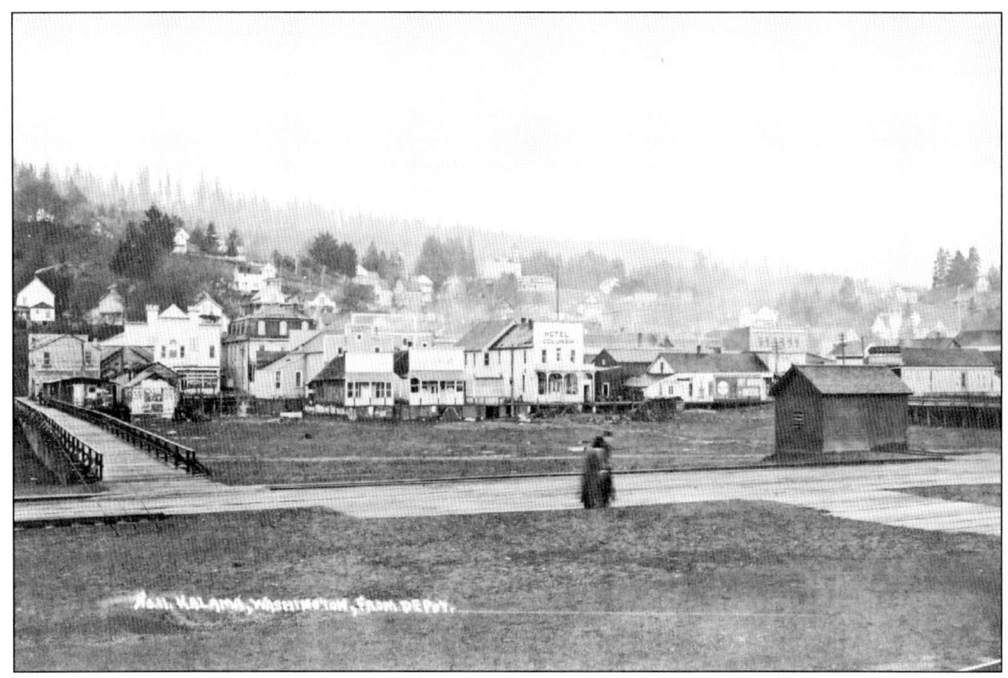

This is a view of Kalama from the train depot, which was located along the waterfront. The photograph was taken in the early part of the 20th century, and the business district is seen thriving. Note that the roads are covered with planks. (Courtesy of Lee Bunn.)

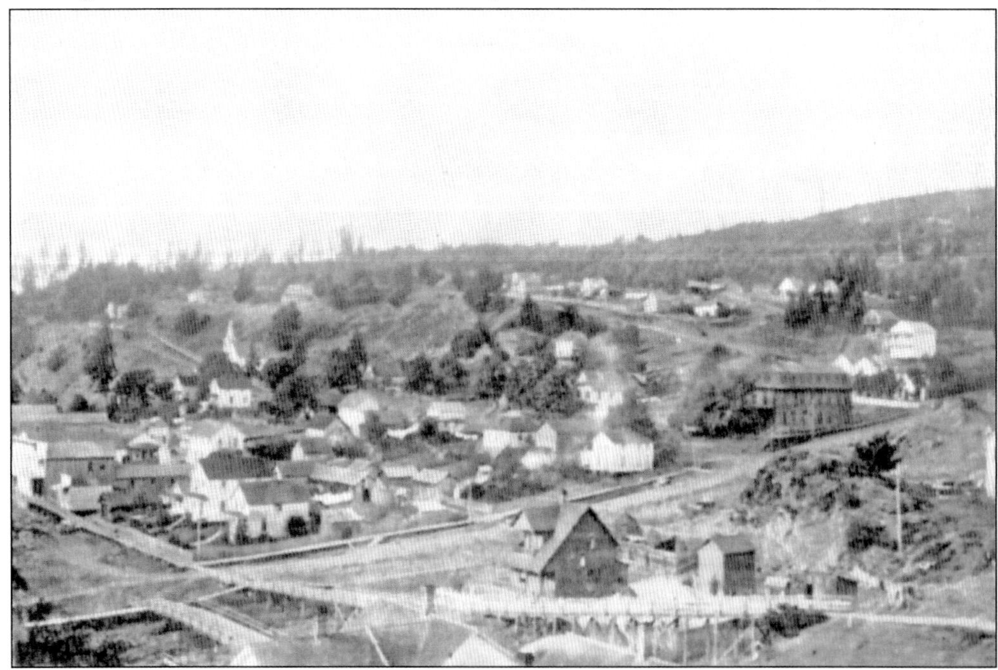

To the right in this picture of early Kalama is the Kazano House. This three-story hotel was built by the Northern Pacific Railroad. It served the Kalama community first as a hotel and then, after it was sold to the city of Kalama, became the Cowlitz County Courthouse. (Courtesy of Cleone Kockritz.)

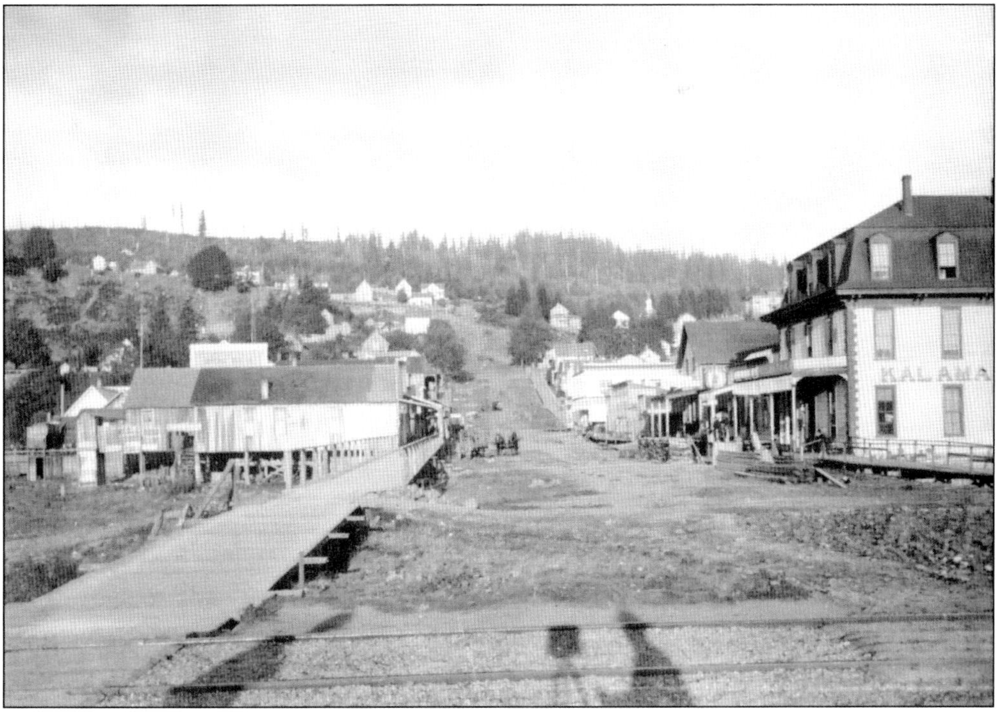

This is Kalama around 1900. The first building on the left was Reardon's Saloon, located on Fir Street. The Kalama Hotel is to the right in the picture. Note the shadow of the photographer at the bottom of the picture. He is taking the picture from behind the rail lines. (Courtesy of Joanna Boatman.)

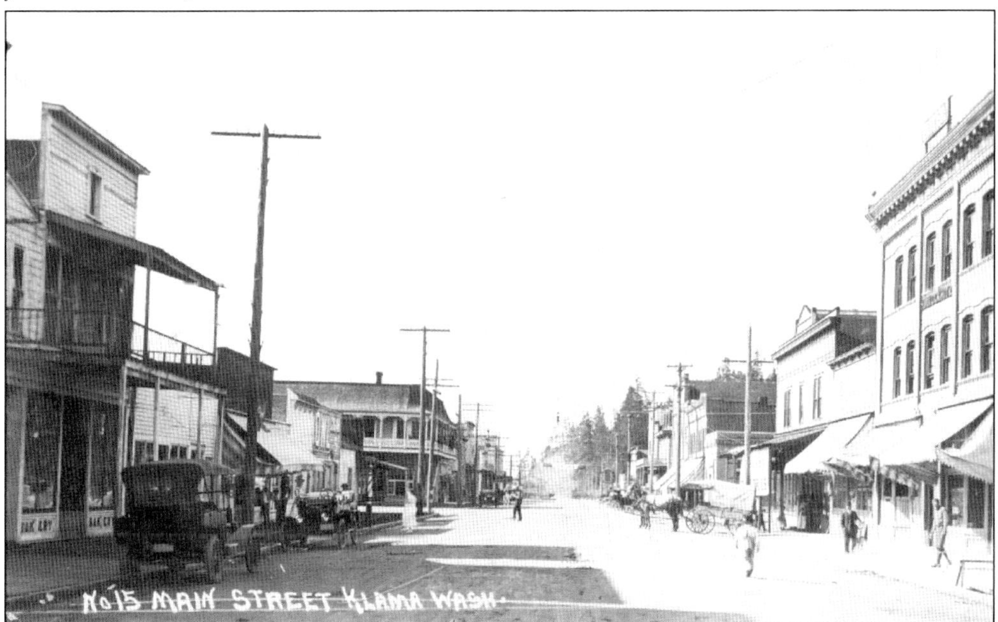

This photograph was taken looking down Kalama's main street (First Street) in the early 1900s. Although cars are making an appearance, many people are still using horses and wagons. The barber pole to the left of the picture identifies the location of the barbershop. (Courtesy of Lee Bunn.)

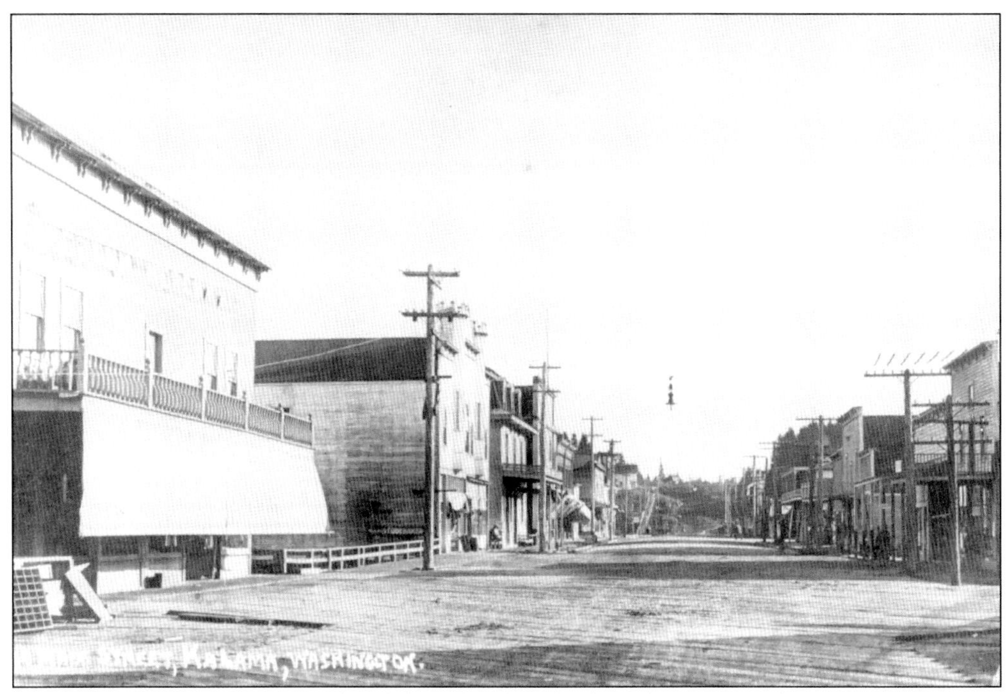

The road in this picture is paved with boards. This plank road went from the business district of downtown Kalama to Cloverdale, which was about 1.5 miles away. (Courtesy of Art Godfrey.)

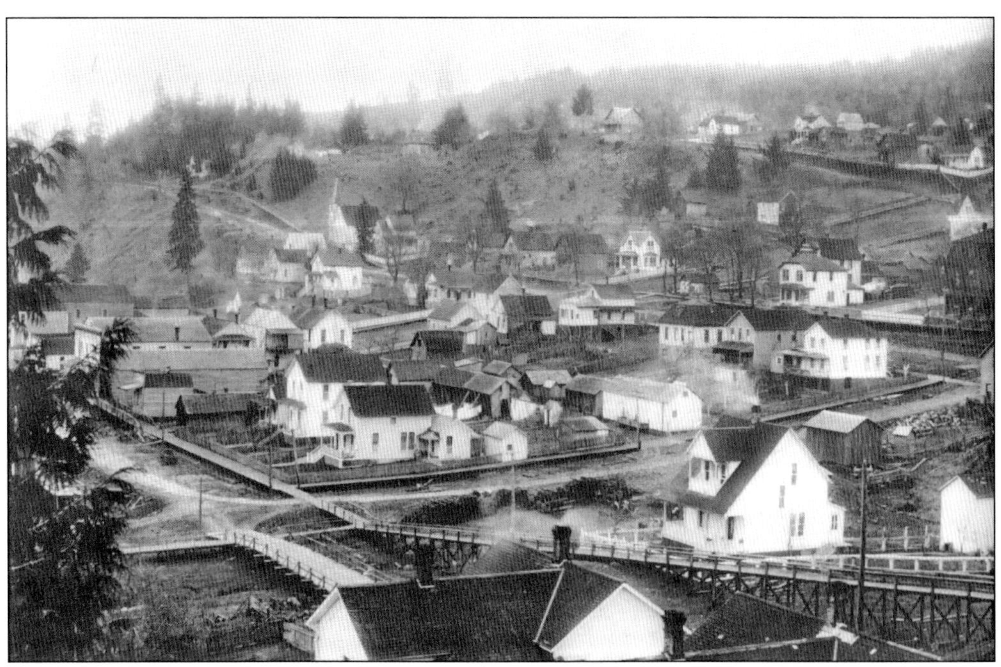

Taken in the early 1920s, this photograph depicts the residential district of Kalama. To the left on the hill is the Congregational church, and the parsonage is the white house in front of it. Elm Street is the road going up what was called Schoolhouse Hill. (Courtesy of Janice Whiteaker.)

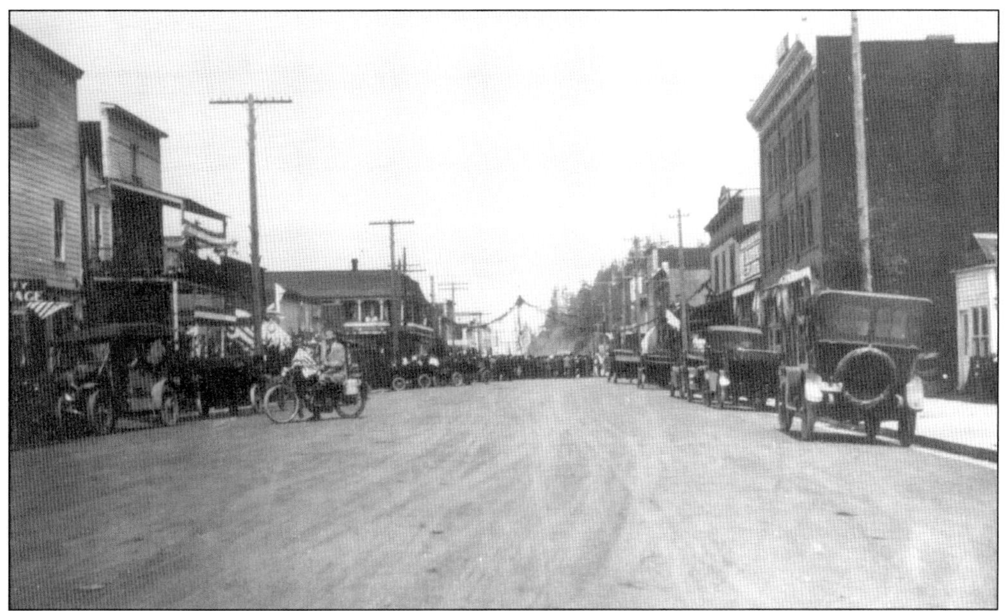

Here, an unidentified man sits astride his motorcycle. Behind him, an event is taking place farther down the street. Bunting is draped across the street, and a crowd has gathered. In the early part of the 20th century, cars are now common, and so are the light poles that line the street. (Courtesy of Cleone Kockritz.)

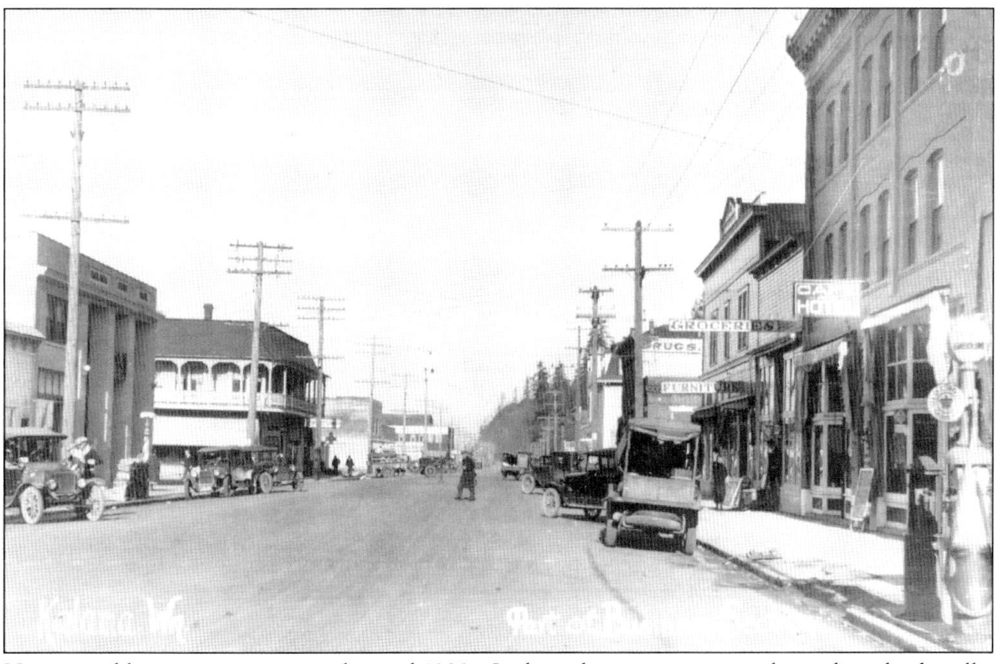

Horses and buggies are gone in the mid-1920s. Light poles are more complicated, and sidewalks have replaced boardwalks. The business district of Kalama is thriving with a wide variety of stores available for its citizens. (Courtesy of Art Godfrey.)

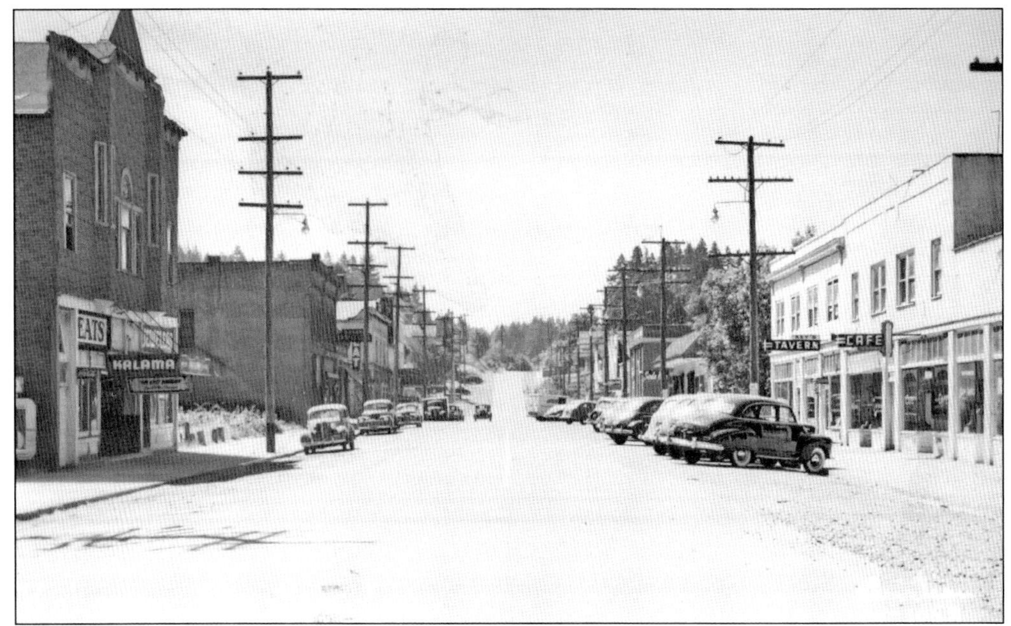

The building at the right was erected by Bob Springer, and the dark structure in the background was an old skating rink. The road is now paved, and sidewalks have been put in. (Courtesy of Lee Bunn.)

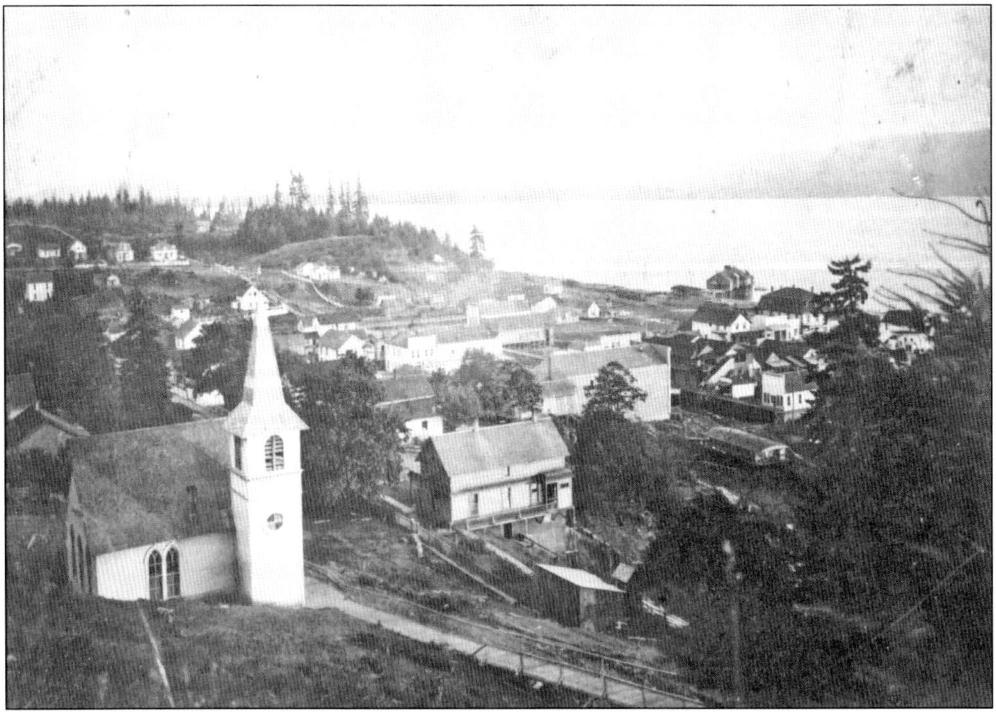

At left in this 1902 picture is the Congregational church, built on the steep hillside behind the city of Kalama. On the right is the LaRoy family's float (boathouse), docked in the Columbia River. (Courtesy of Brian LaRoy.)

Two

People

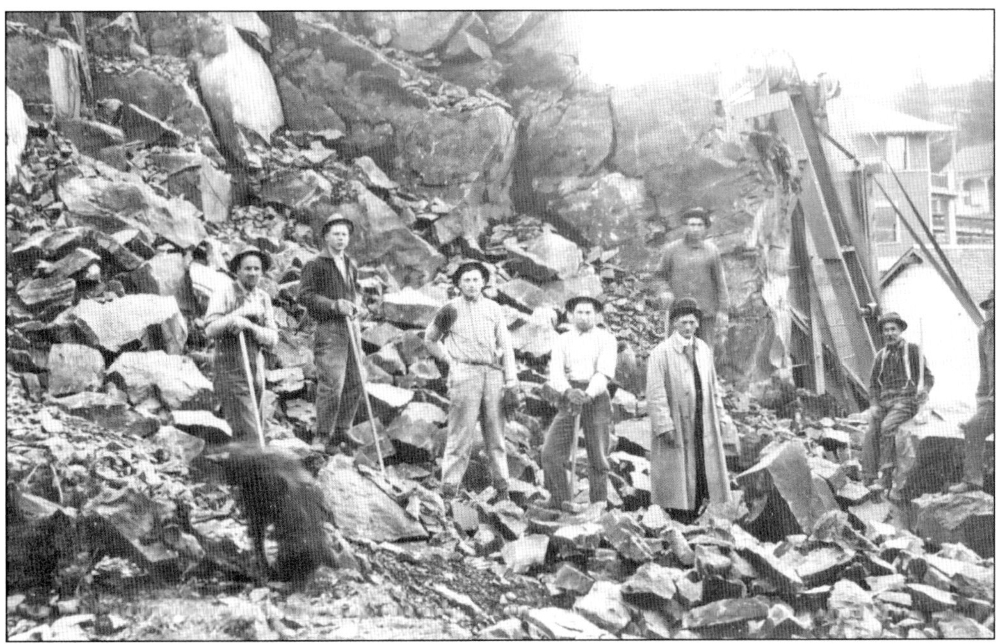

Unidentified men are pictured in a rock quarry located near homes in Kalama. The men are posing with sledge hammers and picks, as much of the work was done by hand. Although the city of Kalama was built on a wide expanse of flatland adjacent to the Columbia River, rocky hills rise up rapidly behind the city, making them an easy and convenient source of raw material. (Courtesy of Janice Whiteaker.)

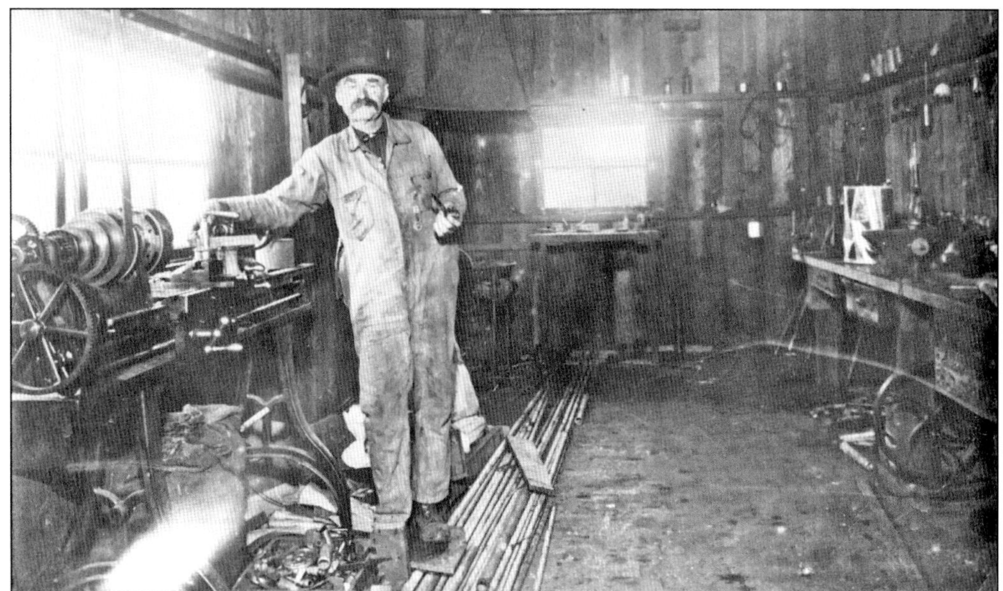

Antone "Tony" Anderson poses in his machine shop beside his tools. There is a forge in the far left background. In this type of machine shop, Anderson could take raw pieces of metal and turn them into usable objects. He could thread pipes, and the forge used coke and coal to make a white-hot fire in which metal and pipes could be bent. Lathes and grinding wheels are also pictured. Anderson was the father of Clarence "Duckeye" Anderson and the grandfather of Wilbur Anderson.

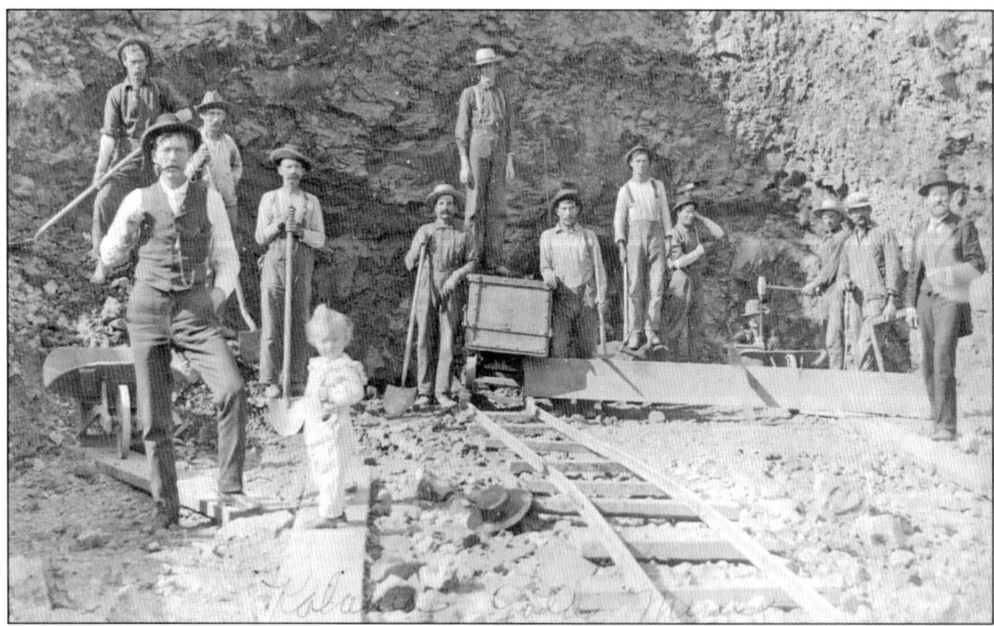

Kalama had a short-lived gold rush in 1903, when a local doctor, Dr. Darnell, found gold in his well. Much of Kalama was dug up, but no gold was found. Here, men pose at the entrance to a gold mine. There were attempts at various kinds of mining in early Cowlitz County, and all were doomed to failure. Investors in this mine were to be disappointed because it was unprofitable. (Courtesy of John Norton.)

This photograph is of early pioneer Mattie Bush. Mattie was considered to be a community beauty and was a member of a prominent local family. Mattie lived in Kalama her entire life and became well known as an eccentric in her later years. (Courtesy of John Norton.)

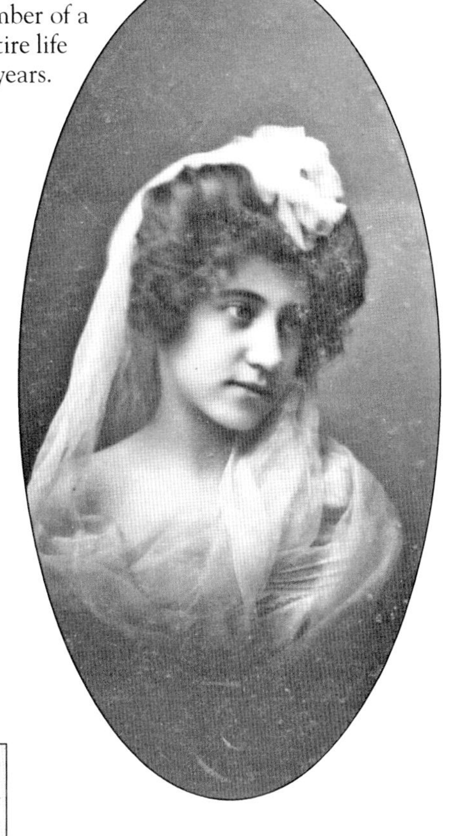

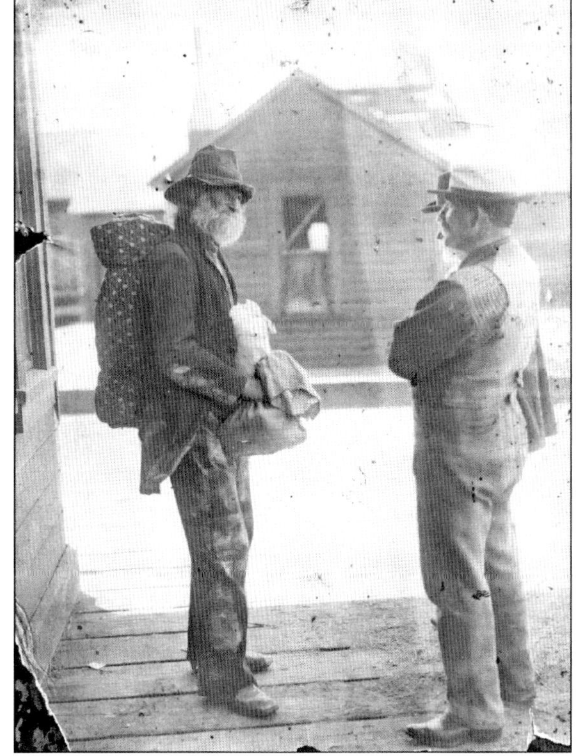

Pictured on the left is "Old Abe," who is "jest travellin." Old Abe is pausing to have a conversation with Harvey Morris as he travels through the city. (Courtesy of Joanna Boatman.)

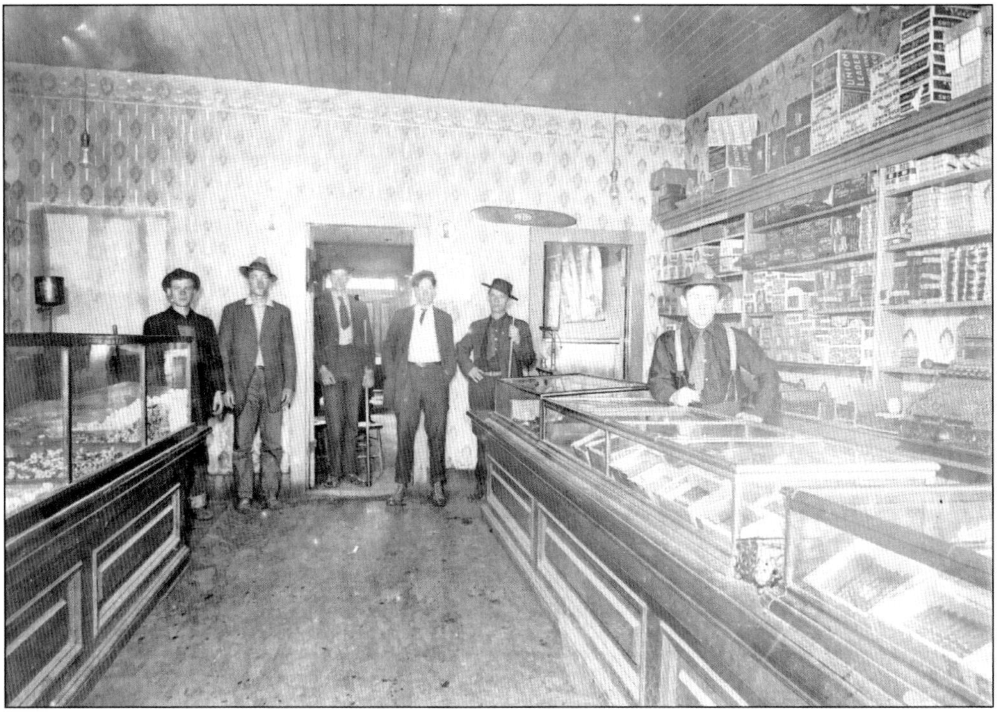

A group of men is gathered in Coffey's Pool Hall about 1913. Curt Whiteaker is behind the counter, and Cliff Whiteaker is standing at the left. At the back of the store is a door to the room with the pool tables. Two of the men—one standing in the doorway to the pool hall and the other at the end of the counter at right—are holding pool cues. (Courtesy of Janice Whiteaker.)

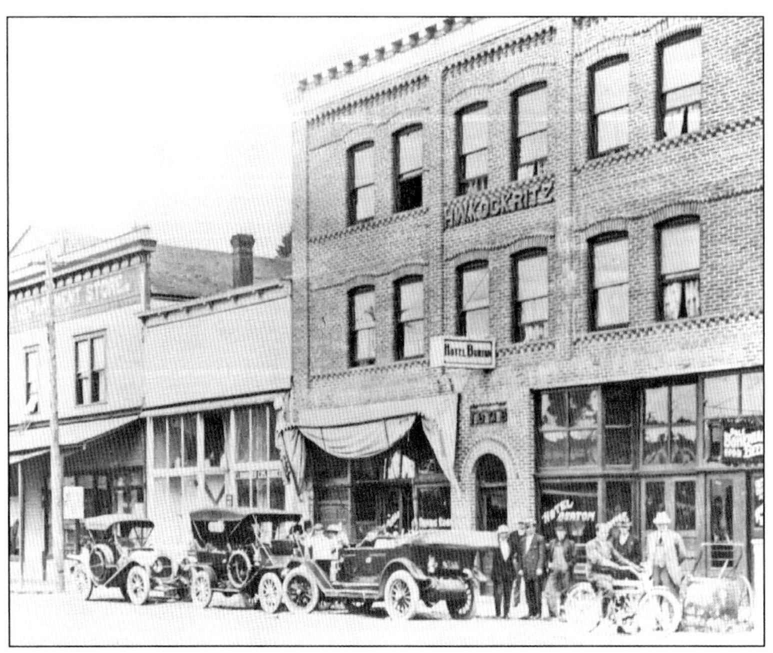

The H.W. Kockritz Building was erected by contractor Herman William Kockritz. The structure was completed in 1908 and was the location of the Hotel Burton. The building is still in use today; in 2015, it is the location of a tavern and pizza parlor. (Courtesy of Cleone Kockritz.)

Before the completion of good highways and connecting rail lines from Vancouver, Washington, to Puget Sound, people used the Columbia River as their watery highway. Here, a group of travelers is on board the little boat *Chief of Kalama*, going either up or down the Columbia to other small communities located along the river. (Courtesy of Catherine Applegate.)

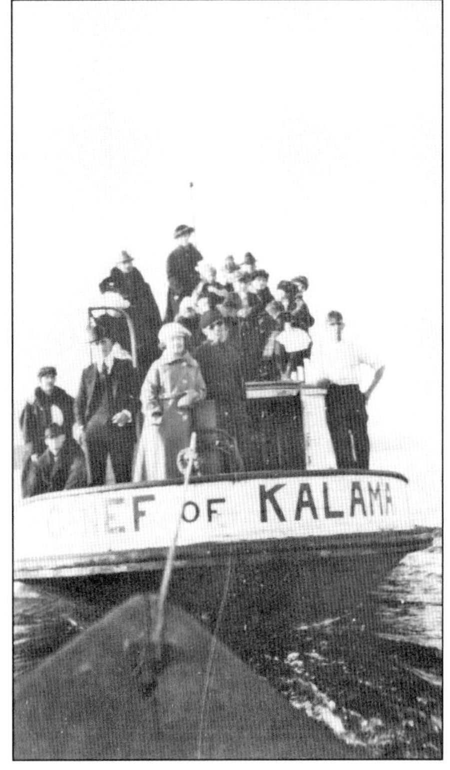

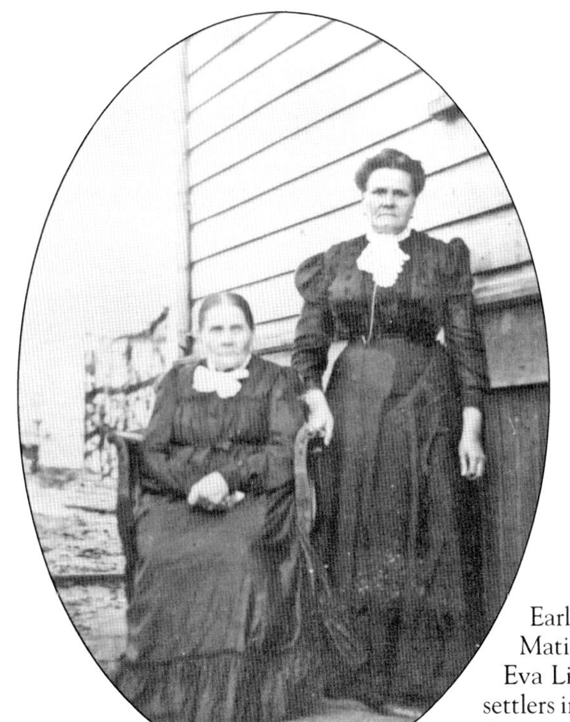

Early Kalama pioneers pose for a formal portrait. Matilda Kockritz is standing beside the seated Eva Lindstrom. The Kockritz family were early settlers in Kalama, and their descendants still live in Kalama and are active in community affairs. (Courtesy of Cleone Kockritz.)

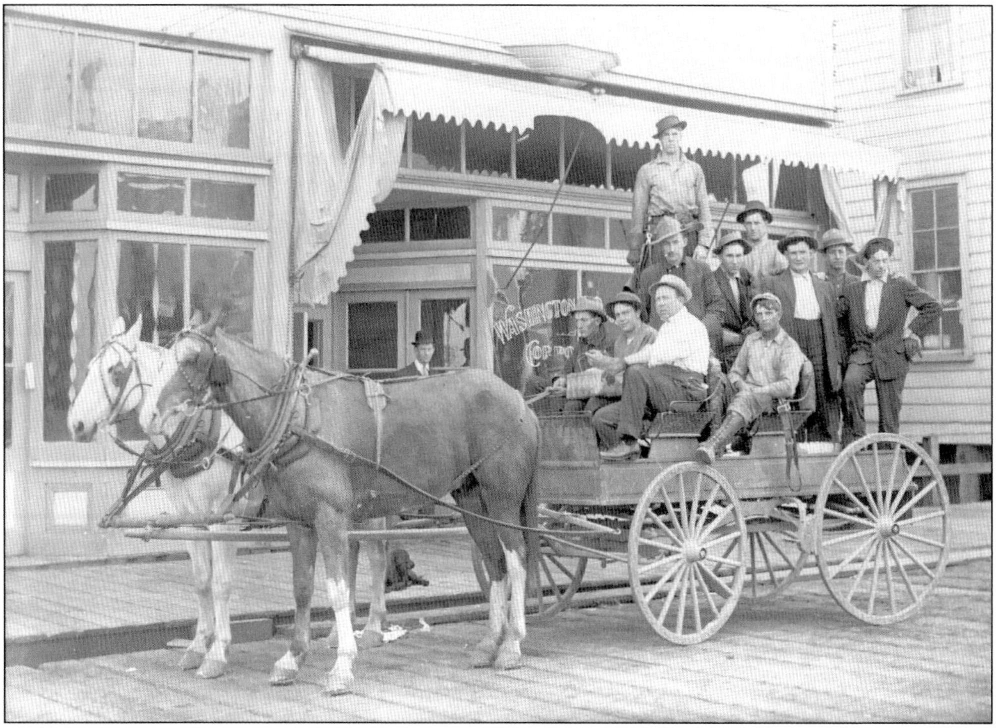

A group of men is posing on a buckboard on a street in the business district of Kalama in the late 1800s. The road is a boardwalk, and a dog is lying on the sidewalk behind the horses' legs. (Courtesy of John Norton.)

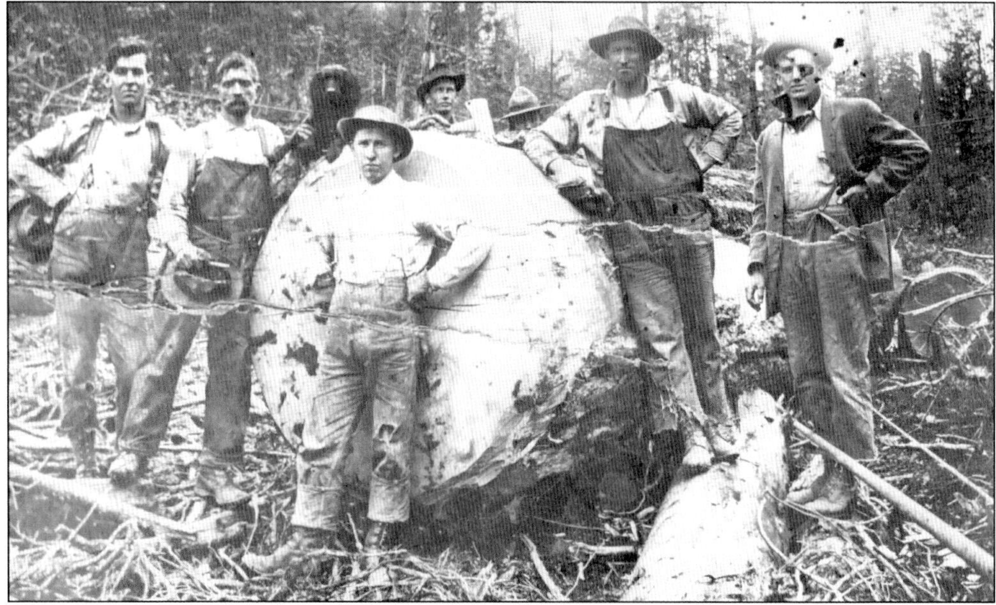

Logging was an extremely dangerous profession in the late 1800s and early 1900s. Men who "worked in the woods" were often injured or killed. These old-time loggers do not have safety gear. Safety procedures and safety equipment were to come in the future. But even in the 21st-century, logging is still considered one of the ten most dangerous professions in the United States.

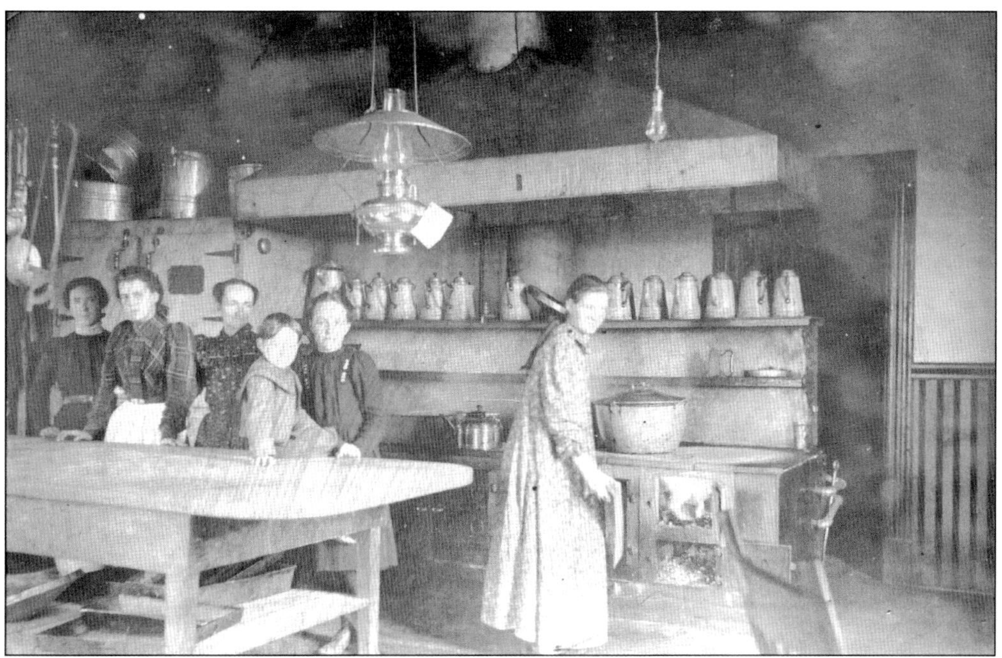

Dickie Morris, the sister of early pioneer Duke Morris, works in the Kalama Hotel kitchen in the early 1900s. Dickie is standing by the stove. (Courtesy of Joanna Boatman.)

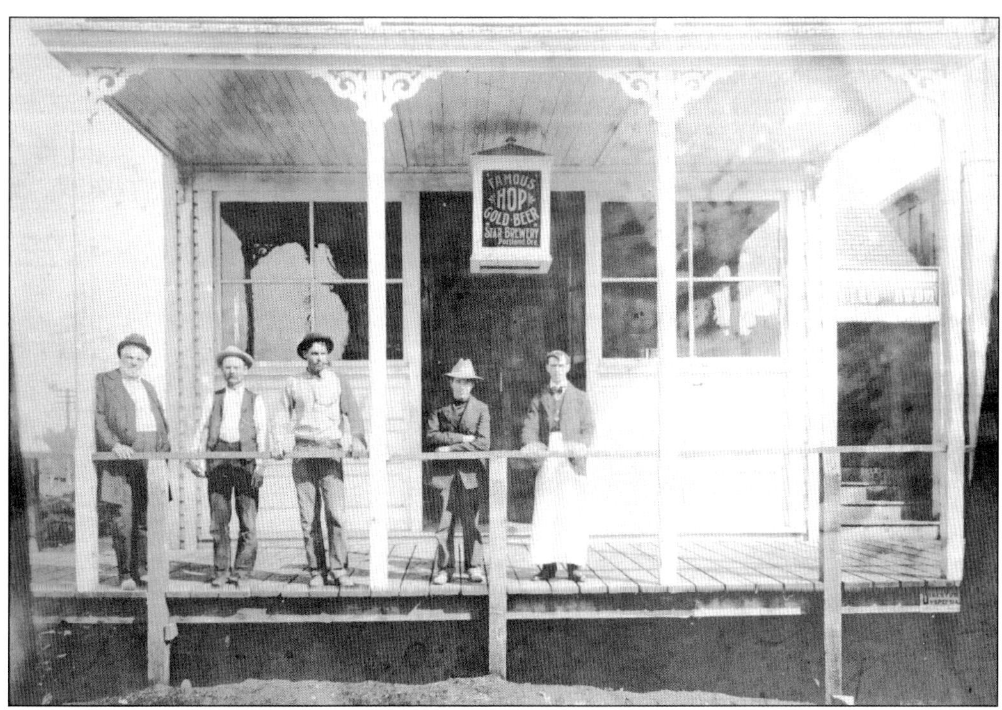

Kalama in the late 1800s and early 1900s had several successful saloons. Pictured is a group of men posing on the porch of a Kalama saloon, which is advertising beer from the Star Brewery.

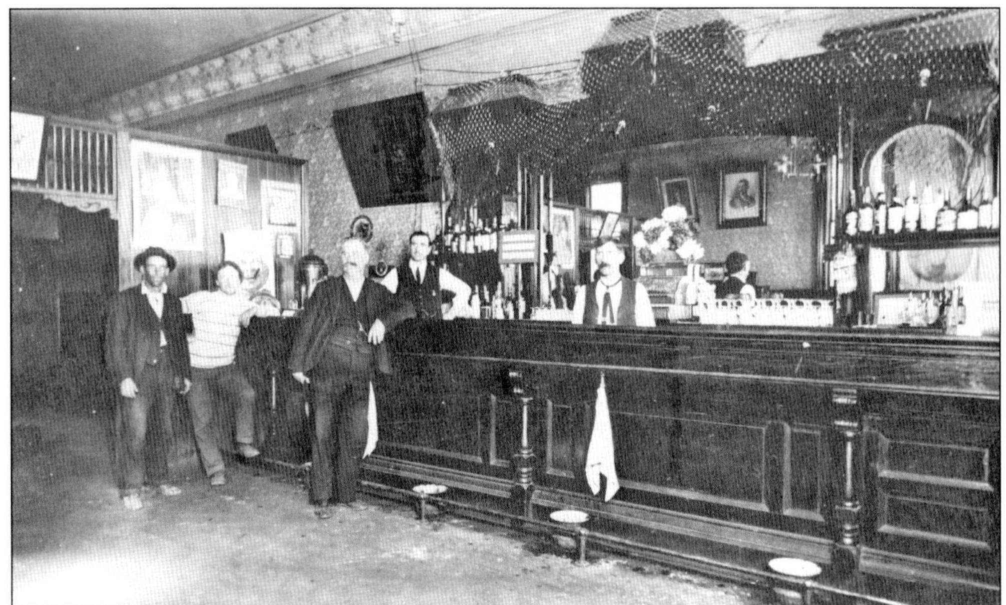

The interior of the Kockritz Hotel bar is pictured in the early 1900s. One man leans on the bar and rests his foot on the brass rail. At this time, Kalama had several saloons. The building that housed the Kockritz Hotel is still in use on First Street. (Courtesy of Joanna Boatman.)

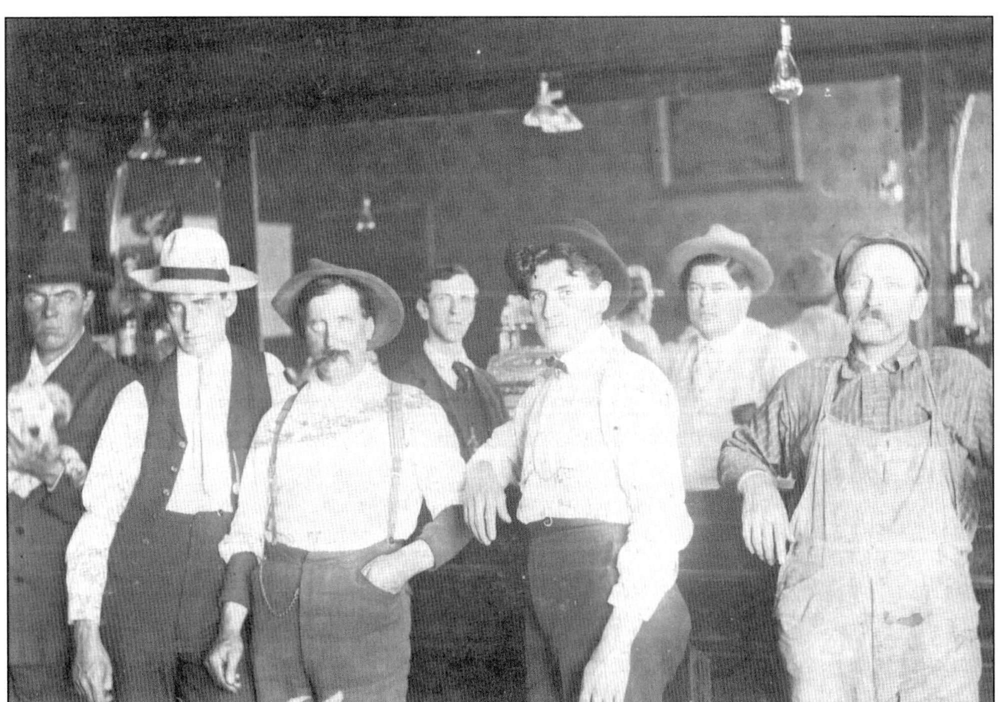

Hanging over the bar is an early electric light. Kalama was fortunate that an electric company was providing electricity to the city by 1903 and local citizens were quick to embrace the technology. Unlike most modern drinking and eating establishments, this saloon allowed its patrons to bring their dogs in for a drink. (Courtesy of Joanna Boatman.)

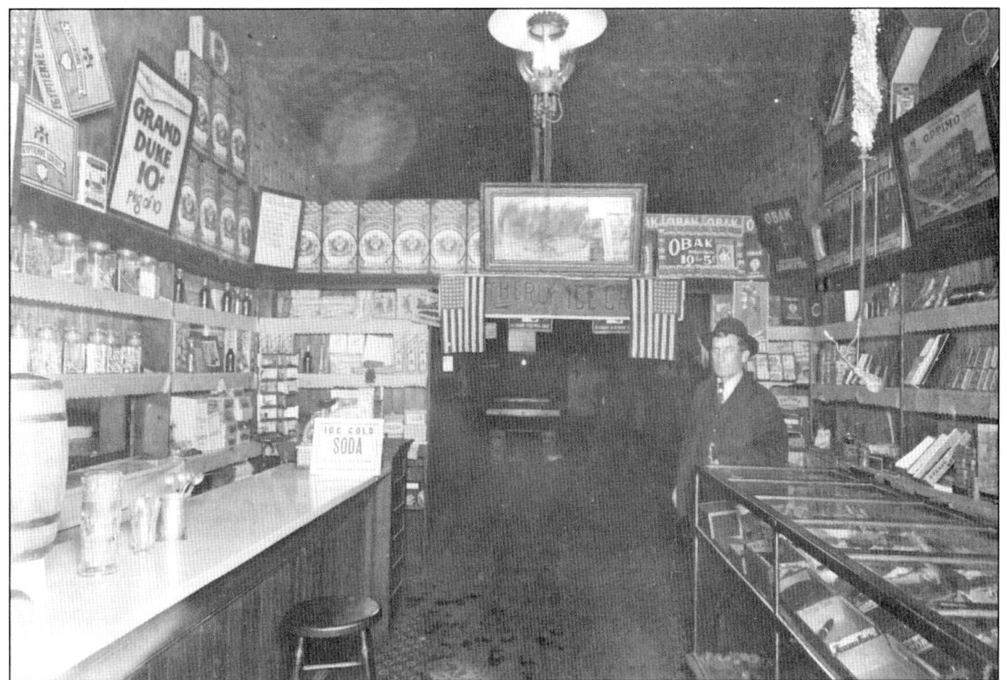

This general store boasts a soda fountain, and behind the soda fountain in large jars is a wide selection of penny candy. At the back of the store is a doorway leading to a pool hall. (Courtesy of John Norton.)

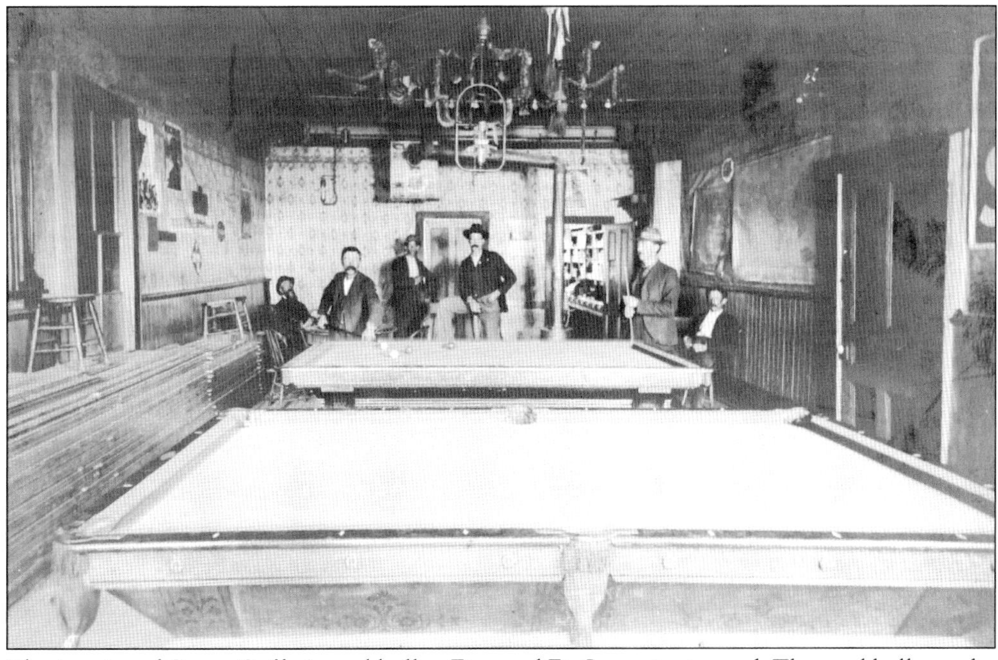

The interior of Green Coffey's pool hall at First and Fir Street is pictured. The pool hall was the first home of Kalama Telephone. Kalama Electric Power and Light owned the phone company originally, but Coffey purchased the business in 1911. He also served as the city fire chief. (Courtesy of Catherine Applegate.)

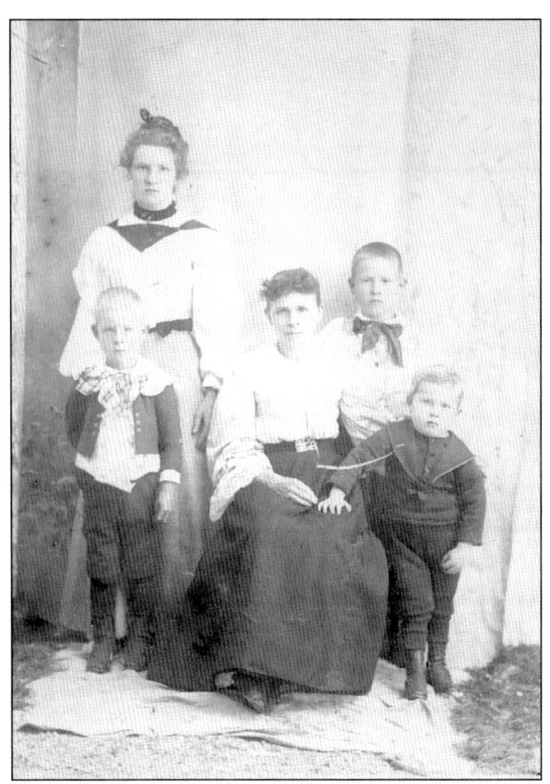

Pictured are, from left to right, (first row) James, Mollie, and William Curtis; (second row) Hattie Whiteaker Webster and her son John. The Whiteakers settled in Kalama in the early 1900s. (Courtesy of Janice Whiteaker.)

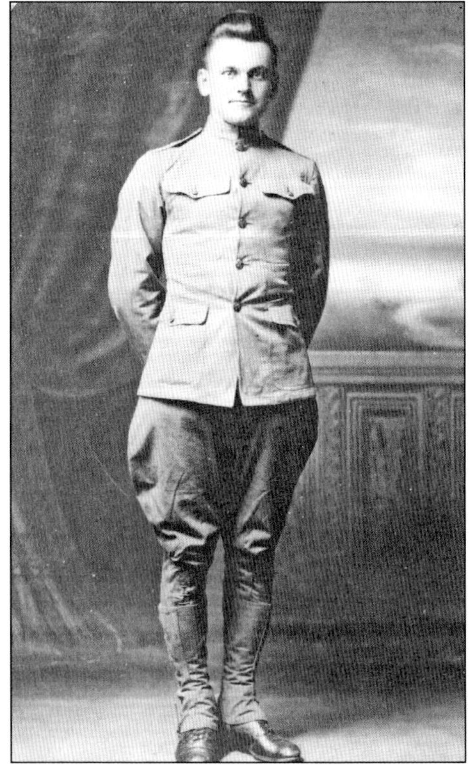

Dilbert Schauble poses in his World War I uniform. The Schuable family were early settlers in Kalama and lived on Spencer Creek, which is a rural area north of the city of Kalama. (Courtesy of Pat Kennedy.)

Mary England Comer was a resident of Kalama in the early 1900s. She was a homemaker who lived most of her life in Kalama and was known to her family as "Mudge." (Courtesy of Elouise Hutton.)

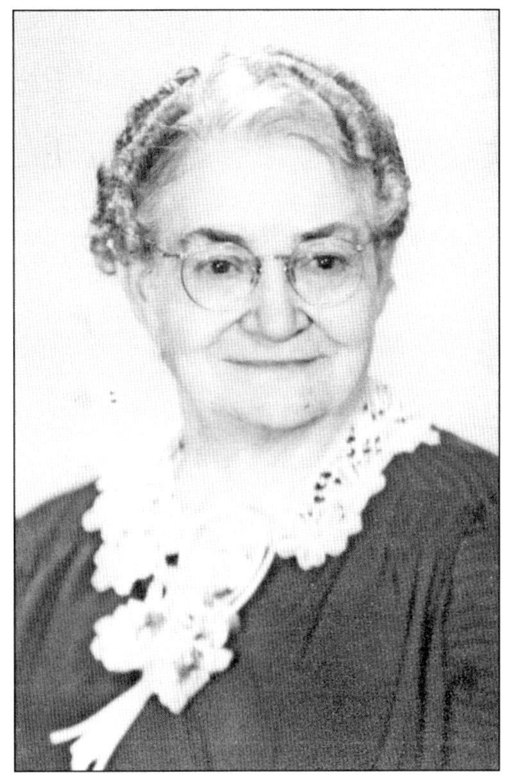

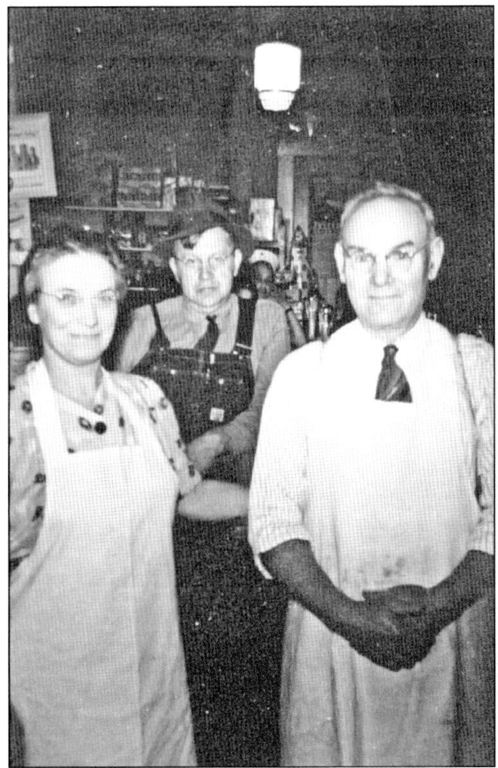

Minnie Downs and John Downs, owners of the Candy Kitchen, are pictured in their store in the 1930s. The gentleman between them is identified only as Ed. The Candy Kitchen had a soda fountain, and candy was made in the back of the store. It was also the location of a bus station.

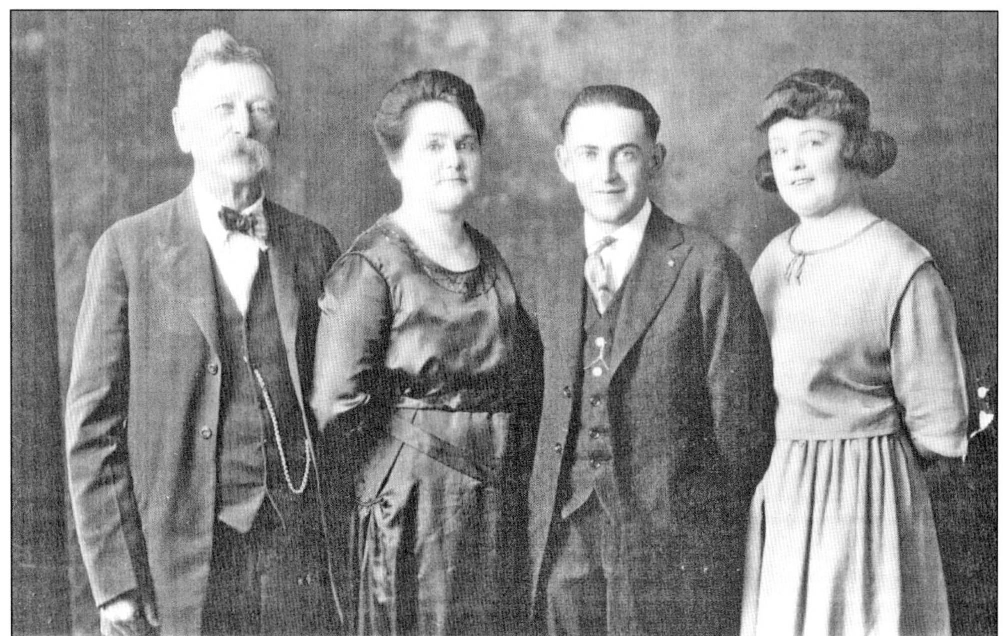

The Coffey family owned and operated the Kalama Phone Company, which is still the phone company for the city of Kalama. Pictured are, from left to right, Green Coffey, Eva Coffey, Darrell Coffey, and Vera Coffey. (Courtesy of Catherine Applegate.)

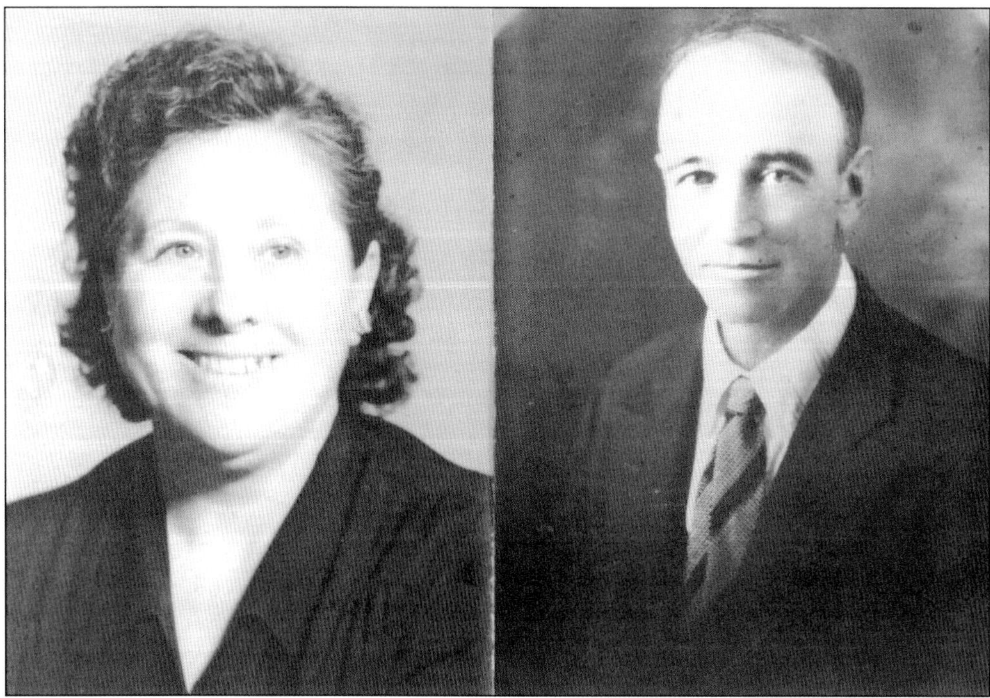

Early Kalama residents Ida Grace Comer and Lewis Melvin Comer are seen here. Lewis logged with horses up China Garden and Green Mountain. Later, he purchased ice from Doty Fish and delivered it to customers in Kalama and the surrounding area. Ida was Lewis's wife. (Courtesy of Elouise Hutton.)

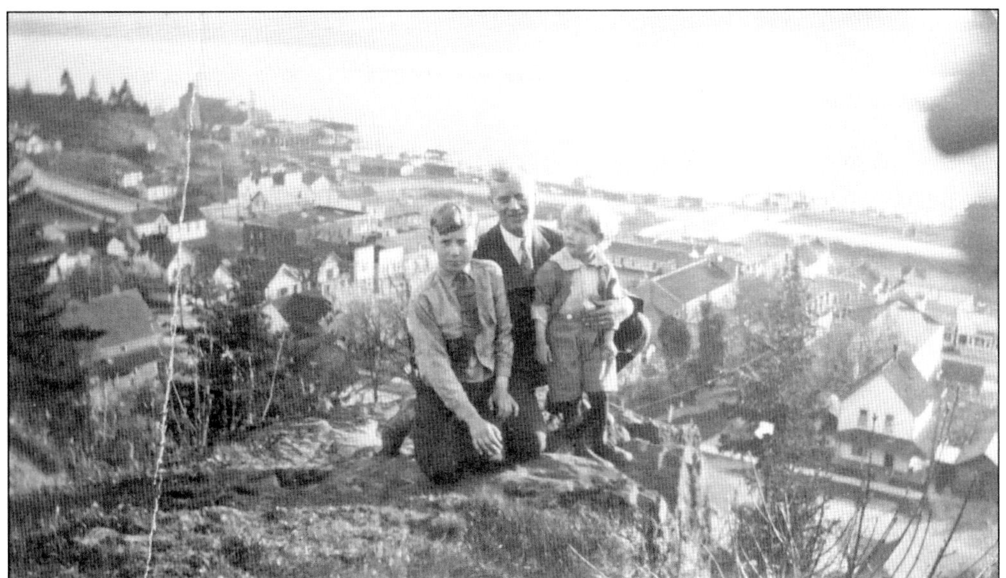

In 1923, an unidentified man and his children pose on the hillside overlooking the city of Kalama. Beyond is the Columbia River, the fourth-largest river in the United States by volume. (Courtesy of Art Godfrey.)

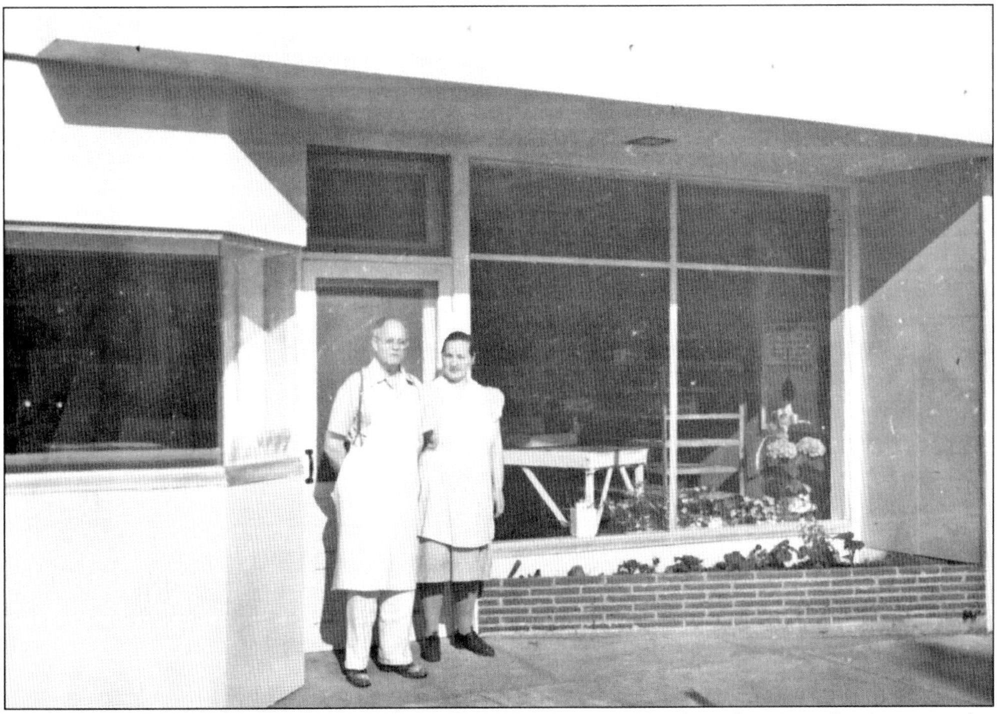

Otto and Ellen Englemann pose in front of their bakery located in the city of Kalama in the 1930s. The couple was very active in Kalama community affairs. They made bread in a brick wood-fired oven and delivered it to local homes and businesses.

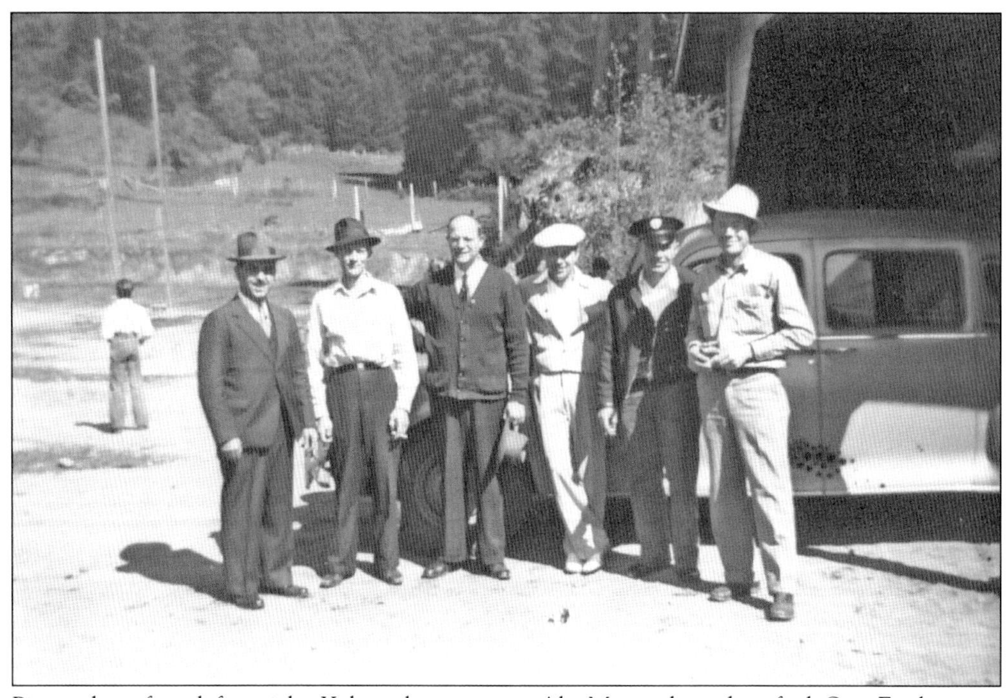

Pictured are, from left to right, Kalama businessmen Abe Moawad, unidentified, Otto Englemann, two unidentified, and Herman Gray.

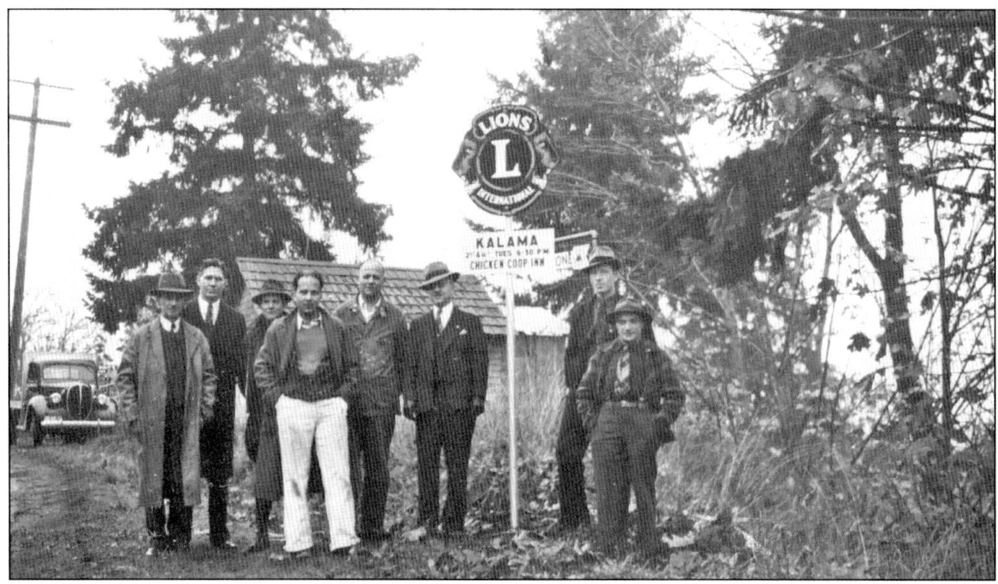

Members of the Kalama Lions Club pose by their new sign welcoming visitors to the city of Kalama. Vern Smith is the gentleman in the white pants, and beside him to the right is Otto Englemann. The sign says they met at the Chicken Coop, a local restaurant specializing in fried chicken.

To the left is Don Merz, the owner of the Burger Bar. Helping him to cut cake is Kalama marshal Frank Boatman. They are enjoying a party being held at the fire department. The Burger Bar still serves the Kalama community and is still owned by the Merz family. (Courtesy of Joanna Boatman.)

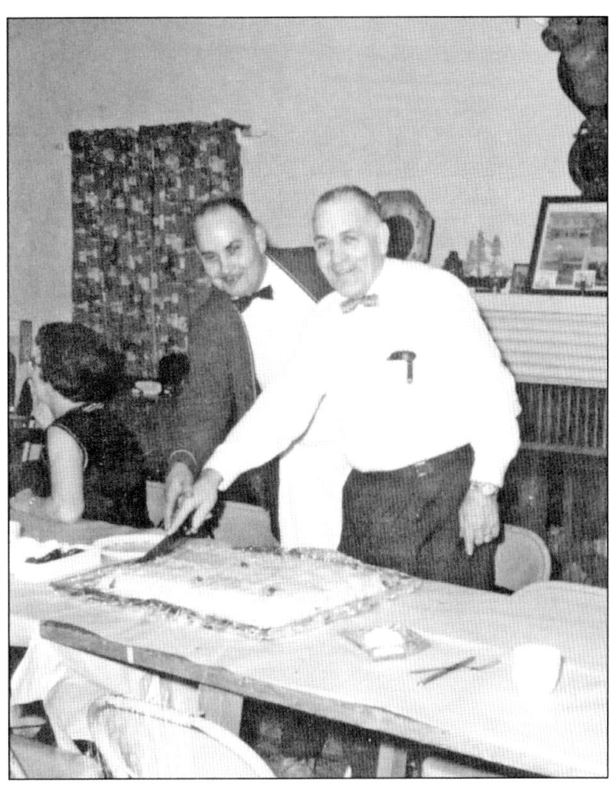

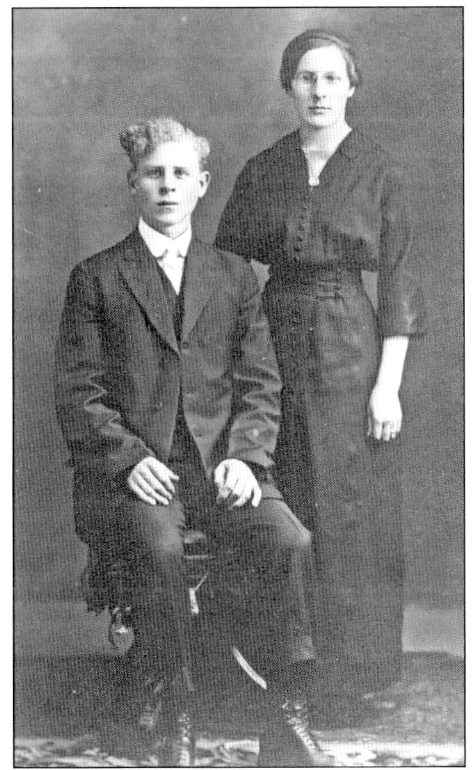

Pictured are J.R. Whiteaker and Elizabeth Sinner. They were married in 1911 and lived in a small house on what was called the Kalama Flats with their sons Royal, Bill, Clyde, and daughter Treva. J.R. grew up in Kalama and played clarinet in the first Kalama High School band; he later logged and ran a dairy farm. (Courtesy of Janice Whiteaker.)

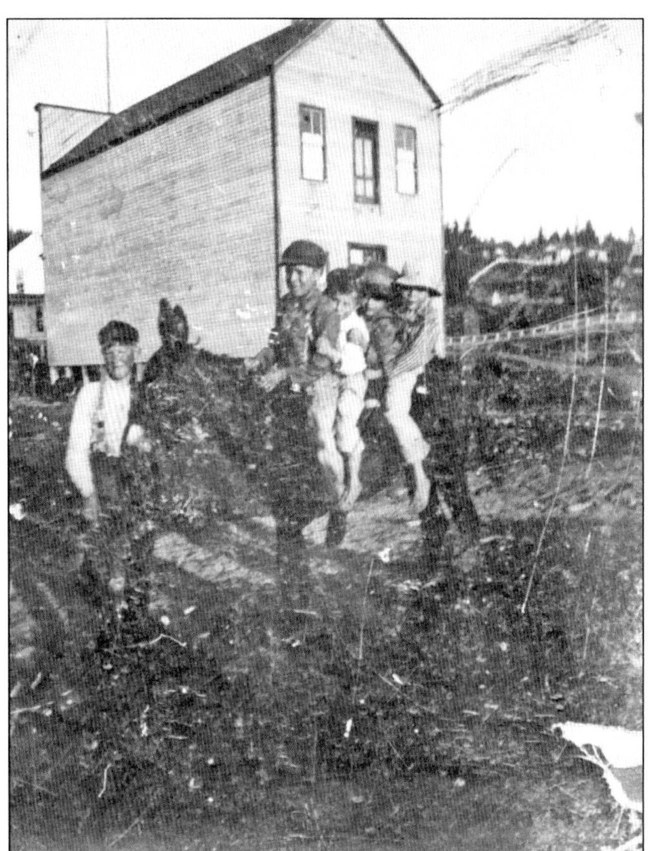

Four barefooted children are sitting on the back of a very patient donkey. An older boy is holding the reins. In an age without radio, television, or the Internet, children had to make their own fun.

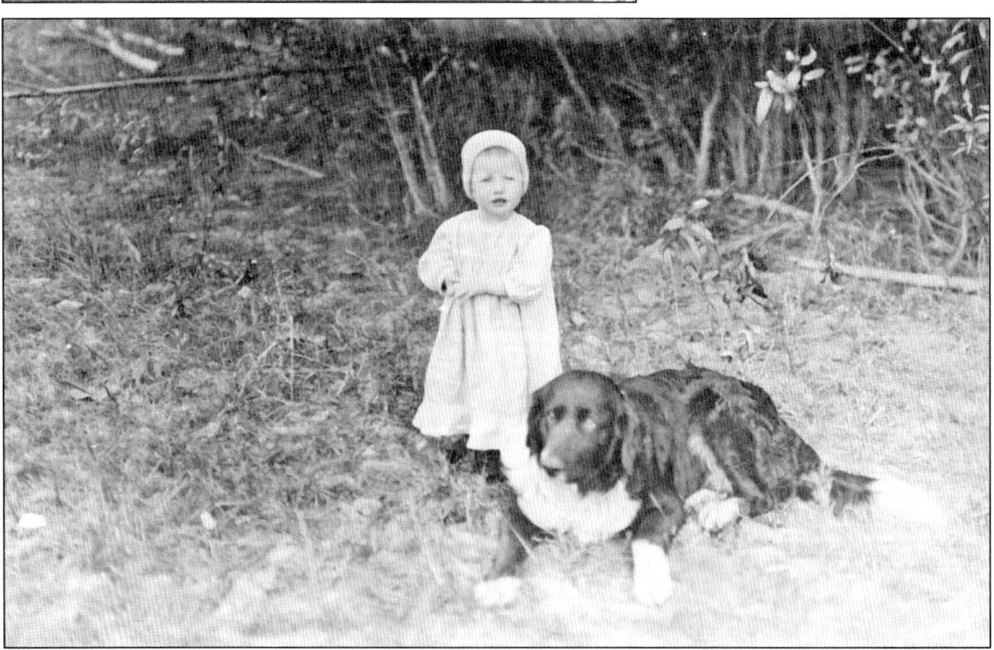

An unidentified little girl in a bonnet and a long dress poses with her dog for the photographer. (Courtesy of John Norton.)

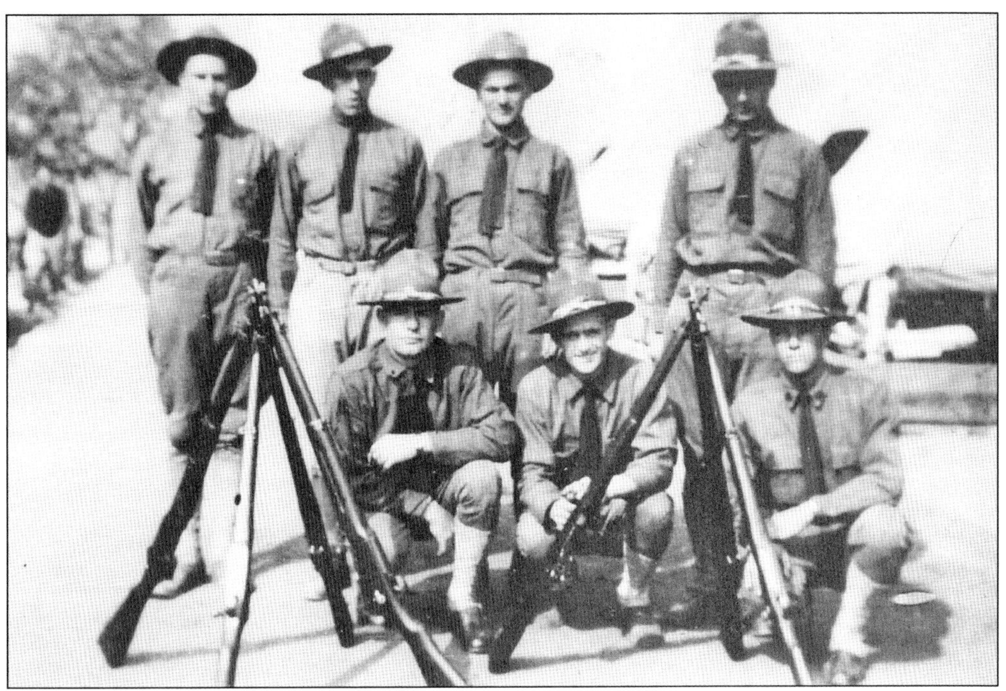

Around the time of World War I, a group of Kalama soldiers, also known as doughboys, poses with their rifles. To the far right is Kalama resident Harold Buck. (Courtesy of Pat Kennedy.)

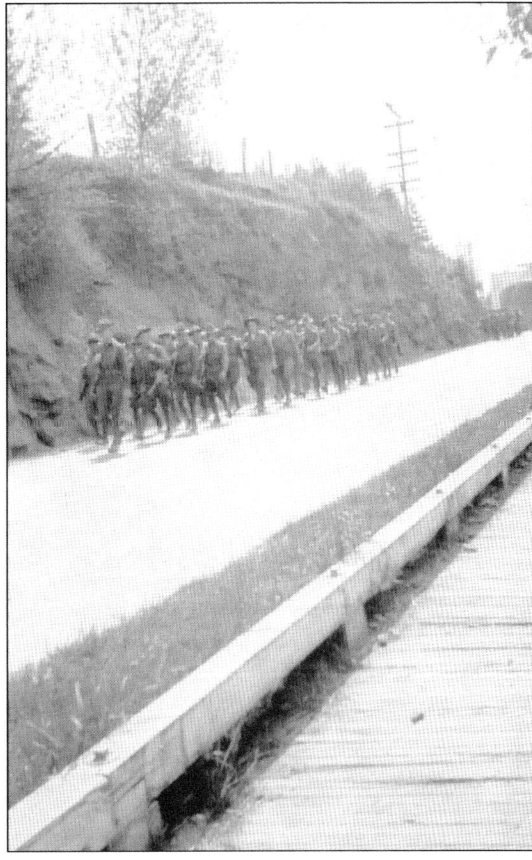

These World War II soldiers billeted at Fort Lewis, Washington, go by Kalama on a training march.

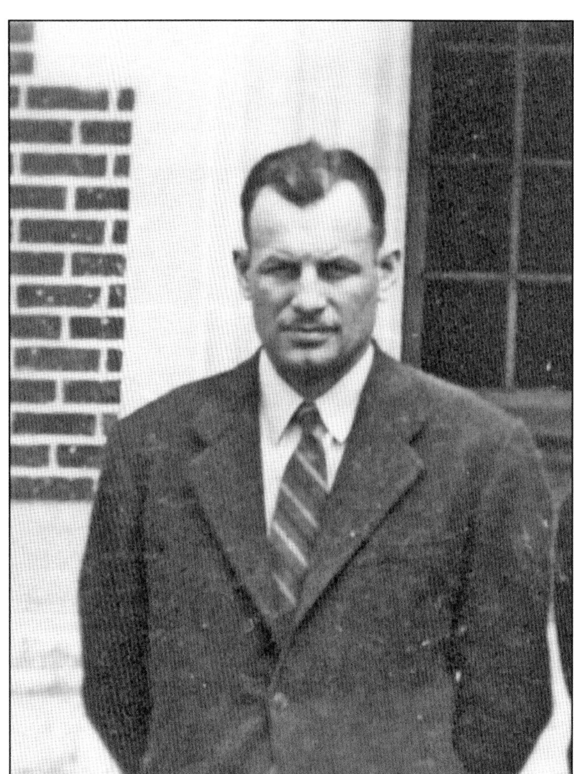

Pictured is Virgil Simmons. Virgil was born in Kalama, taught school at Kalama, and coached the Kalama High School football and basketball teams for many years.

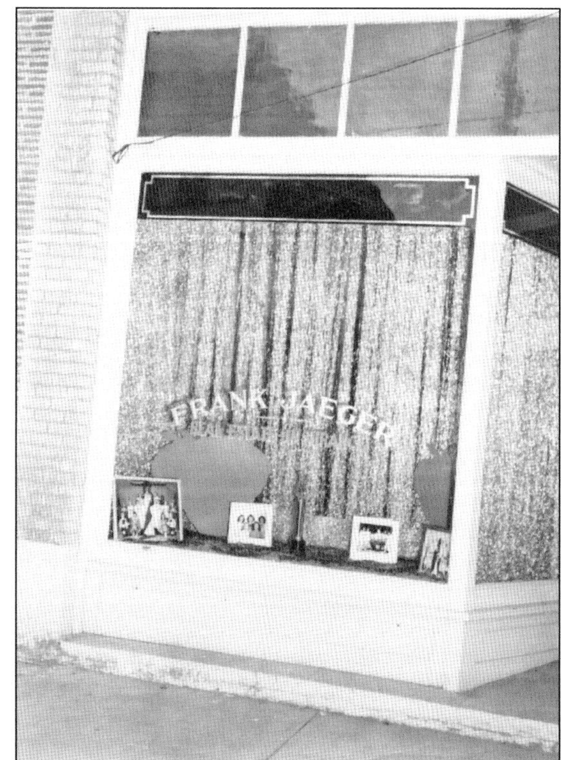

Here is the real estate and insurance office of Kalama resident Frank Jaeger. He was an active member of the Kalama community.

Young Frank Boatman poses for the photographer in 1904. He grew up to be an avid horseman and Kalama's town marshal. The Boatman family was always active in community affairs, and Frank's daughter Joanna was elected mayor of Kalama in 1958. She was the only woman mayor in the state of Washington at that time. (Courtesy of Joanna Boatman.)

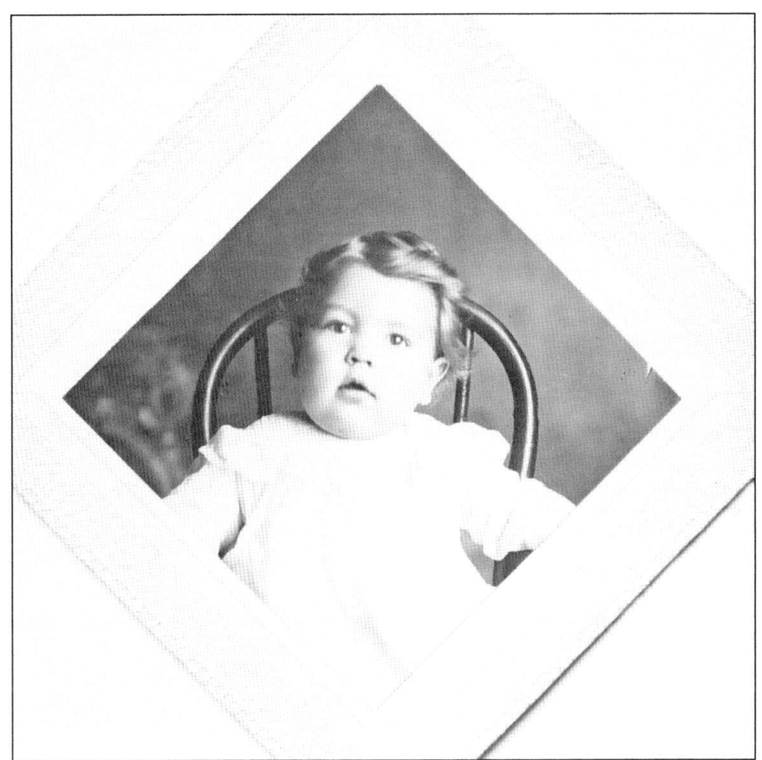

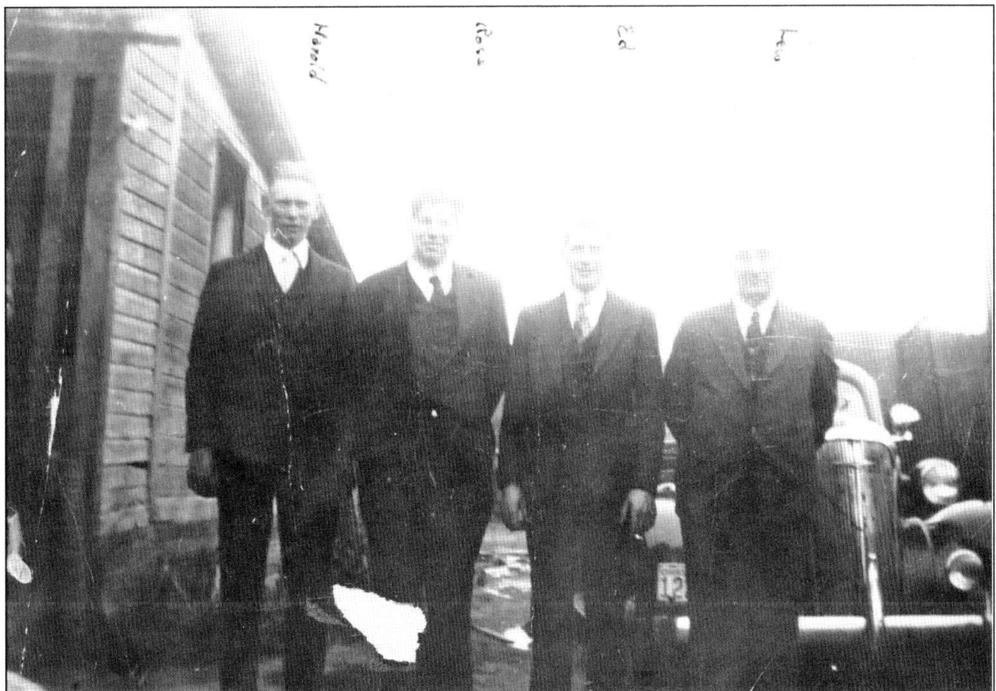

The LaRoy brothers were commercial fishermen. They ran a fish trap at the Kalama River until fish traps were outlawed. From left to right are Harold, Ross, Ed, and Lew LaRoy. (Courtesy of Brian LaRoy.)

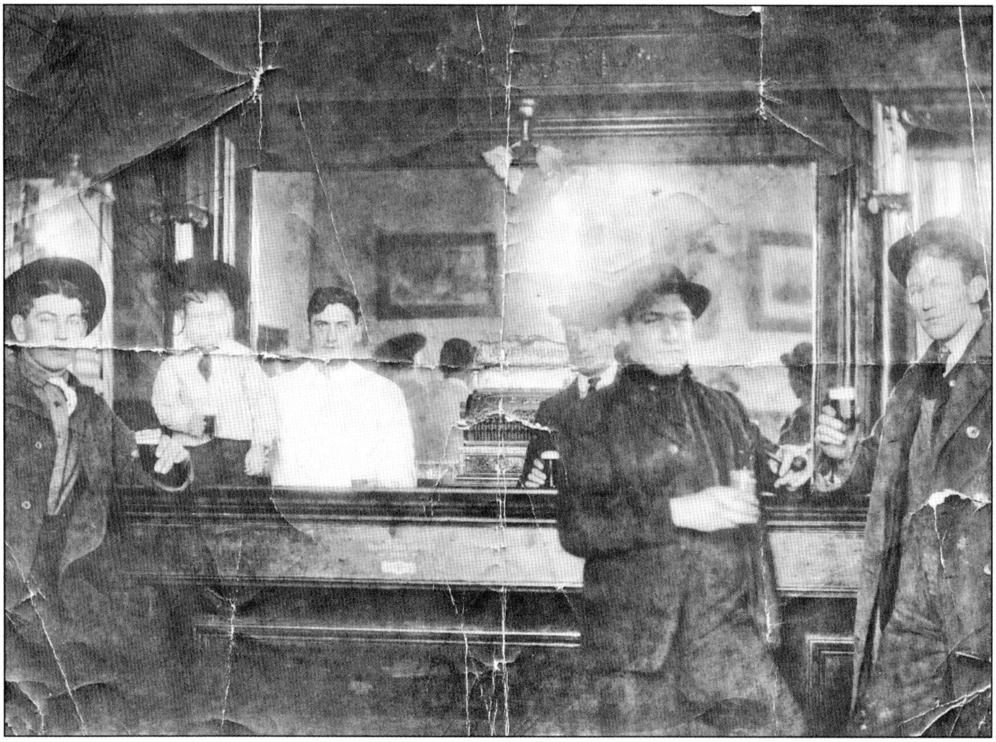

Small glasses of beer are being enjoyed by habitués of this turn-of-the-century saloon in Kalama. Saloons were bastions of male bonding. Ladies did not go to saloons. (Courtesy of John Norton.)

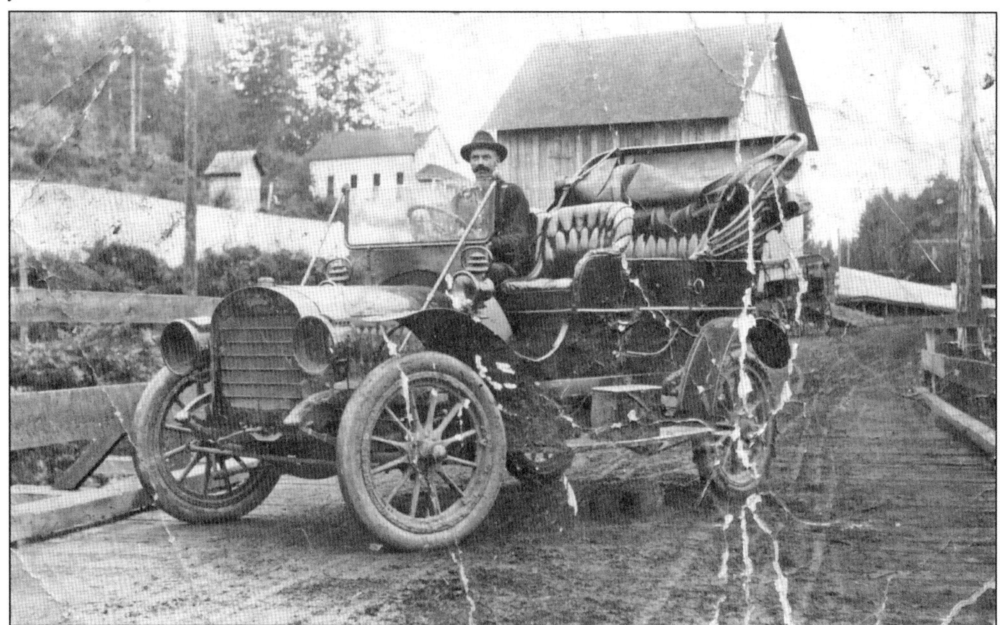

Axel Stridel came to Kalama in the late 1800s. He was a blacksmith and later moved to Carrolton (Carrolls), Washington, where he operated a smithy with his partner Olaf Halbom. Stridel is seen here posing in his new car on a road near Kalama. (Author's collection.)

Three

LOGGING

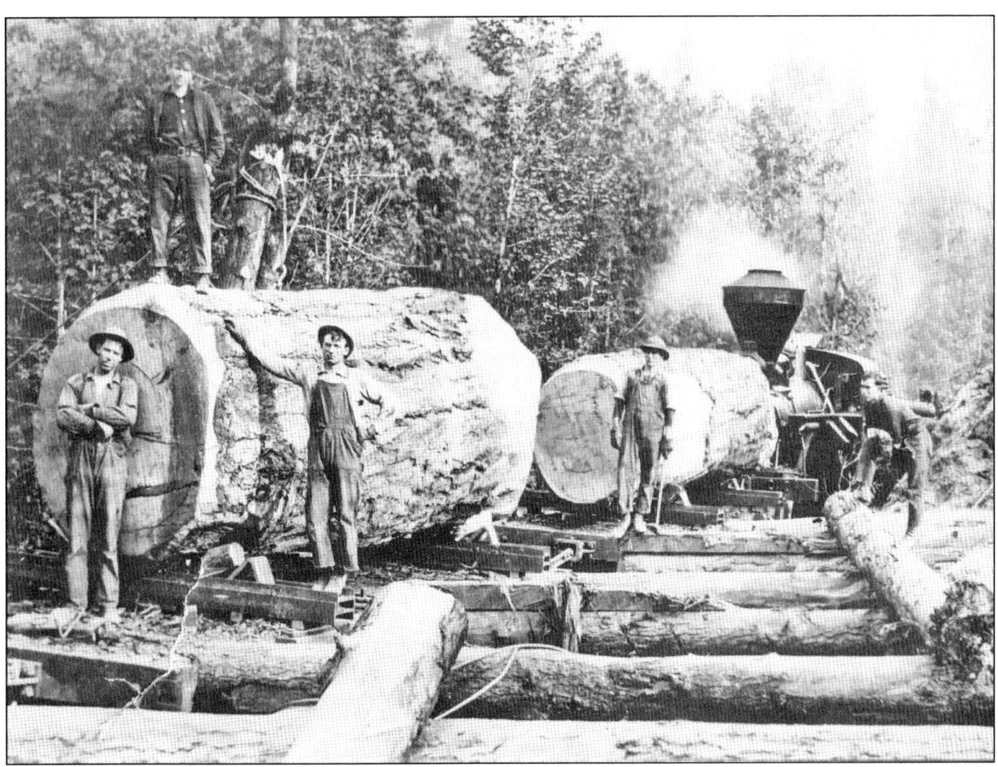

Logging was king in the early history of the Pacific Northwest. These loggers are felling what is called old-growth timber. Old-growth timber comes from forests that have never been harvested before. In the early history of logging, it was common for men to cut down trees that were so large that one log would be all that a logging truck could carry to a sawmill. It was also common for timber companies to lay rail line into the woods to help them bring trees to market. Today, many of these old, abandoned rail lines are used as hiking trails and for recreation.

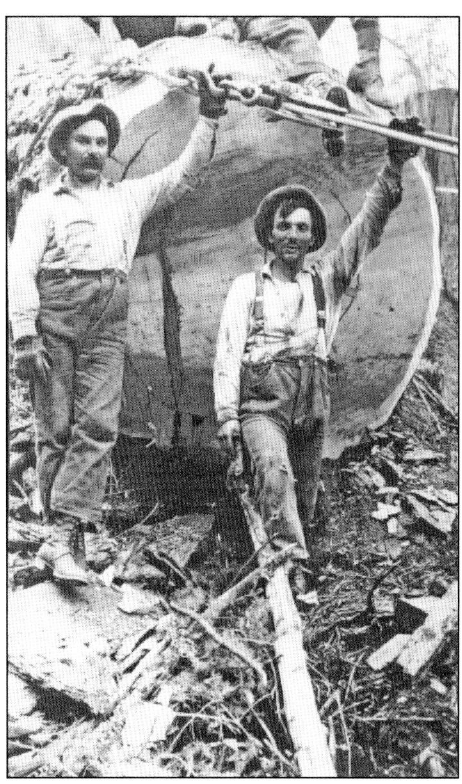

According to locals, they are not lumberjacks; they are loggers. Two loggers stand in front of a harvested old-growth tree. Logging was hard physical work, and the men pictured appear to be tired and happy for an opportunity to take a break to pose for the photographer. (Courtesy of Joanna Boatman.)

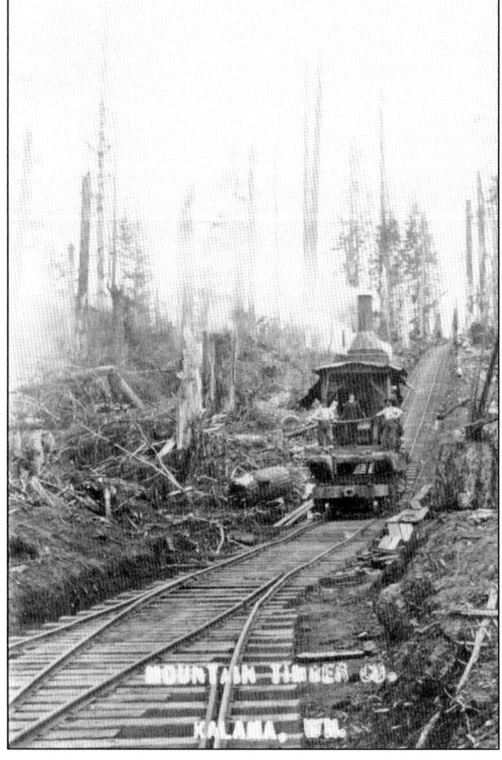

Mountain Timber was a logging company working in the Kalama area in the early 1900s. Like many logging companies of the time, Mountain Timber laid railroad into the woods to facilitate the transport of logs. This little engine on the tracks is called a shay.

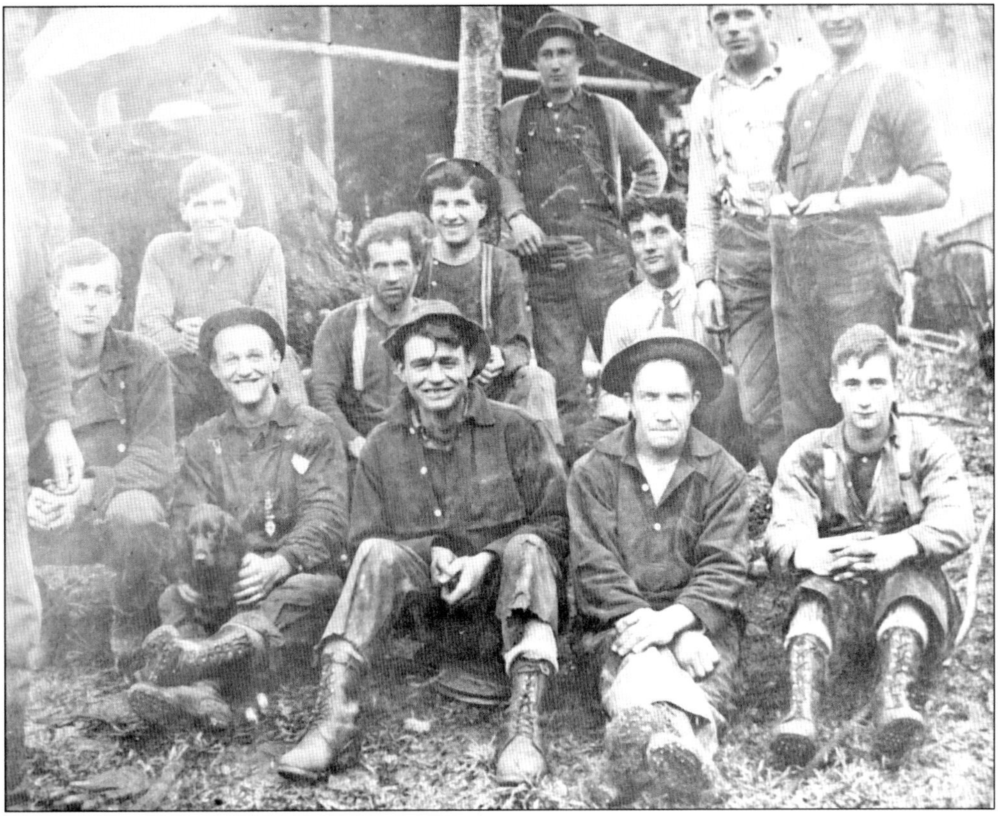

In the past, men who worked in the woods would stay at logging camps during the week. They were provided with rough lodging and meals. These men are wearing what are known as cork boots. The soles of the boots are studded with sharpened cleats to allow loggers to run safely across slippery logs without falling. Identified in the first row are John Keller (far left) and Frank Modrow (third from left); the others are unidentified.

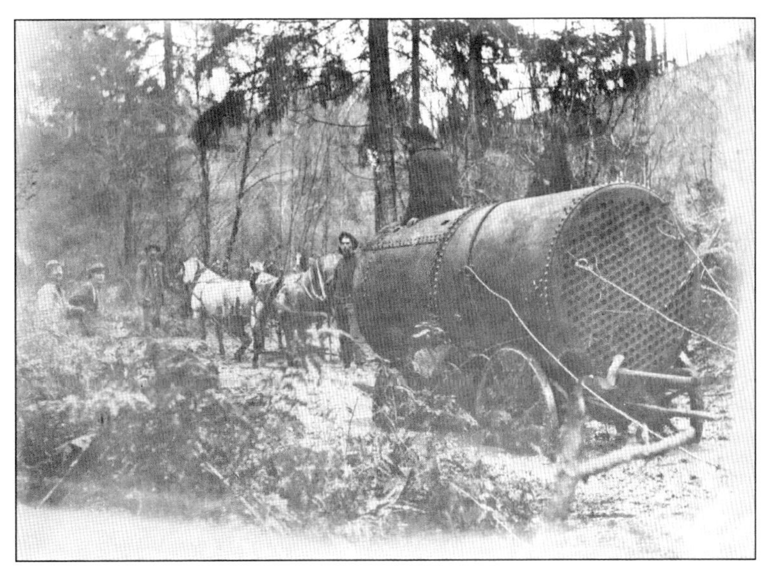

Pictured is a steam donkey, which is a steam-powered winch. Steam donkeys were usually fitted with a boiler and equipped with skids (sleds made from logs) to aid them in moving logs from one location to the next. This steam donkey is unusual because it is mounted on wheels. (Courtesy of Joanna Boatman.)

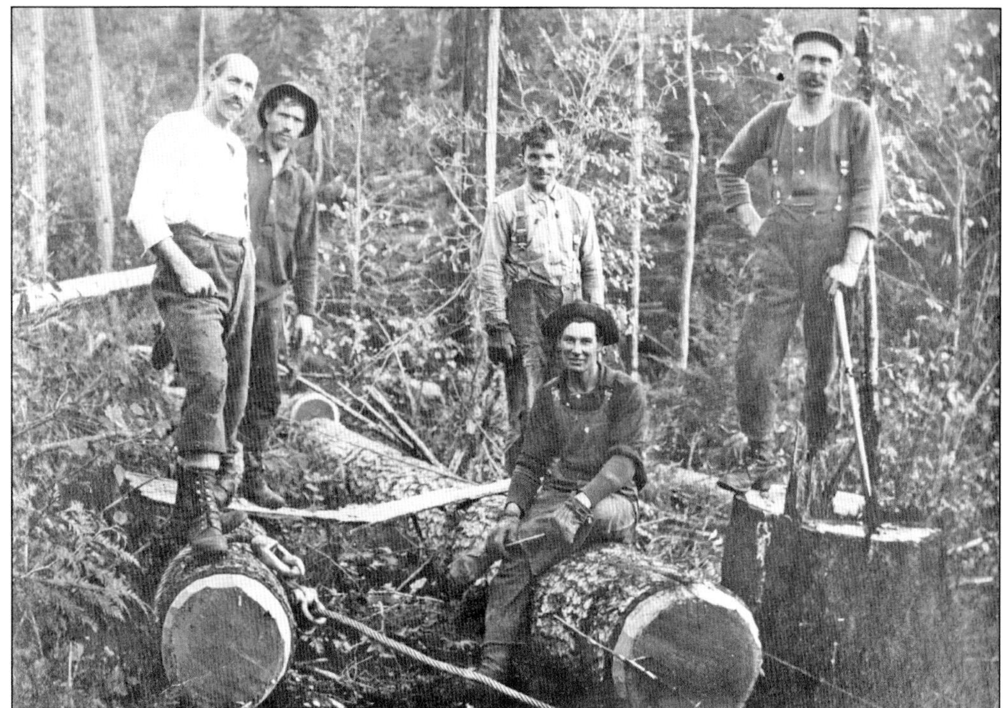

The forests of the Pacific Northwest are temperate rain forests, and as a result, they have a lot of undergrowth. The loggers are wearing very short pants as long pants are a hazard when logging. One man is leaning on his double-bladed ax, which was standard issue for any working logger.

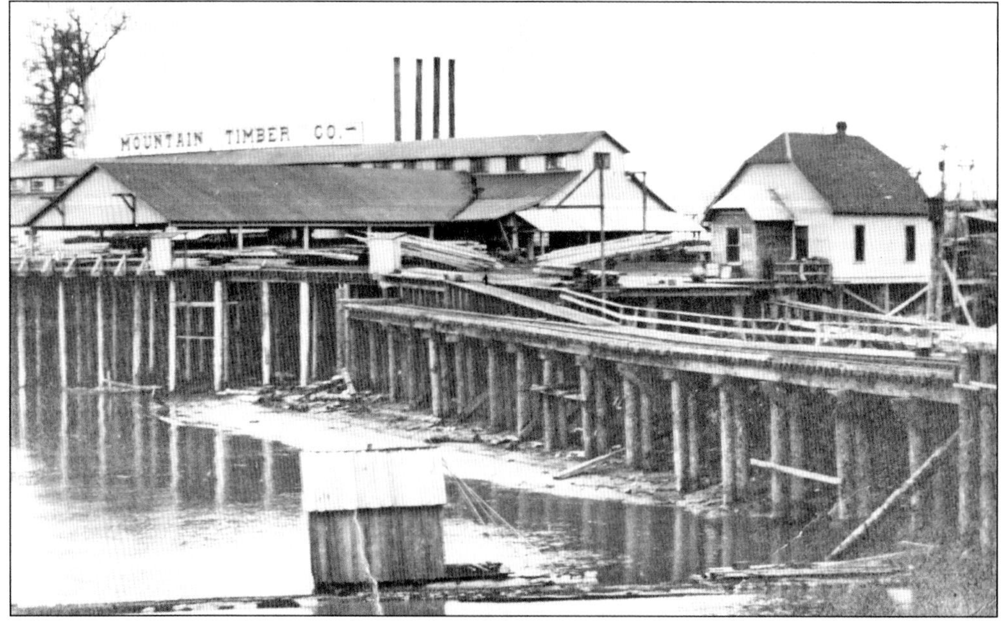

Mountain Timber Company was started in Kalama in 1910. The milling of logs was one of the most important industries in the Pacific Northwest in the late 1800s and early 1900s. This mill was located by the Columbia River for ease of transportation of the finished products—cedar shakes and milled lumber.

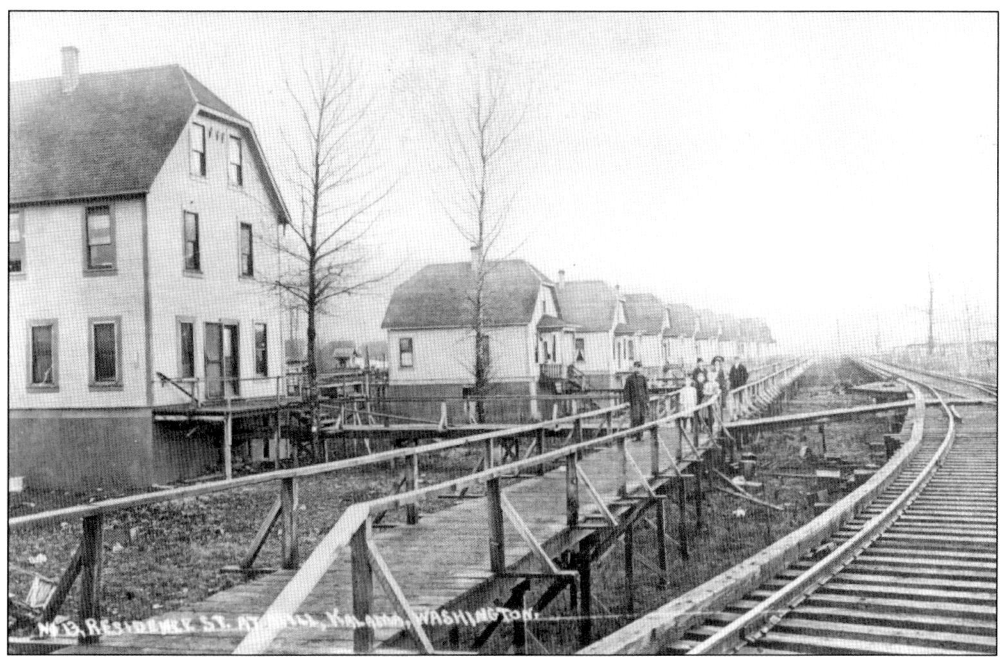

Mountain Timber Company provided houses on the Kalama flats for its employees. The houses were located near the Mountain Timber Company, which is seen in the distance in the right of the photograph. (Courtesy of Lee Bunn.)

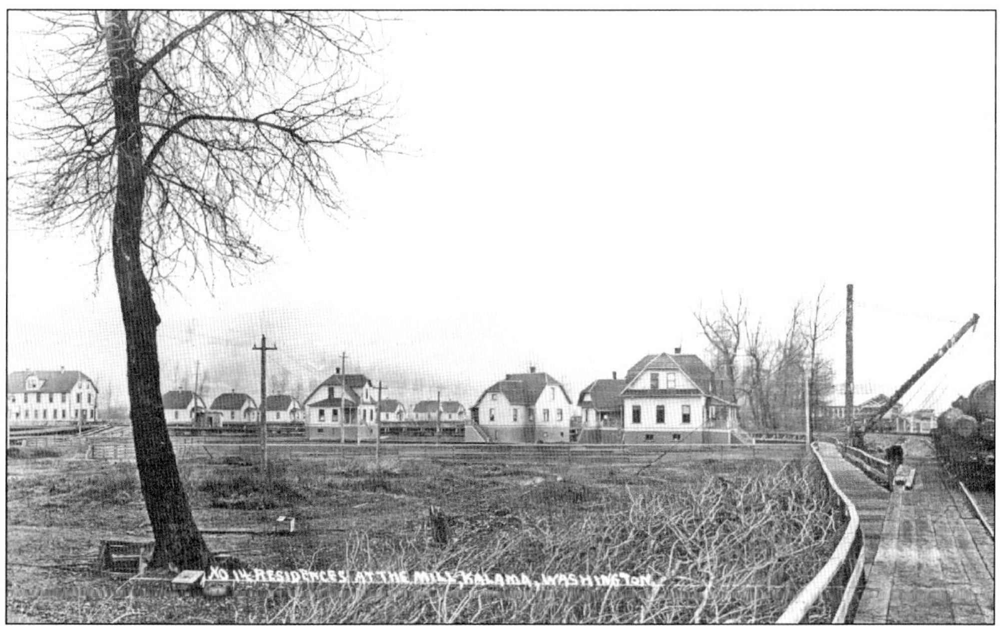

Mountain Timber provided wood-frame houses, and the first floors of the homes were about 15 feet off the ground to protect them from flooding. In early spring, the Kalama flats flooded during freshets. This melting of snow in the spring swelled local rivers, causing high water and sometimes flooding. Elevated boardwalks built near the rail line going to the Mountain Timber Sawmill kept pedestrians above the mud and high water. (Courtesy of Art Godfrey.)

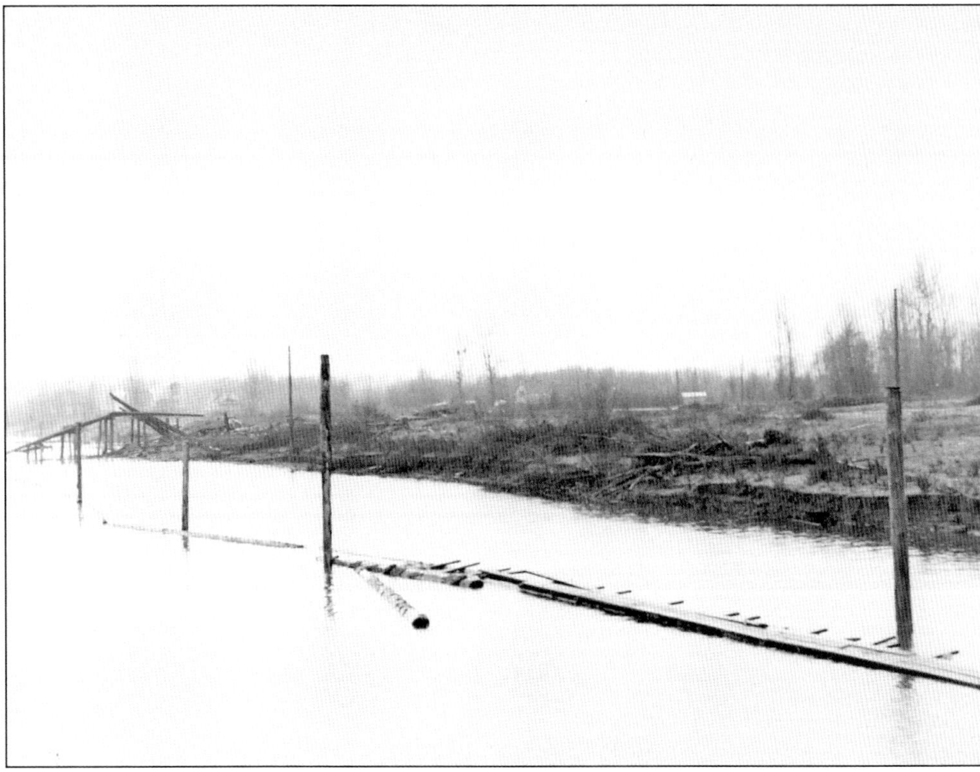

Pilings situated along the riverbank are used to moor logs and watercraft. Log rafts are created by lashing the logs together, or logs are lashed together to from a little enclosed area of water for storage. Logs are stored this way until they are ready to be used.

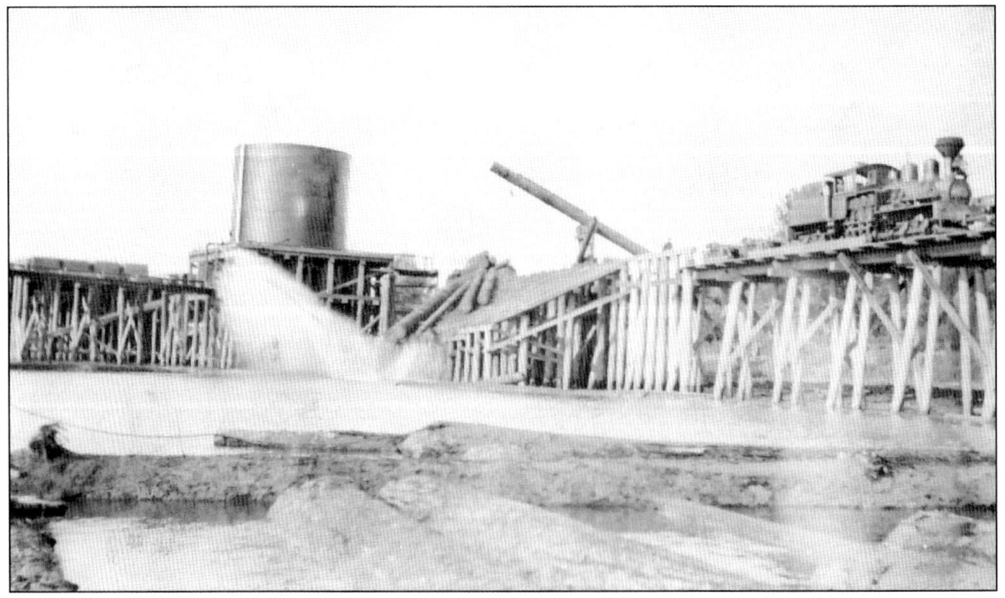

Pictured are logs splashing into a log pond where they will be stored until ready for use. A little steam logging shay is being used to bring logs to the sorting yard so the crane can lift them to the location where they are needed. (Courtesy of Lee Bunn.)

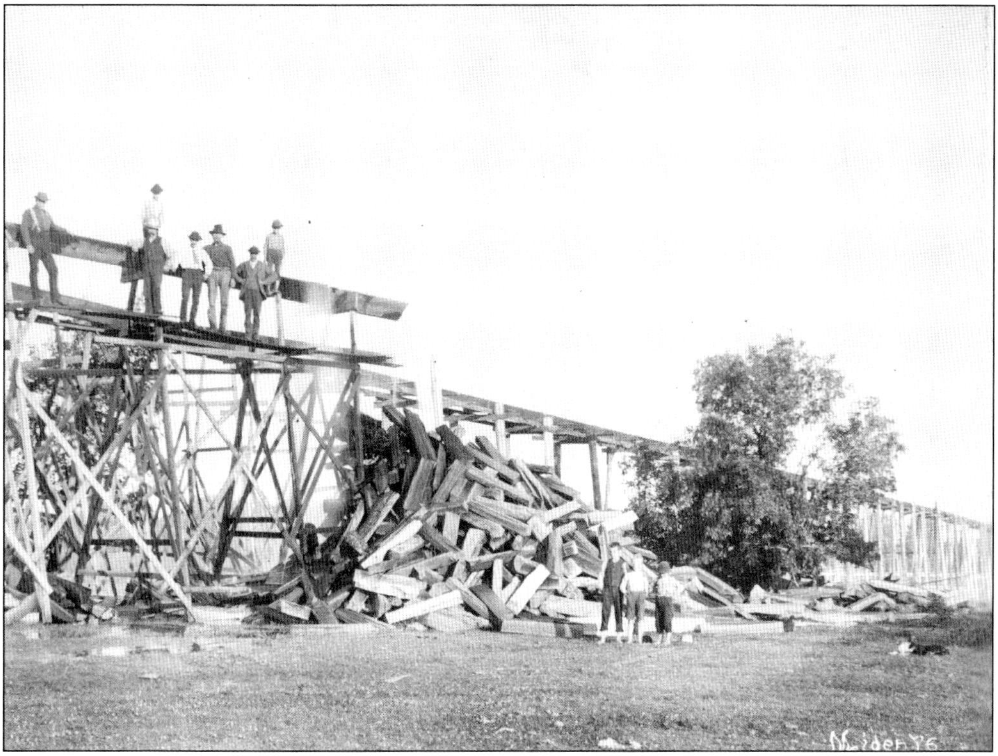

The men are pictured with what appear to be slabs of cedar. Cedar was commonly used for making fence posts and shakes for roofing. The trestle in the background probably belongs to Mountain Timber Company. (Courtesy of John Norton.)

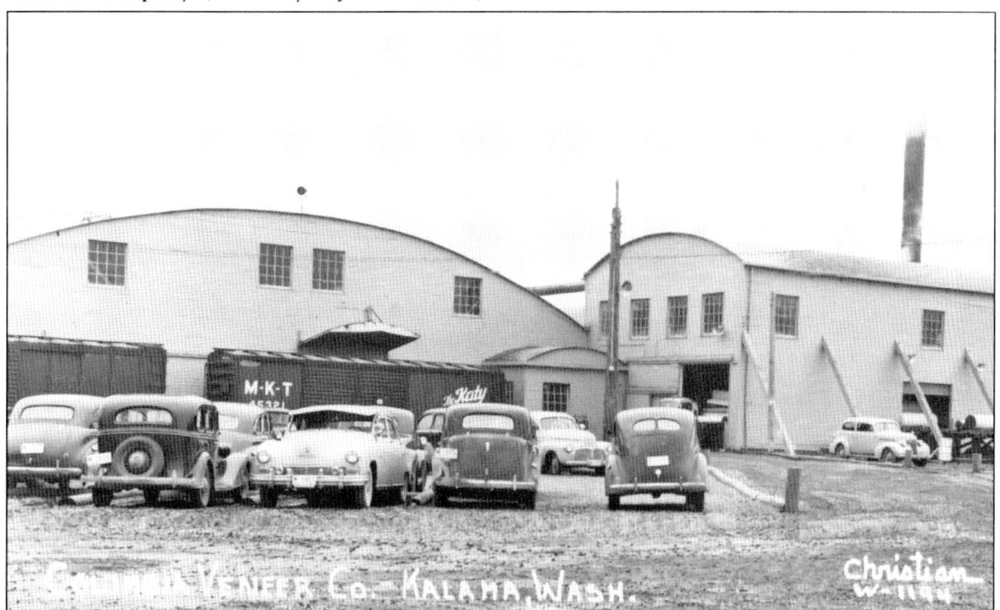

The Columbia Veneer Company employed hundreds of people in Kalama. The business made plywood, and many men worked for the company their entire lives. Columbia Veneer later became Pope and Talbot. (Courtesy of Lee Bunn.)

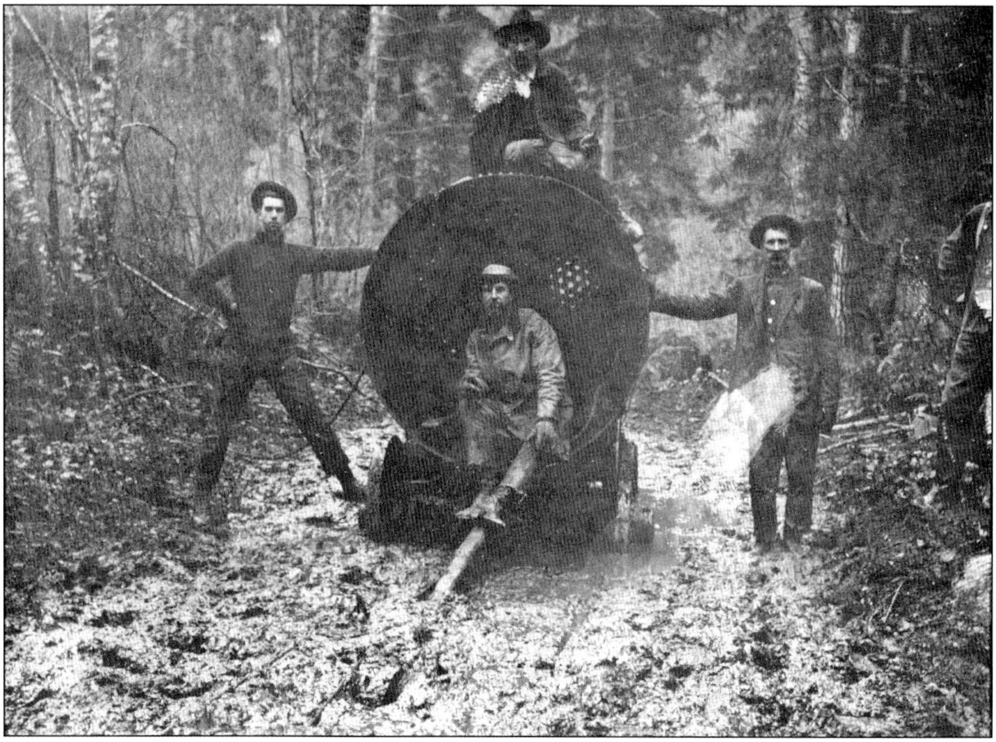

Here, a group of loggers poses with a steam donkey. (Courtesy of Joanna Boatman.)

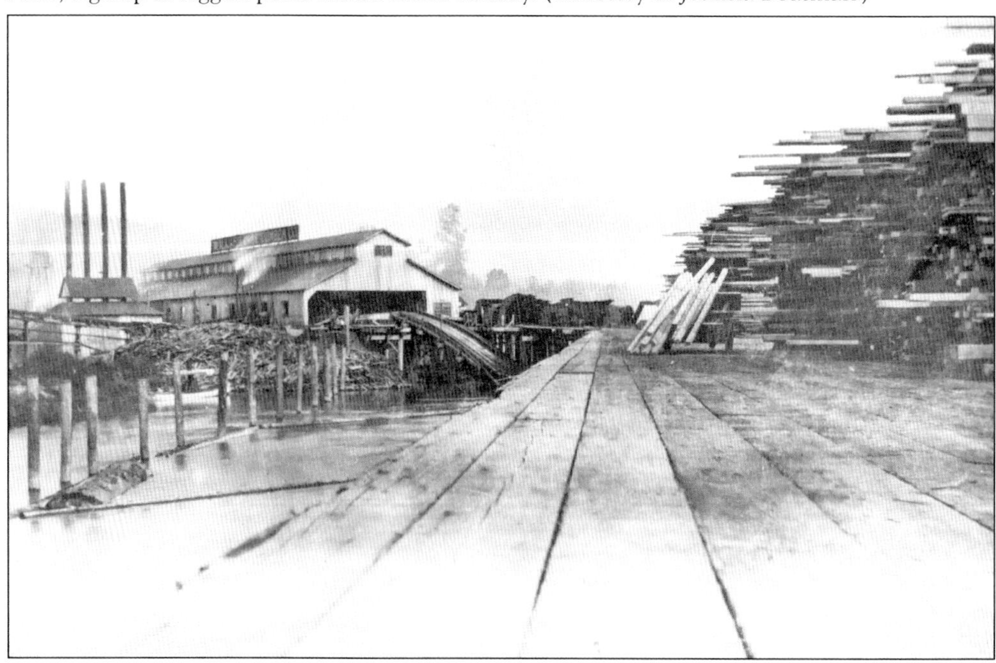

The Willard Case Lumber Company was located on the Columbia River. This sawmill was purchased by the Mountain Timber Company in 1910. Mountain Timber also had a logging operation, and the purchase of this mill meant it controlled the product from harvest through manufacturing and sales.

Four

FISHING

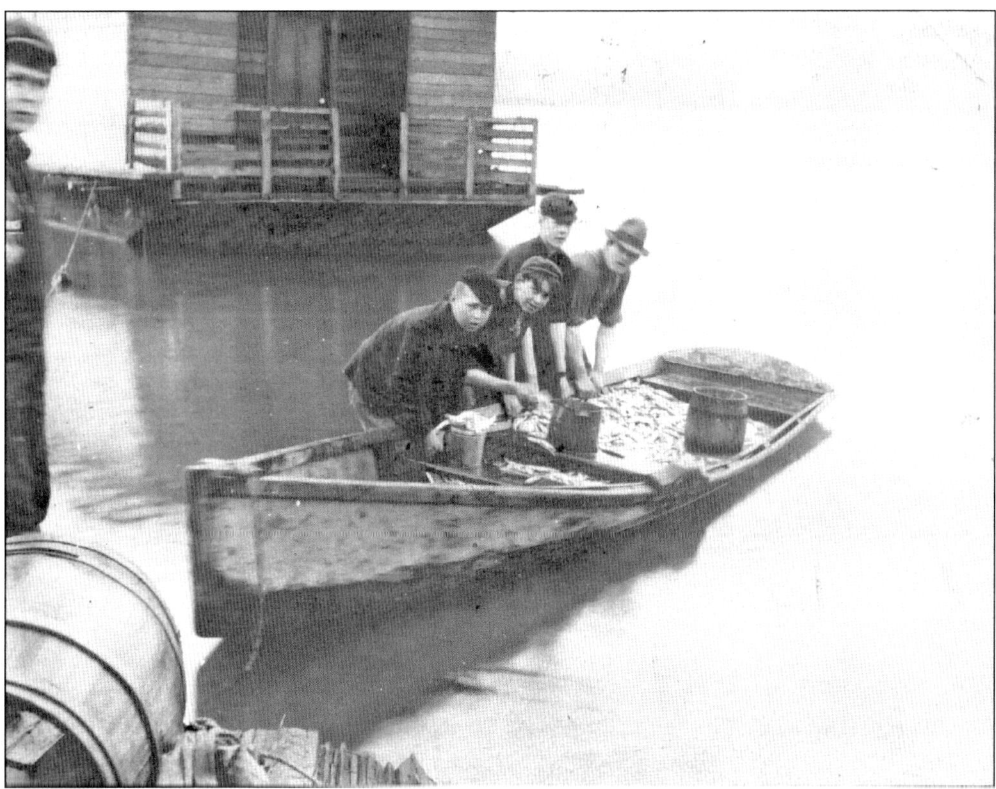

These fishermen have been smelt dipping. Smelt are a small, oily fish officially named eulachon. The fish are so oily that a dried smelt can be lit and burned for light, which led to the nickname "candlefish." Once a year, these fish return in great schools and navigate up the Columbia River and then into its tributaries to spawn. The runs of smelt were so great that, in the past, one could put a dip net into the water and barely be able to lift the net back into the boat because of the weight of the fish netted. (Courtesy of John Norton.)

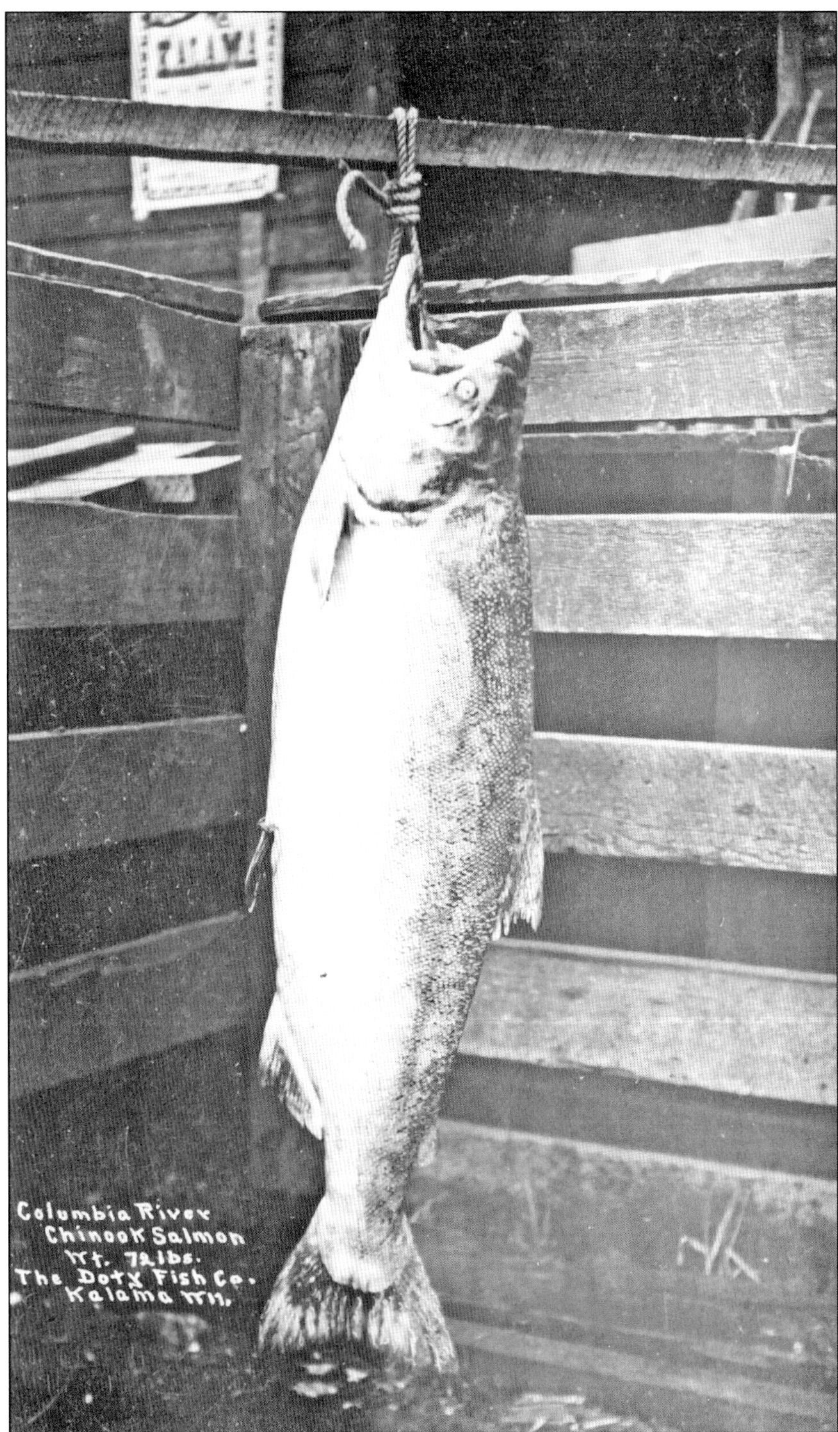

Pictured is a Columbia River chinook salmon. The text on the picture indicates the fish weighs 72 pounds. In the past, it was not uncommon to get a "June hog" that weighed 100 pounds. The building of dams has made salmon fishing extremely regulated, and a fish this large is a thing of the past. (Courtesy of John Norton.)

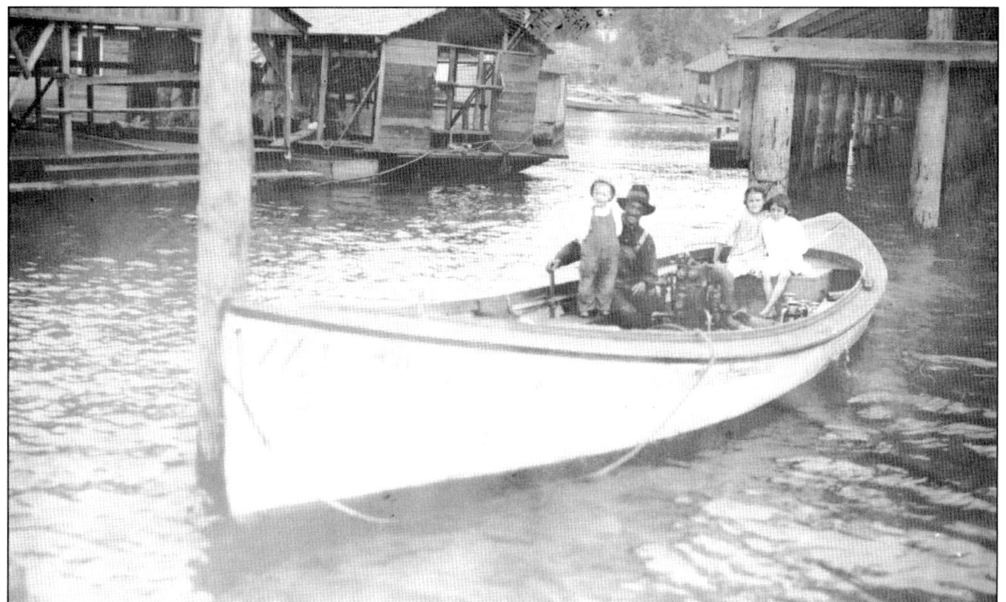

A family enjoys an outing in a fishing boat. The Columbia and the Kalama Rivers provided early pioneers with not only a means of employment but also recreation. This mixed use of both rivers continues today. (Courtesy of John Norton.)

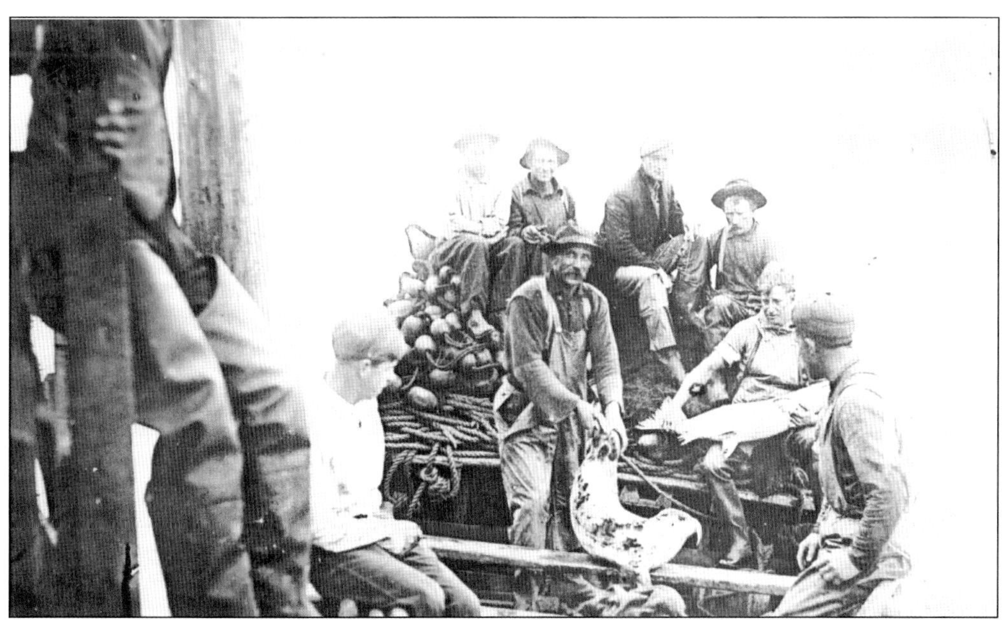

In the back, fishermen sit on their nets. In the front, one man displays his catch of a fish while another displays a seal. Seals and sea lions have commonly swum 100-plus miles up the Columbia River to catch salmon. (Courtesy of Janice Whiteaker.)

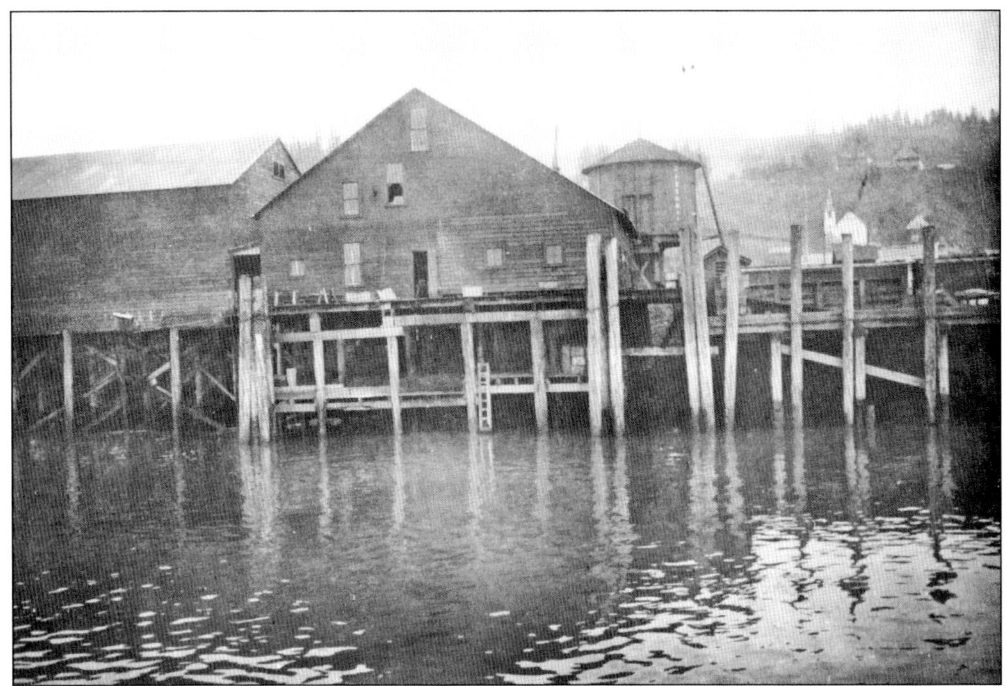

The Doty Fish Company was located on the Columbia River. The building was constructed by a Mr. Ruckles. Doty Fish not only processed fish but also shipped them for many of the other canneries located on the Columbia River. (Courtesy of Joanna Boatman.)

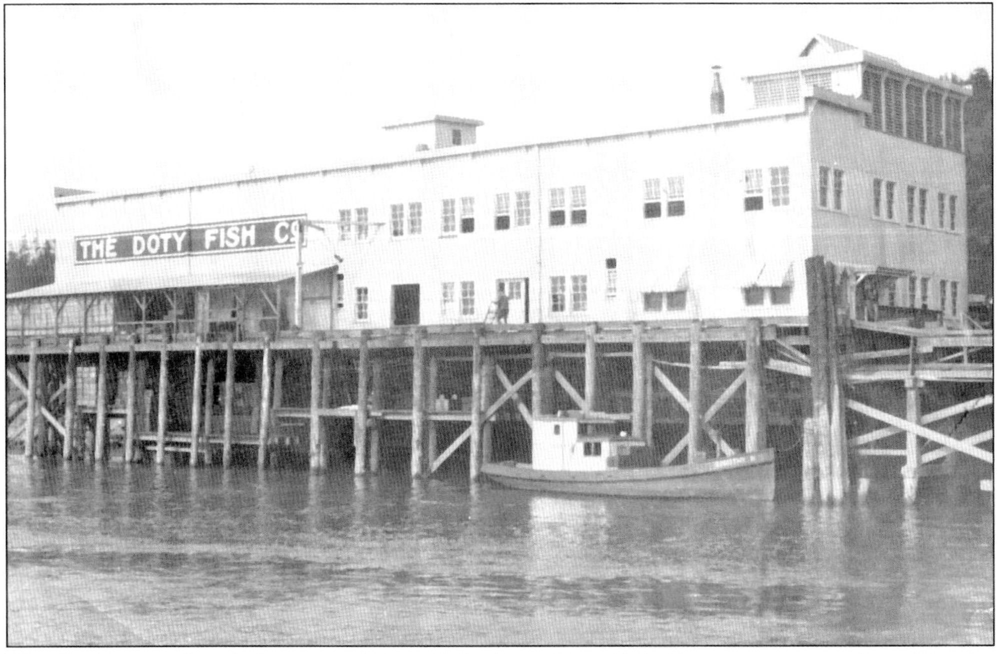

This building replaced the original Doty Fish plant. Doty Fish Company was purchased by the New England Fish Company, which built a dock (pictured at the right) that allowed fisherman to come and moor their boats right at the fish plant to conveniently unload their catches. (Courtesy of Joanna Boatman.)

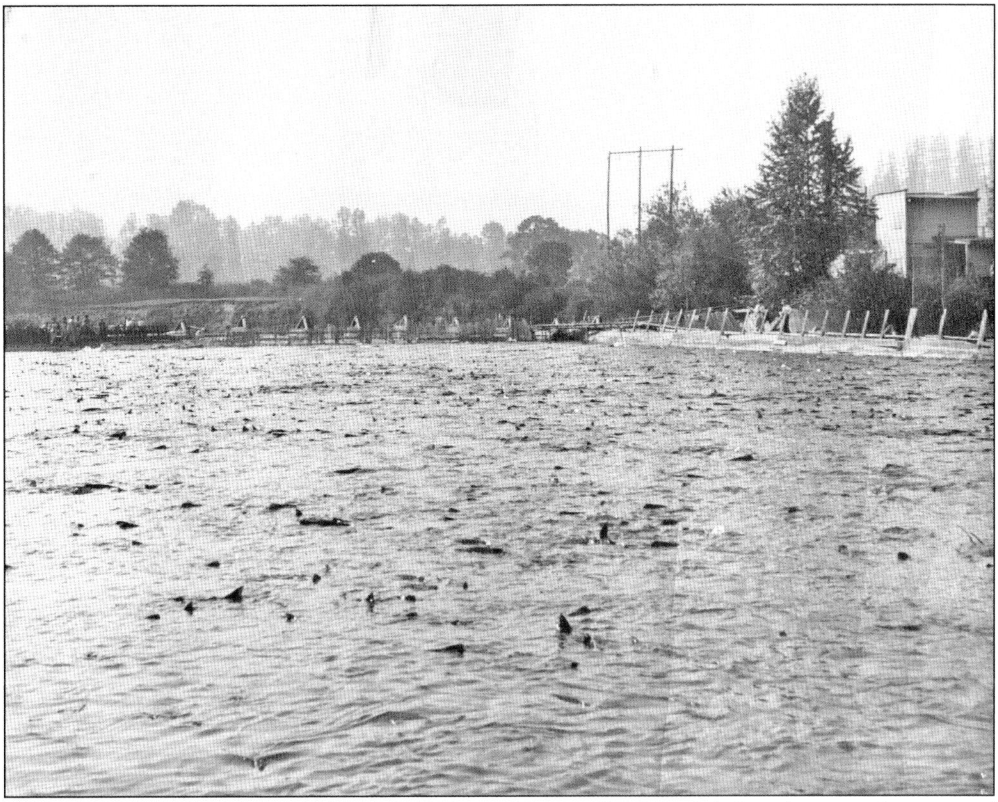

The Lower Kalama Fish Hatchery, built in 1895, was the first fish hatchery in the state of Washington. Salmon returning to the river of their birth to spawn are being netted in a pond so their eggs can be used to produce hatchlings. (Courtesy of John Norton.)

Fish hatchery workers are pulling the netted salmon in close to shore so they can catch the fish easily to get the roe. In the wild, salmon die after they spawn. Fish hatcheries commonly catch these returning spawning salmon to insure future healthy runs of fish. (Courtesy of John Norton.)

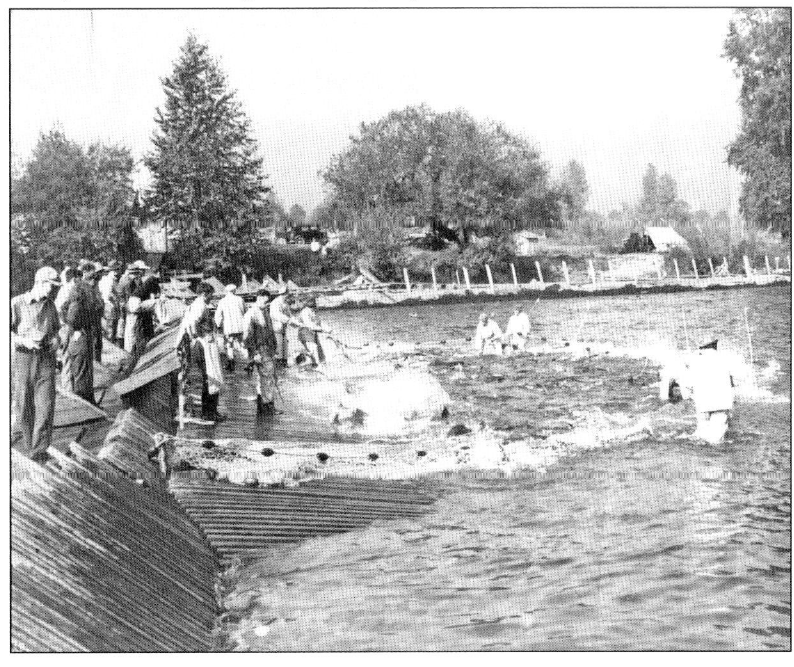

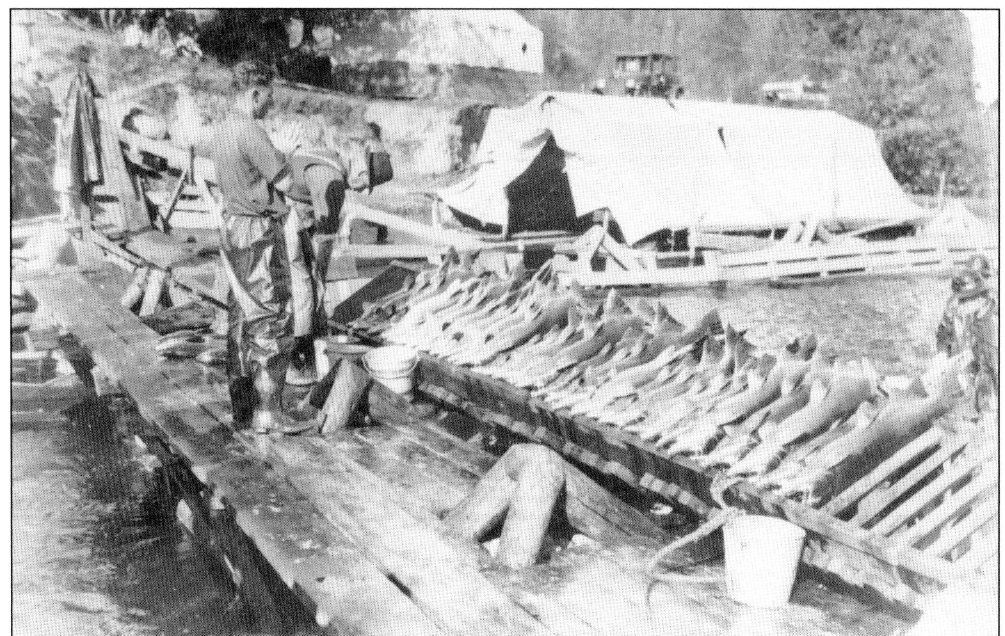

The salmon have been laid out on a rack. The fish hatchery workers take the eggs out of the female salmon. Sperm will be taken out of the male salmon and used to fertilize the eggs. The fertilized eggs will then be taken to the fish hatchery to be hatched, raised, and released. (Courtesy of John Norton.)

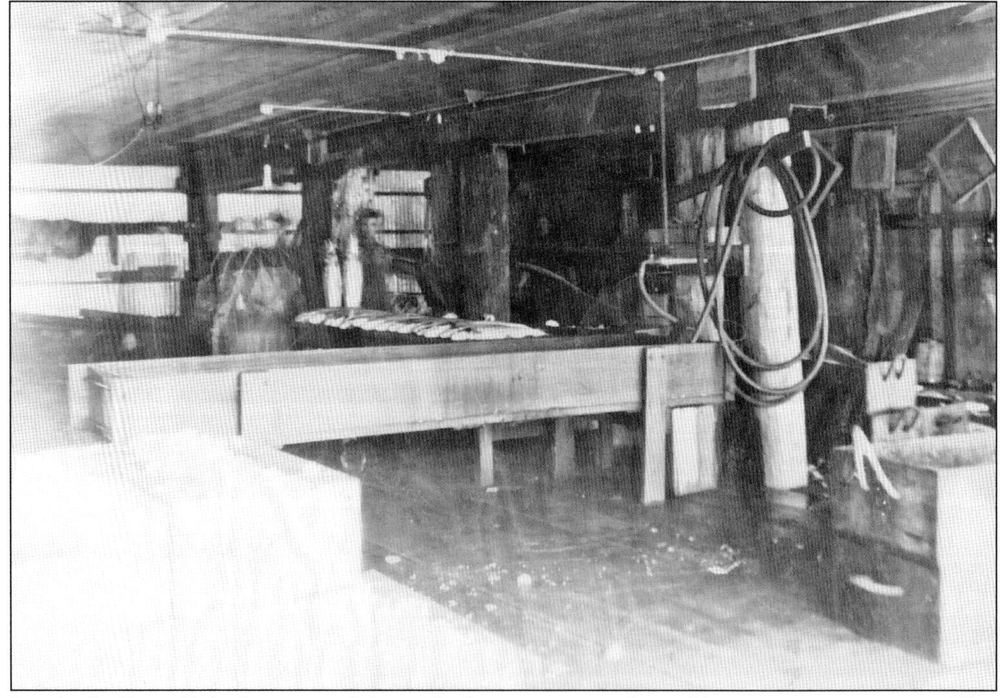

Inside the Doty Fish Company, fish are laid out on a wooden table awaiting processing. This operation has made the floor wet and slick. Doty Fish was owned and operated by C.W. Doty, an early settler and businessman in Kalama.

Five

The Port of Kalama

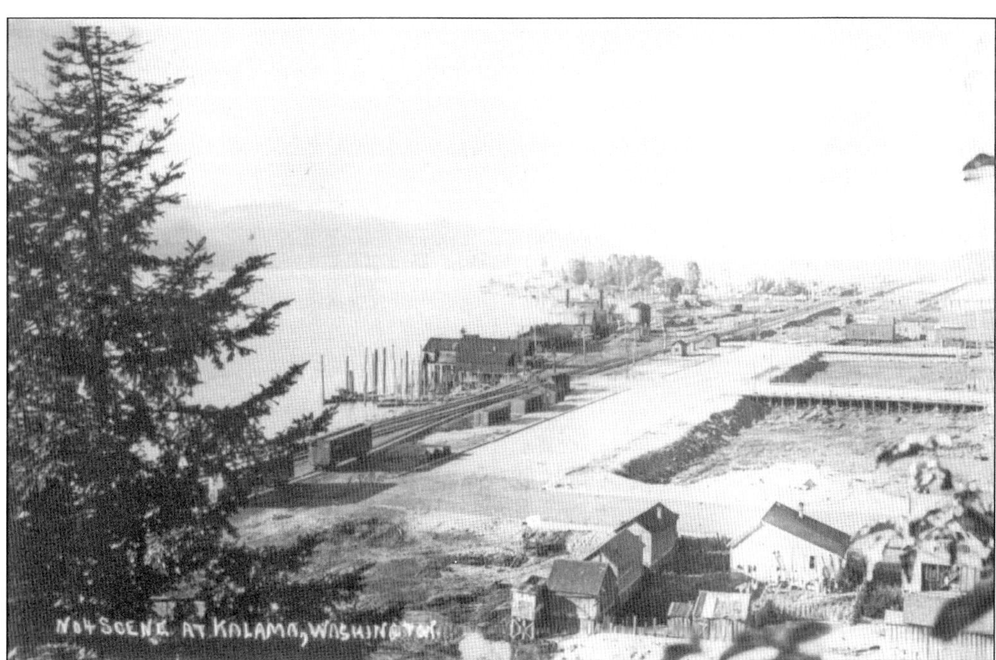

In 1929, understanding the need to improve shipping conditions, the citizens of Kalama voted to form a port district. The port property included what was known as the Kalama River Watershed, which included territory from the community of Carrolls to an area known as Martin's Bluff. The creation of a port district enabled the construction of a dock. Companies exporting logs, veneer, shingles, and lumber were the main businesses to lease property in the beginning.

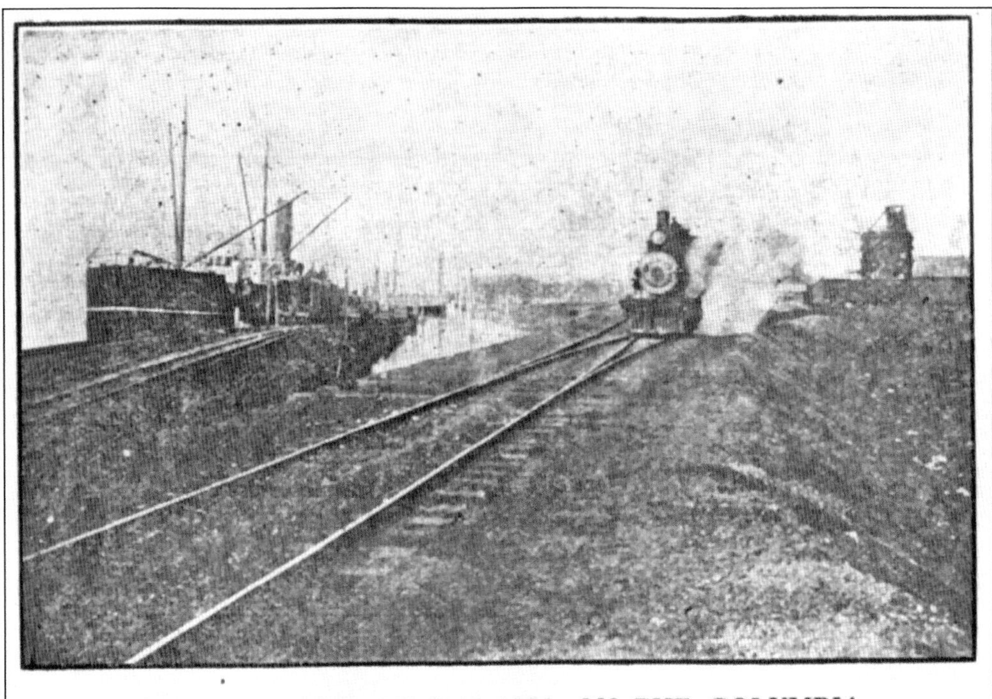

This early picture illustrates the location of the railroad's right-of-way by the waterfront at the Port of Kalama. The port district had 600 acres available for development. The first business to lease from the port in 1924 was the C.W. Fisher Company. (Courtesy of John Norton.)

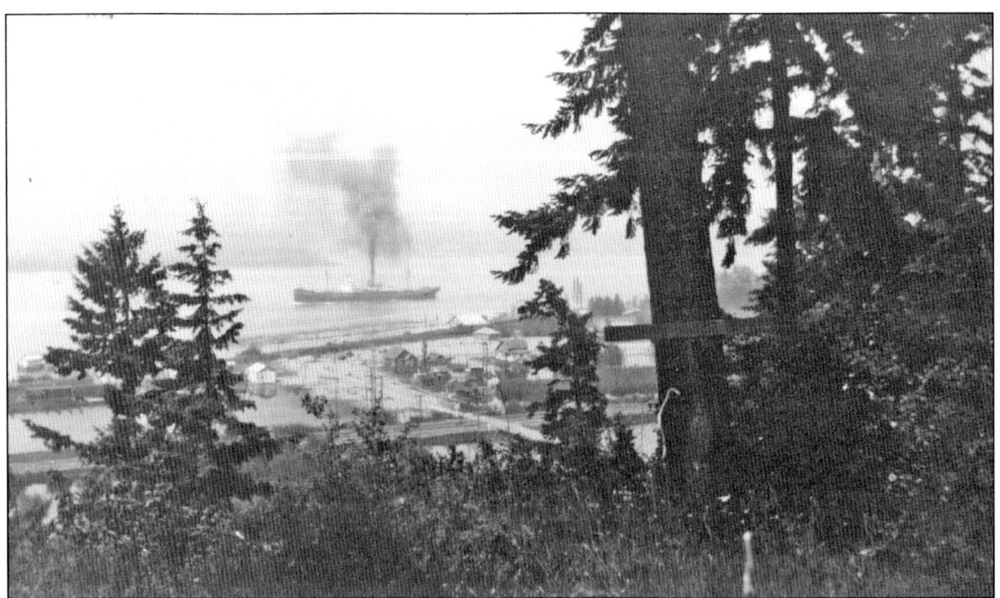

This view from a hill behind the city of Kalama shows an early Kalama waterfront. Shingle mills were the predominant industry at the port in the 1920s and 1930s. One shingle company was the Blue Ribbon Shingle Mill. (Courtesy of Lee Bunn.)

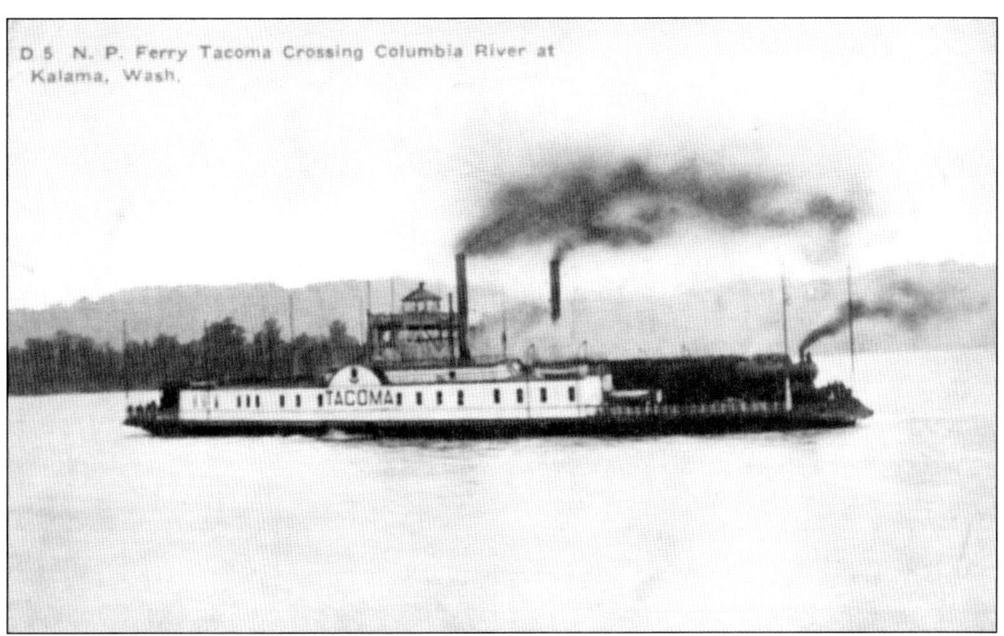

The Northern Pacific Railroad was not completed from Vancouver, Washington, to Puget Sound. There was a rail line from Portland, Oregon, to Goble, Oregon, across from Kalama. In order to get trains to Puget Sound, the Northern Pacific had a rail transport ferry, the *Tacoma*. The *Tacoma* was used to transport locomotives and railcars across the Columbia River to Kalama. (Courtesy of John Norton.)

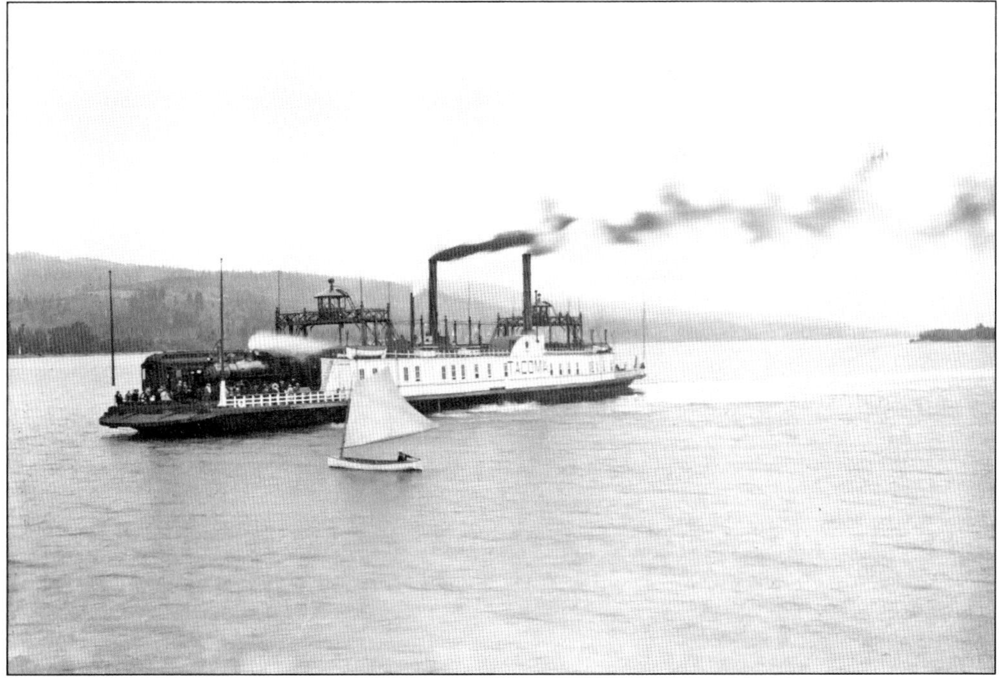

The crossing of the Columbia River by the rail transfer ferry *Tacoma* took about 20 minutes. The locomotive is positioned to the front of the ferry, and beside it are passenger cars. In the foreground is a small fishing boat, which was part of the Butterfly fleet. (Courtesy of Joanna Boatman.)

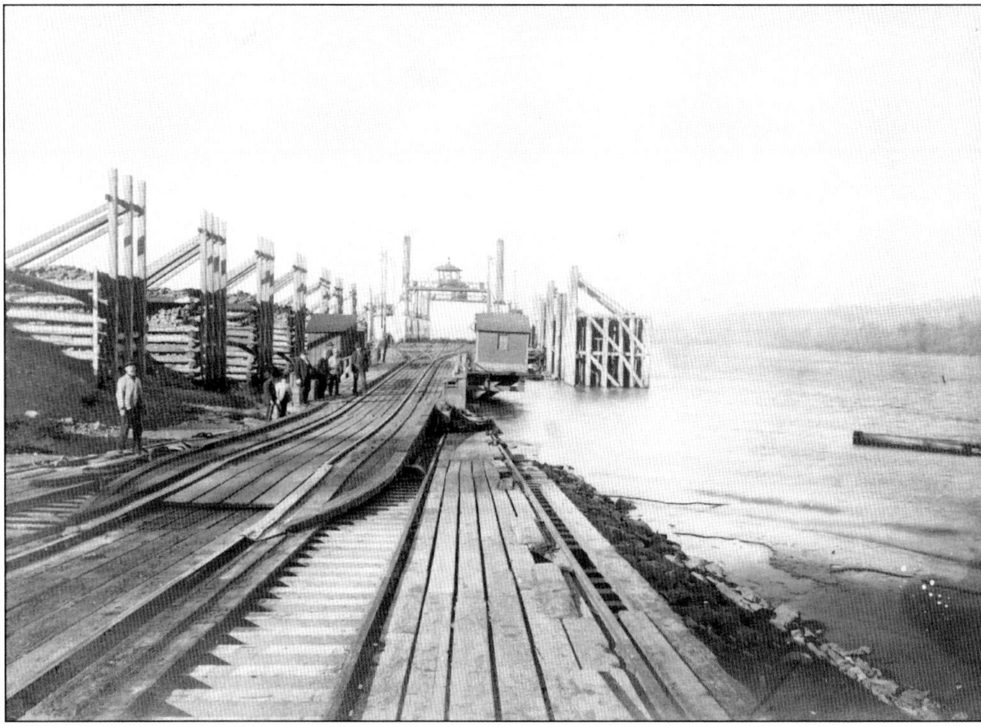

Pictured is the dock for the rail transfer ferry *Tacoma*. The dock was located on the Columbia River across from the small settlement of Goble, Oregon. The locomotive and its cars exited the ferry on these rails. The locomotive was reconnected with its freight and passenger cars and continued north to Puget Sound. (Courtesy of Joanna Boatman.)

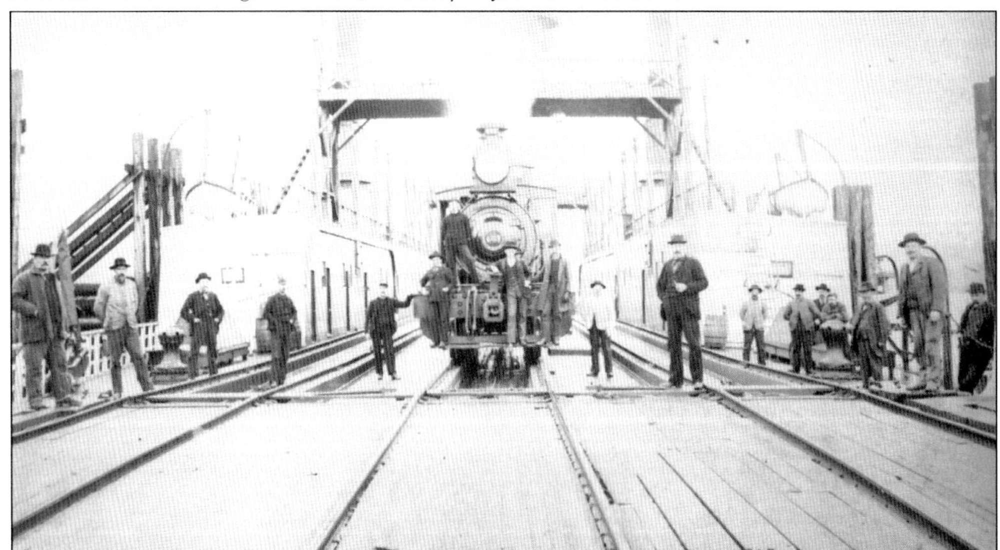

A locomotive is exiting the rail transfer ferry *Tacoma*, having just crossed the Columbia River from Goble, Oregon. The *Tacoma* was in service from 1883 until 1910 and ended its career on Puget Sound. The *Tacoma* was no longer needed when rail lines from Vancouver, Washington, connected with lines at Kalama. This created a single rail line from Vancouver to Puget Sound, eliminating the need to transfer trains across the Columbia. (Courtesy of Joanna Boatman.)

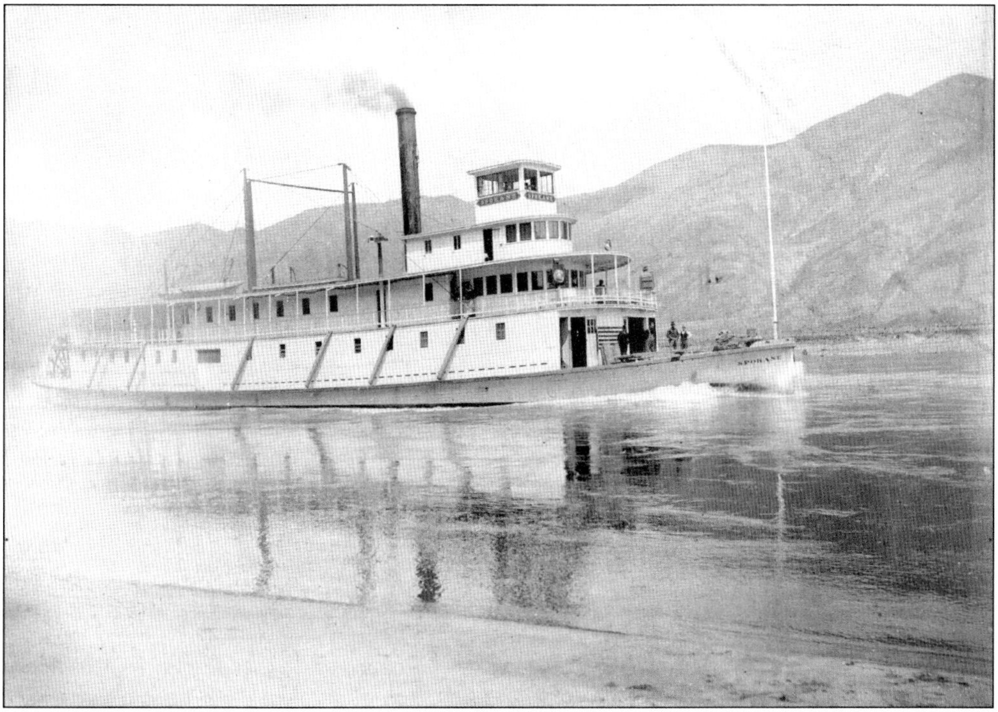

The Columbia River was the main way to transport both people and goods in the 1800s and early 1900s. Pictured is the stern-wheeler *Spokane*. It was built in 1891 and licensed for 125 passengers and had 19 staterooms. The boat ended its career on the lower Columbia River. (Courtesy of John Norton.)

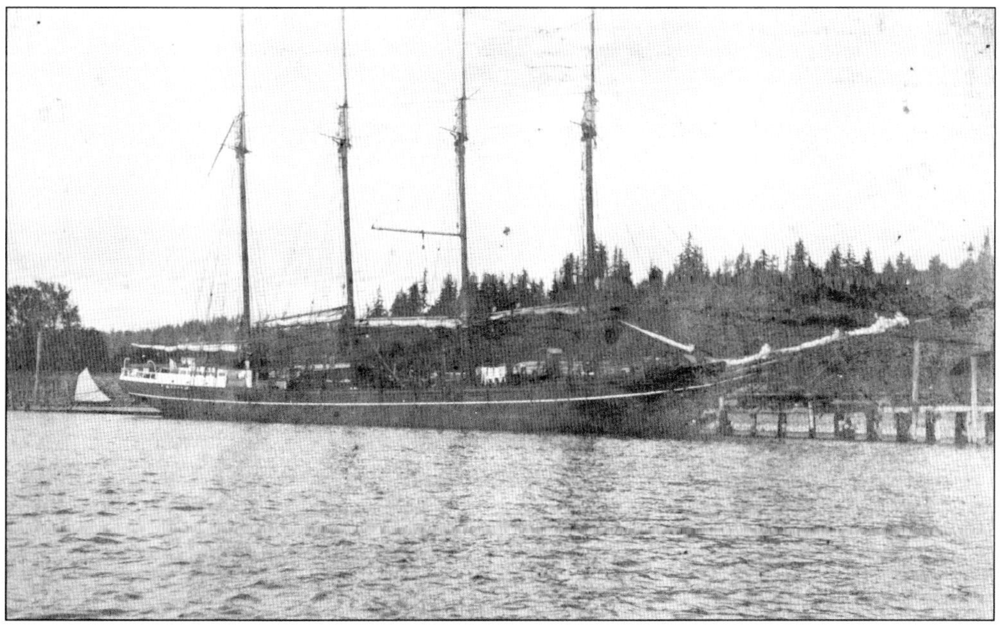

This old four-mast schooner is seen docked at Kalama. It was used for fishing in Alaska. It spent the winter docked at what was called the "Old Salmon Trace," so named because it was the dock where salmon were unloaded. (Courtesy of Joanna Boatman.)

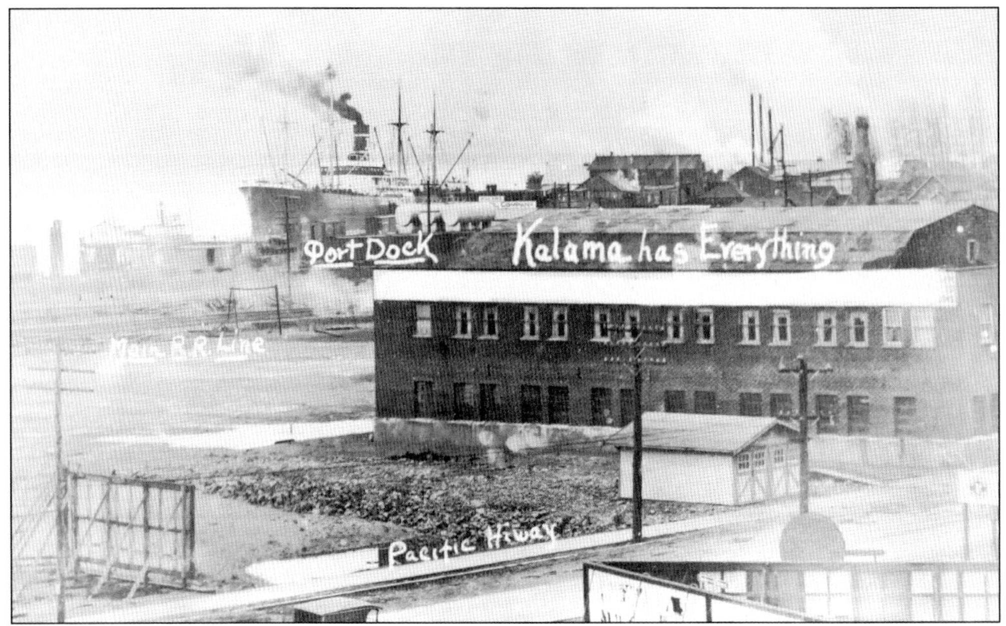

The port of Kalama was blessed with water deep enough to accommodate the docking of larger ships, like the one pictured here. The rail line is situated close to the dock, which helped facilitate shipping. (Courtesy of John Norton.)

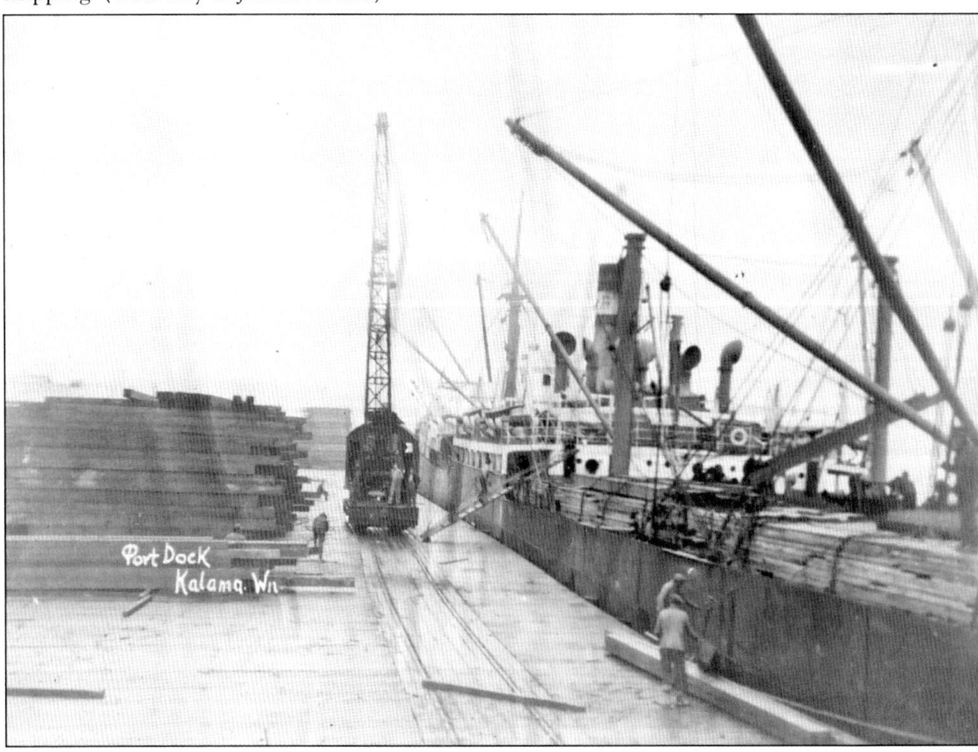

A crane at the Port of Kalama is loading lumber on a ship. The shipping of lumber products was one of the main uses for the port in the early 20th century. One of the primary products being shipped at this time was shakes. (Courtesy Port of Kalama.)

A steam crane is loading rail scrap at the Port of Kalama. In the 1940s, the port was also the site for the partial scrapping of the ship USS *Oregon*, an Indiana-class battleship commissioned in 1893. The *Oregon* served in the Spanish-American War. It was decided at the outbreak of World War II that its value as scrap was more important than its historical significance. (Courtesy of the Port of Kalama.)

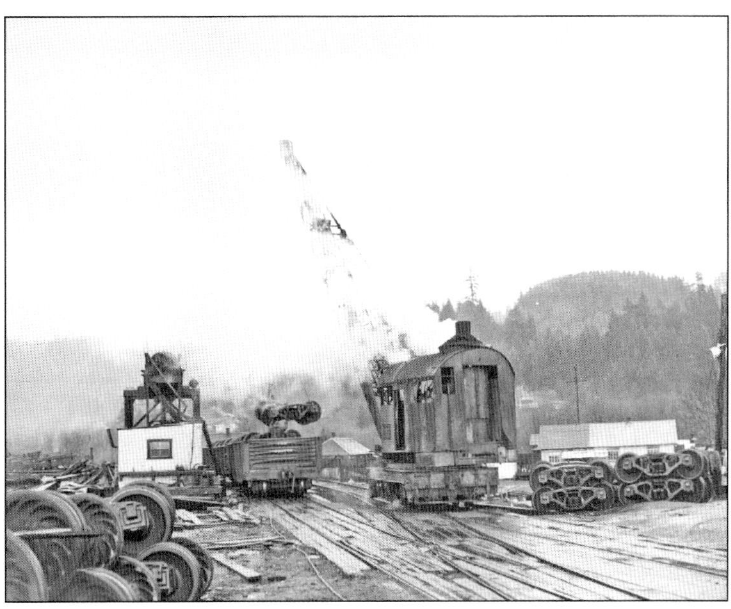

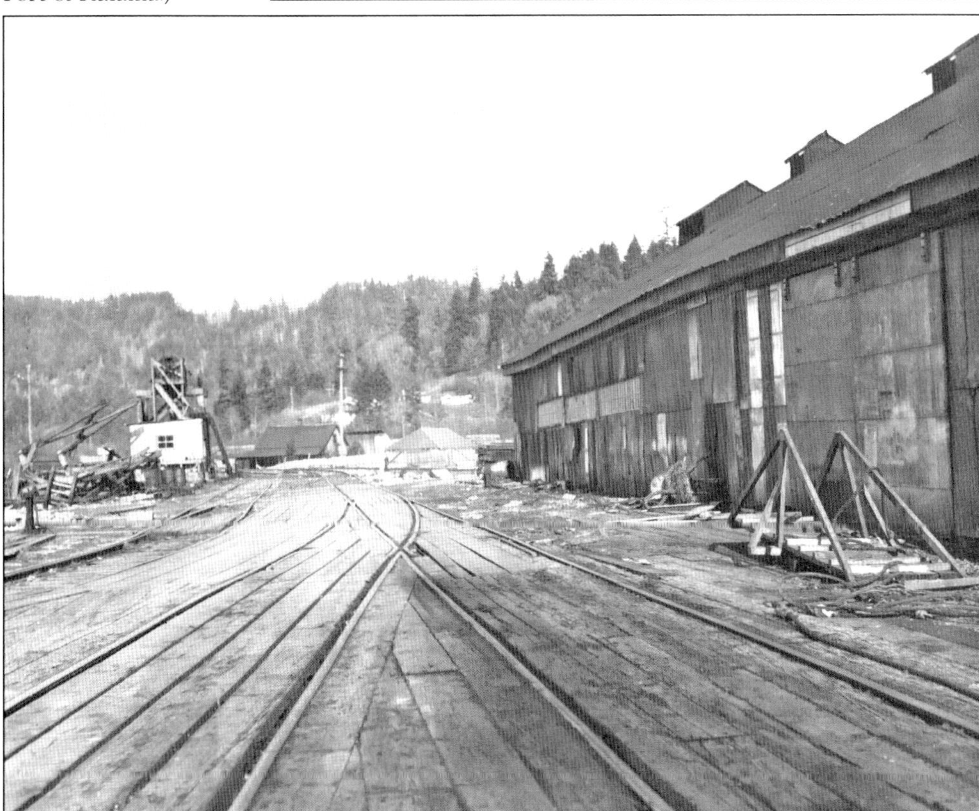

An early-1930s picture of the Port of Kalama shows old port buildings and a rail line. Having a good port capable of handling big ships and easy access to both rail lines and roads made Kalama very appealing to businesses and contributed to the success of the port. (Courtesy of the Port of Kalama.)

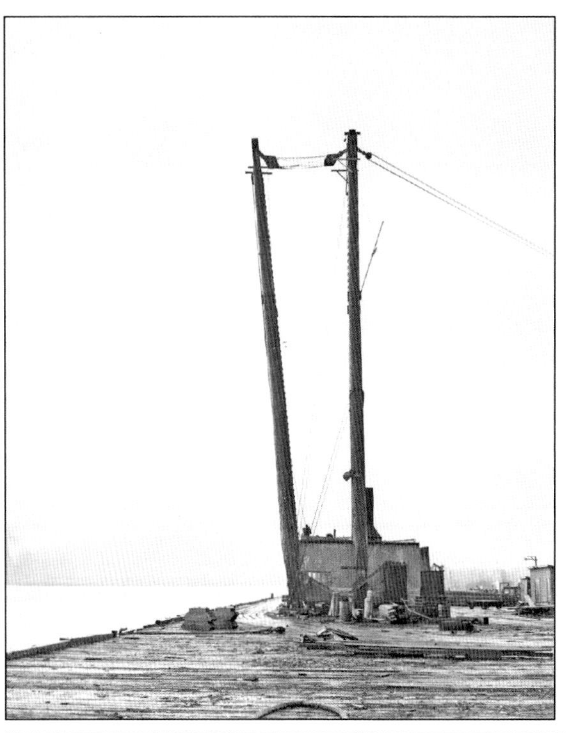

This 1940s photograph shows a crane on the dock at the Port of Kalama on the Columbia River. The Columbia River is the fourth-largest river in the United States by volume and is navigable by large ships to Portland, Oregon; barges can go inland to Lewiston, Idaho. Cranes were and still are used to load and unload a variety of goods at the Port of Kalama. (Courtesy of the Port of Kalama.)

Here are logs tied to the old port docks in the 1940s. Log rafts were commonly used to store logs for future use. It was common in the 1940s to see rafts of logs in the many sloughs of the Columbia River. (Courtesy of the Port of Kalama.)

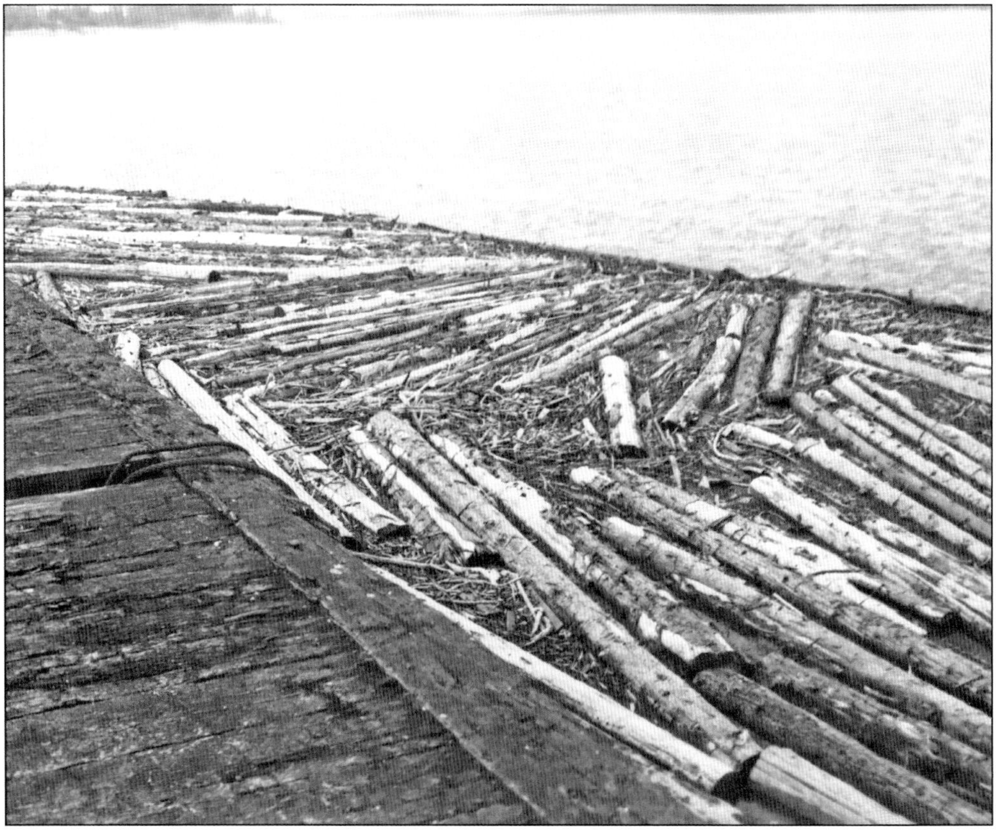

Six

Building Kalama

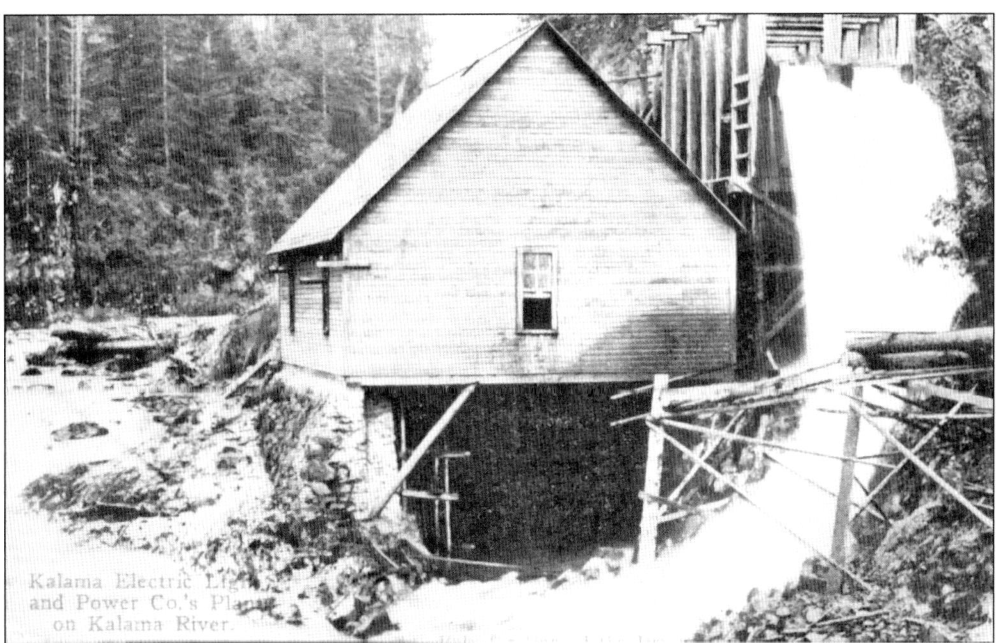

On September 6, 1903, at 6:00 in the evening, citizens with ingenuity and ambition turned on "the juice" of the first hydroelectric power plant to provide the city of Kalama with electricity. The power plant was built on the upper reaches of the Kalama River by Kalama Electric Light and Power. The Kalama was the first river to support a hydroelectric power plant. In the beginning, the power to the town was only turned on only when it started to get dark. Later, the company supplied power to Woodland and Kelso. (Courtesy of John Norton.)

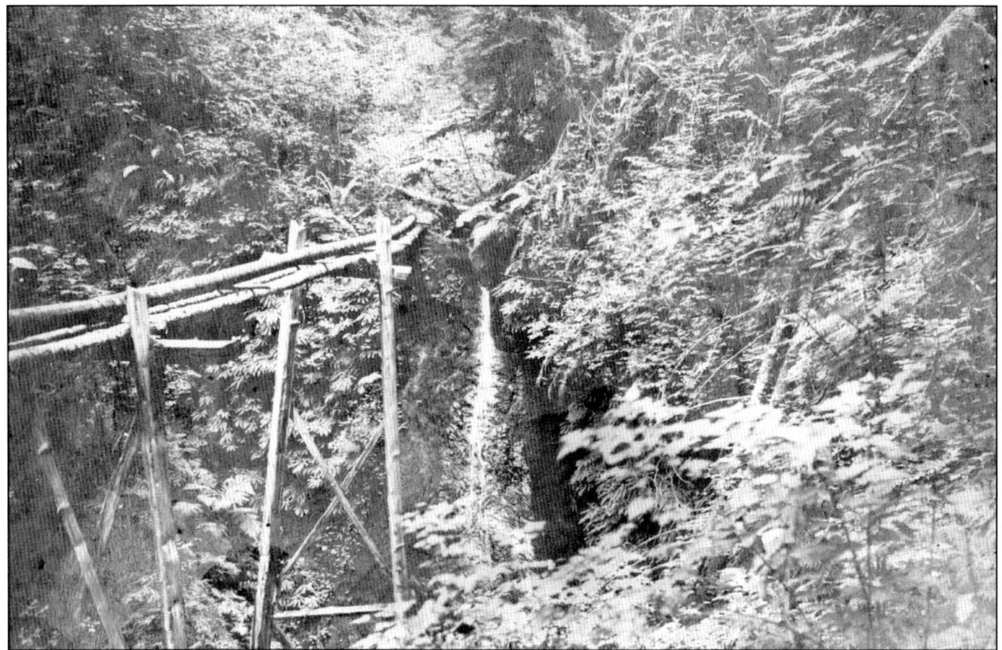

The original water supply for the city of Kalama was taken from a stream called Italian Creek. The water ran through wooden pipes suspended by wire. Later, the city began to get its water from the Kalama River. Kalama is reputed to have the best-tasting water in the United States. (Courtesy of Joanna Boatman.)

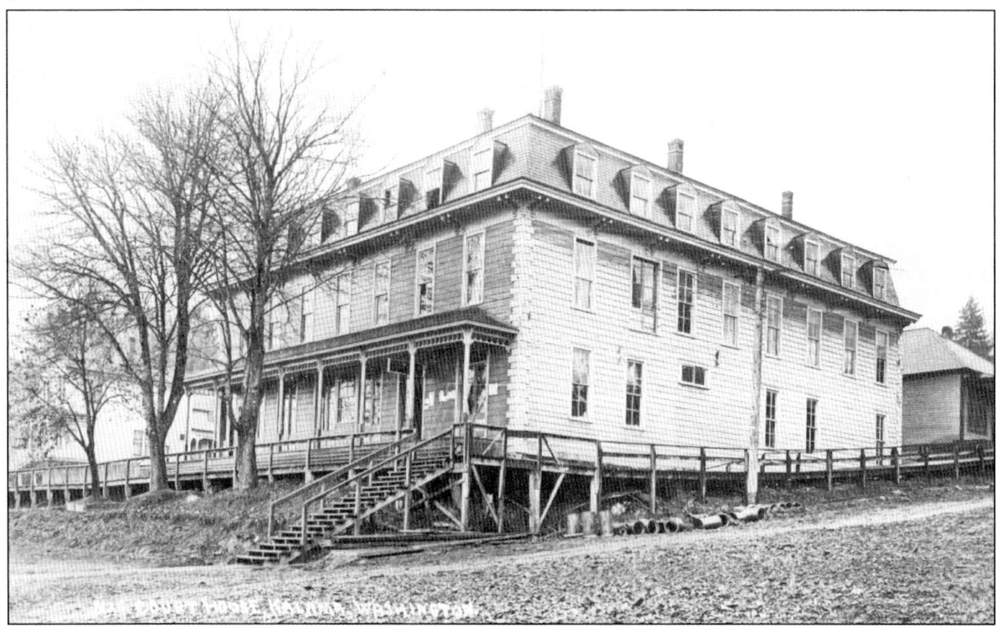

Finished in 1871, the Kazano House was a hotel built by the Northern Pacific Railroad for business, employees, and travelers. The City of Kalama purchased the building from the railroad for $5,000, and it served as the Cowlitz County Courthouse from 1873 to 1922. Some employees lived on the top floor of the structure, and the jailhouse was located in the back. (Courtesy of John Norton.)

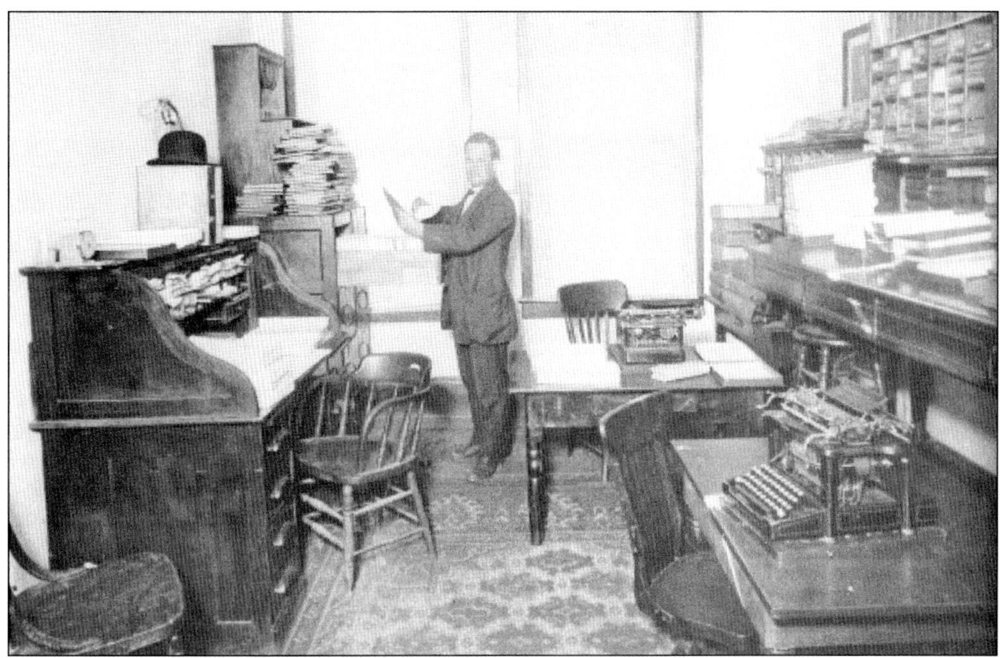

The first Kalama Post Office was located on the waterfront but then moved to a building on First Street. The Kalama Post Office started rural delivery in 1915. Ed Schauble is pictured in the post office in the early 1900s. The Schaubles were a large family and settled in the area known as Spencer Creek. (Courtesy of Pat Kennedy.)

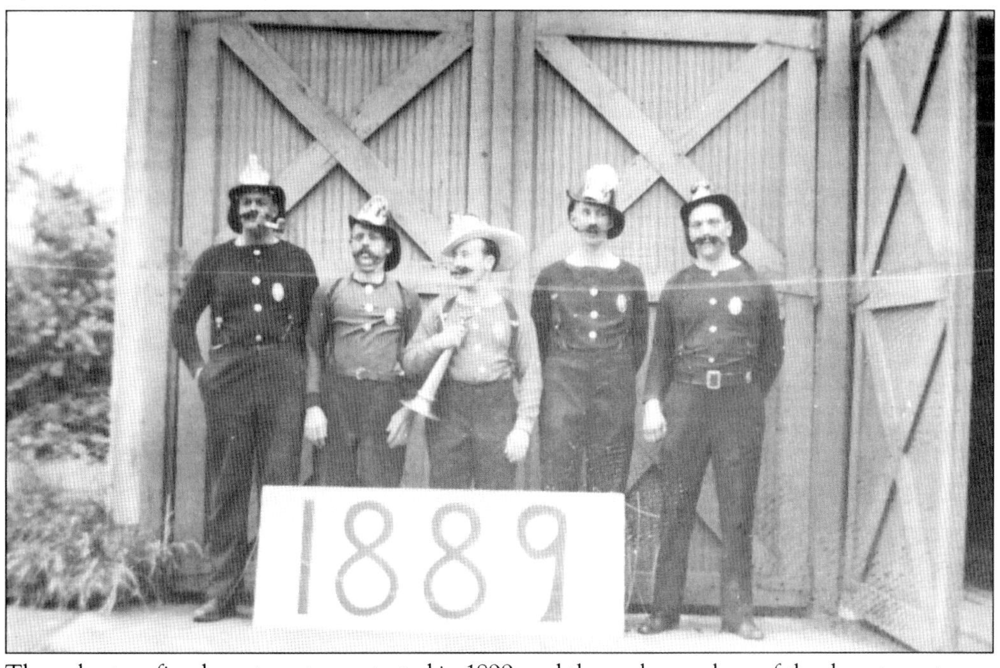

The volunteer fire department was started in 1899, and the male members of the department were required to be between the ages of 15 and 50. The dues to be a fireman were $1 a year. Kalama firemen pictured are, from left to right, Ernie House, unidentified, Monk Gilbert, Ralph Aslin, and Art Spreadborough. (Courtesy of Catherine Applegate.)

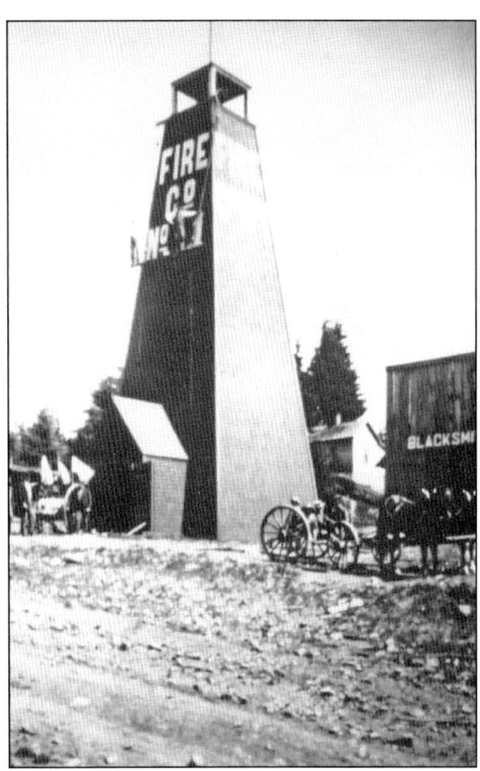

This is the Kalama fire tower built in the 1800s. Hoses used to fight fire were made out of cloth, and this tower was where the hoses were hung to dry. The tower was located up the hill from the Kalama flats and was adjacent to a local blacksmith.

A fire truck is seen parked in front of the Kalama Fire Department in the 1930s. Standing on the back of the truck are Darrell Coffey (left) and Willard Owens. Lyle Ficklyn stands in front of the truck. (Courtesy of Catherine Applegate.)

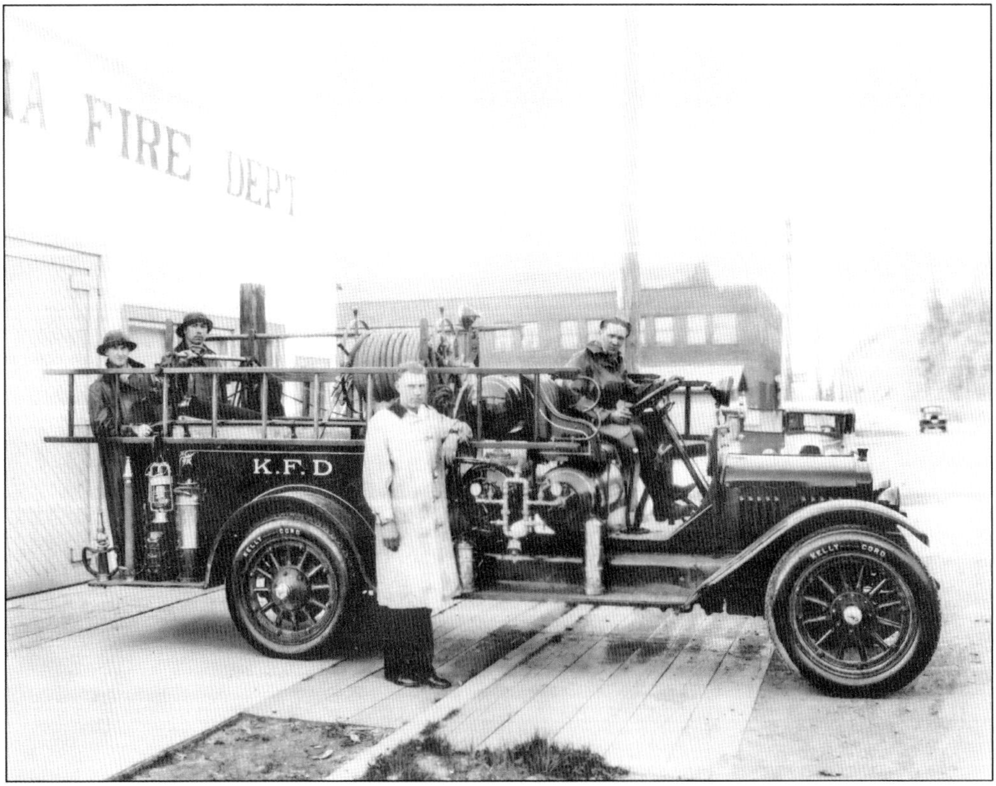

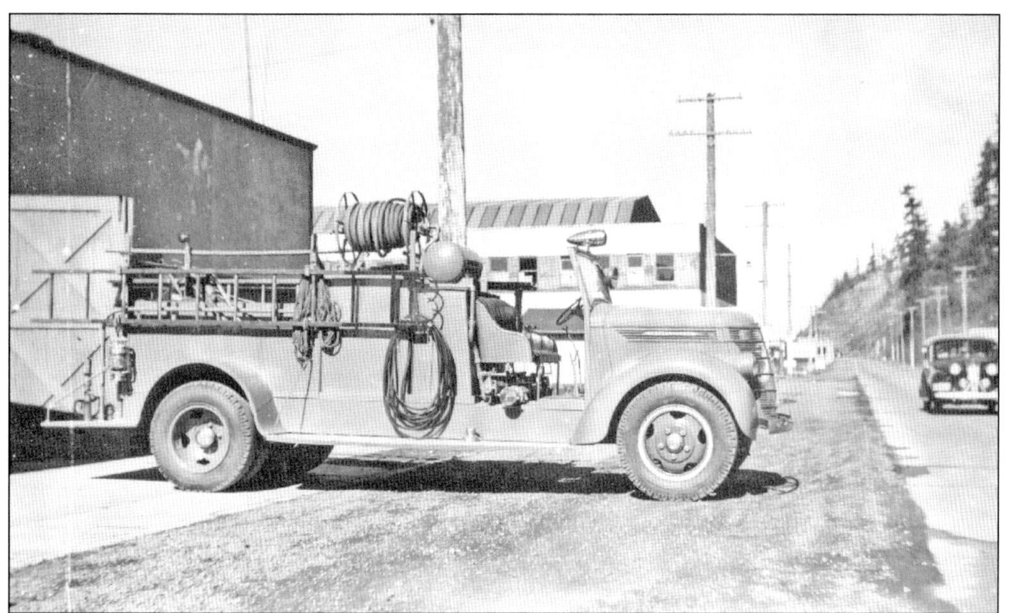

A Kalama fire truck is ready to go out on call. Kalama's firemen were volunteers at this time and were on call 24/7. An active and committed volunteer fire department was critical to how Kalama survived several devastating fires, one of which destroyed its business district.

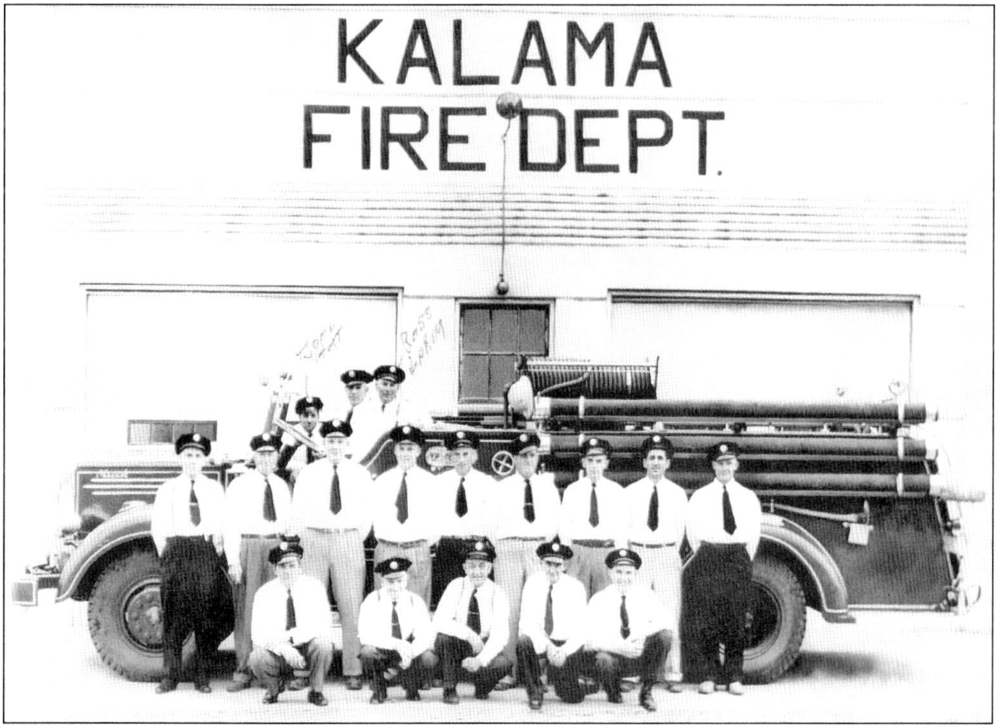

In the 1930s, a group of Kalama volunteer firemen poses in front of a truck. Most of the buildings constructed in Kalama were made of wood, which made them very susceptible to fire. Perched in the truck are, from left to right, John Hart, unidentified, and Ross LaRoy; the others are unidentified. (Courtesy of Brian LaRoy.)

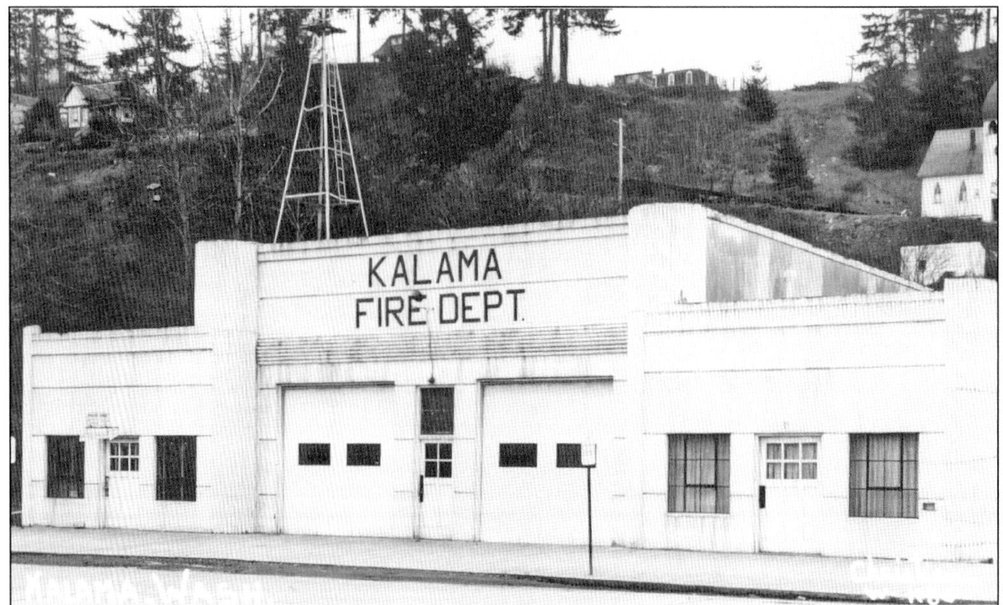

The Kalama Fire Department was located on First Street until 1982, when it moved across the street into newer, more modern facilities. This building was refurbished and became the location of city offices, the city council chambers, and the library. The city offices later moved to the Heritage Building, but the library and the city council chambers remain in the old fire department.

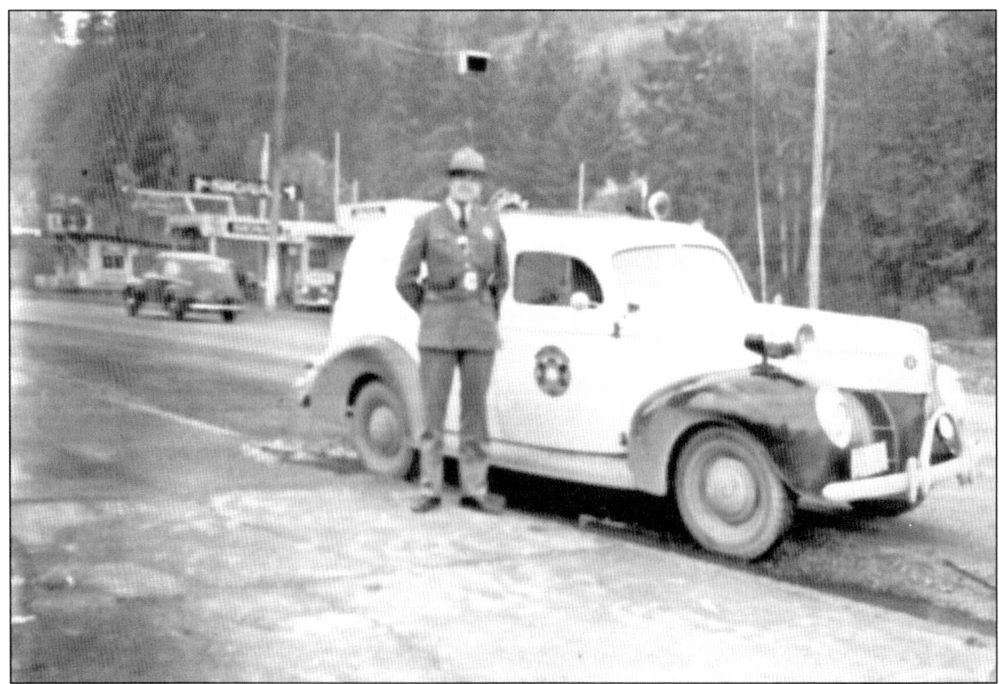

This 1930s photograph shows Washington State patrol officer Ted Bishop. Kalama had its own police force within the city limits. County residents were served by the Washington State Patrol and the Cowlitz County Sheriff's Office.

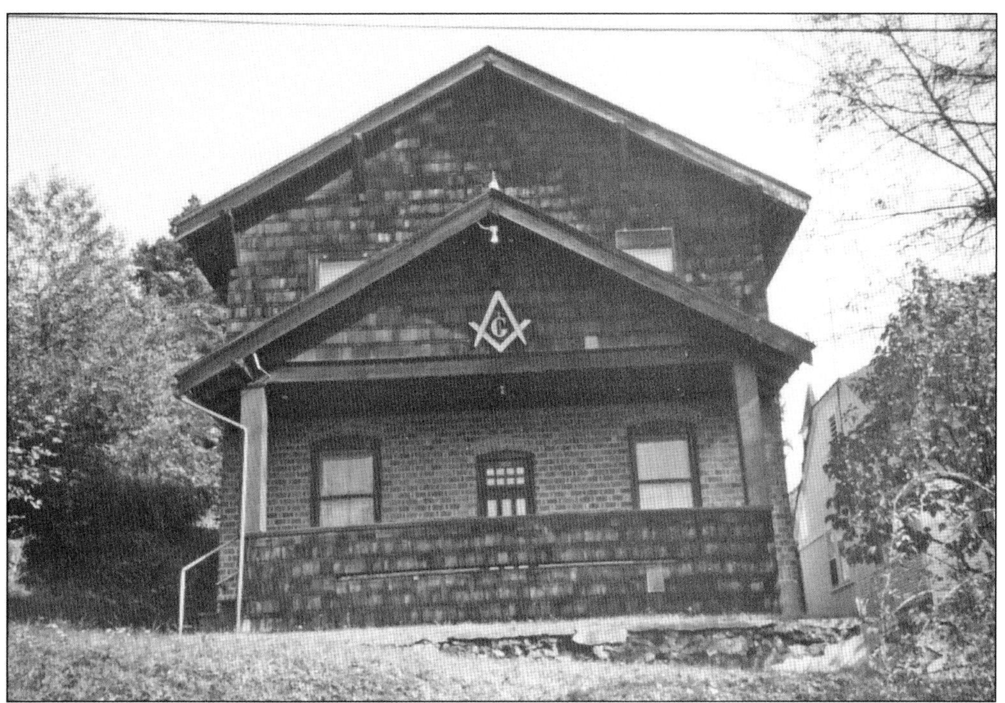

The Masonic lodge in Kalama was chartered on September 21, 1871. In 1872, Kalama Masonic Lodge No. 17 had 27 members, and its master was Lewis VanFleet. The lodge built a Masonic hall in the 1800s and constructed the Masonic temple, pictured in 1922, using materials from the original hall. Today, the former Masonic hall is a private residence.

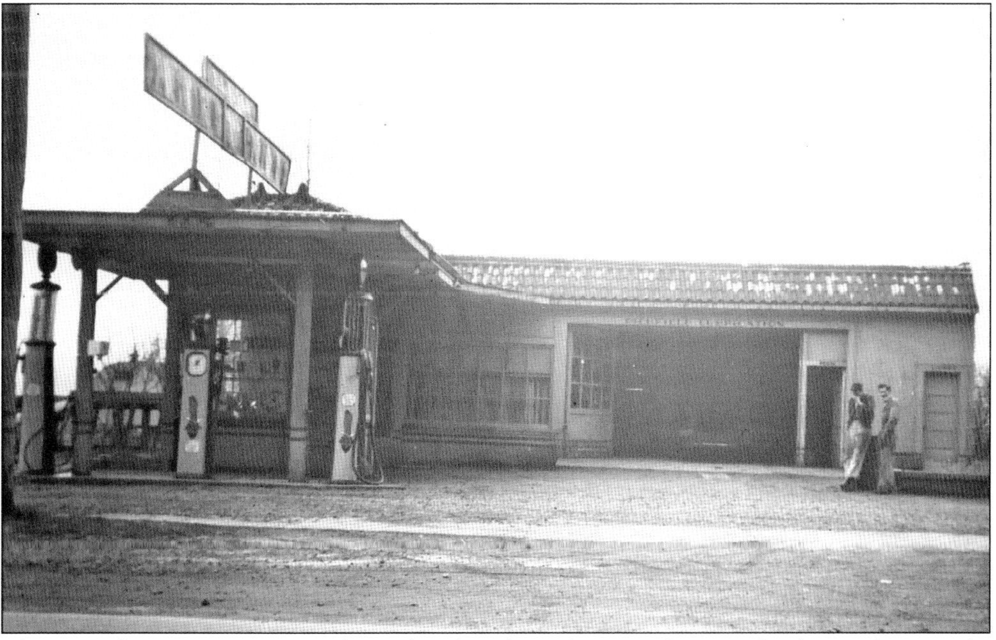

There is only one service station located within the Kalama city limits today, but in the past, the city had many service stations. This is representative of the kinds of gas stations found in the city in the early and mid-20th century.

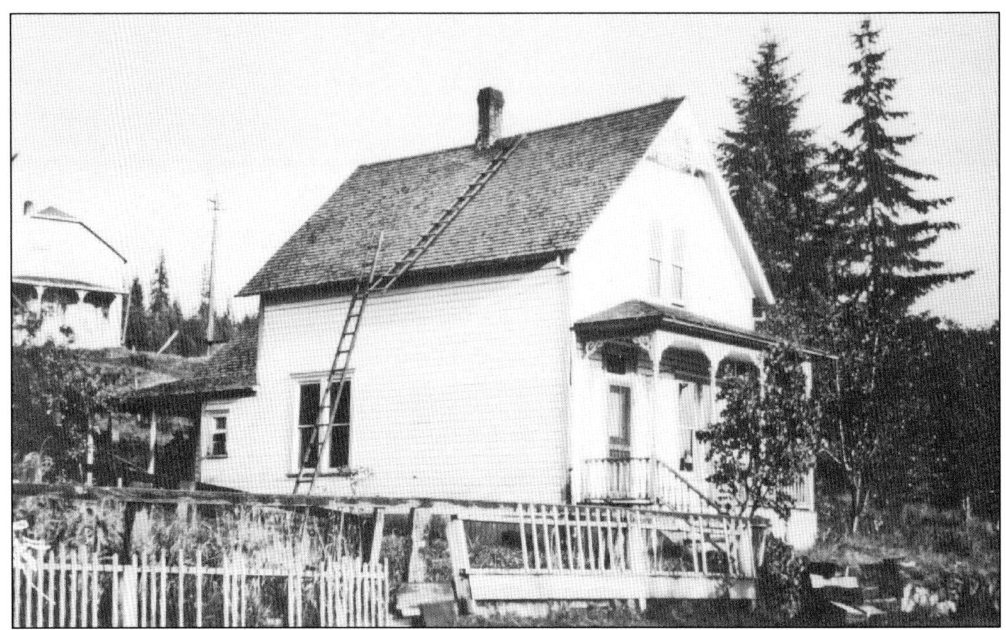

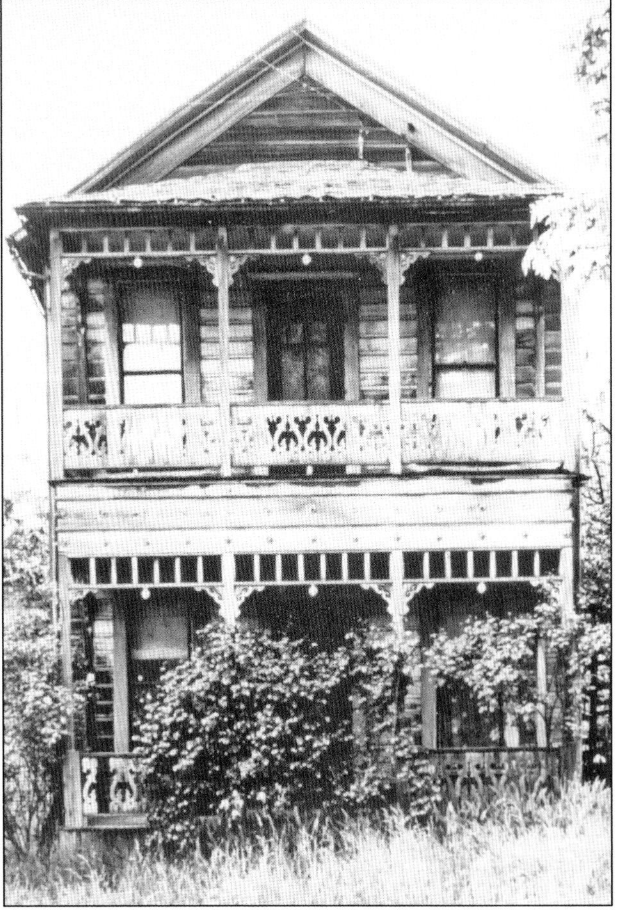

This house is typical of the kind of wood-frame construction commonly used for houses and buildings in the Pacific Northwest from first settlements to the present. This dependence on wood-frame construction makes communities like Kalama prone to problems caused by structural fires.

This house was built by a Civil War veteran named Duvall. Later, it became the residence of George Gore, who was one of the captains of the rail transfer ferry *Tacoma*. The home is located adjacent to the community building on Elm Street.

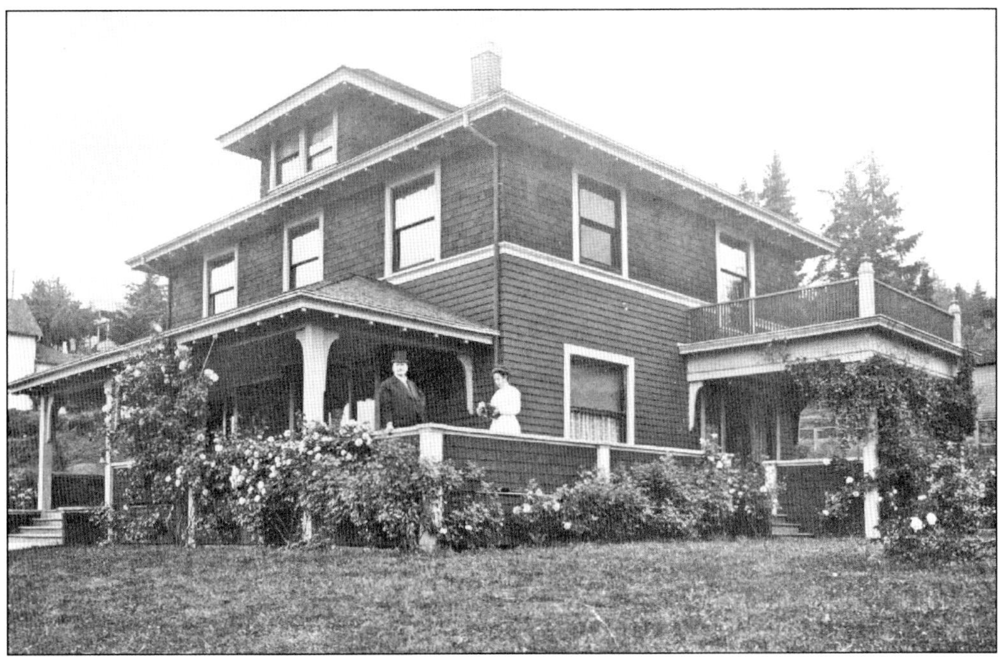

Built in the 1930s, this was the Billeau family's home. It later became known as the Galloway house. It is located on the corner of Third and Elm Streets in Kalama. (Courtesy of Lee Bunn.)

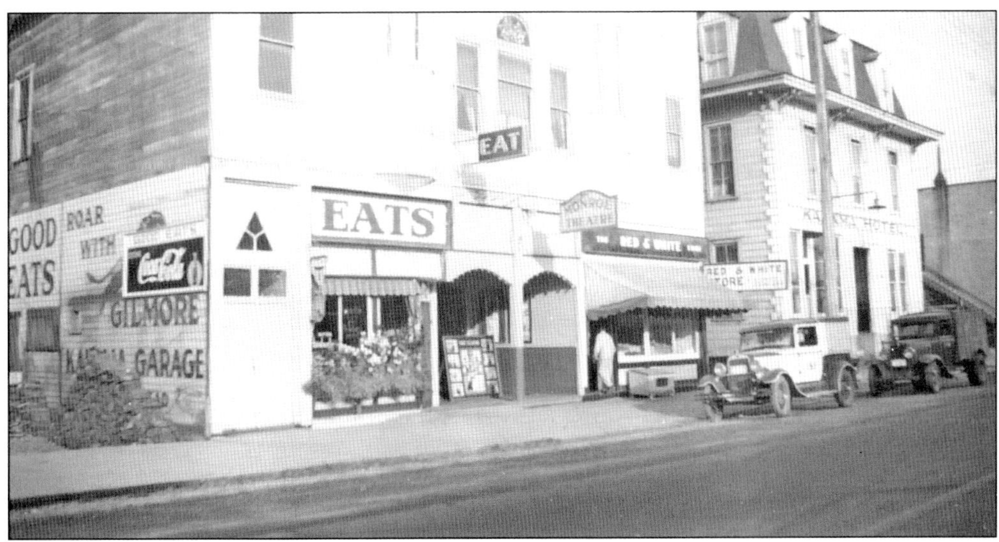

This is a street scene of early Kalama. From left to right are Clyde Long's Café, the Monroe Theatre, Shorty Comer's Store, and the Kalama Hotel. (Courtesy of Art Godfrey.)

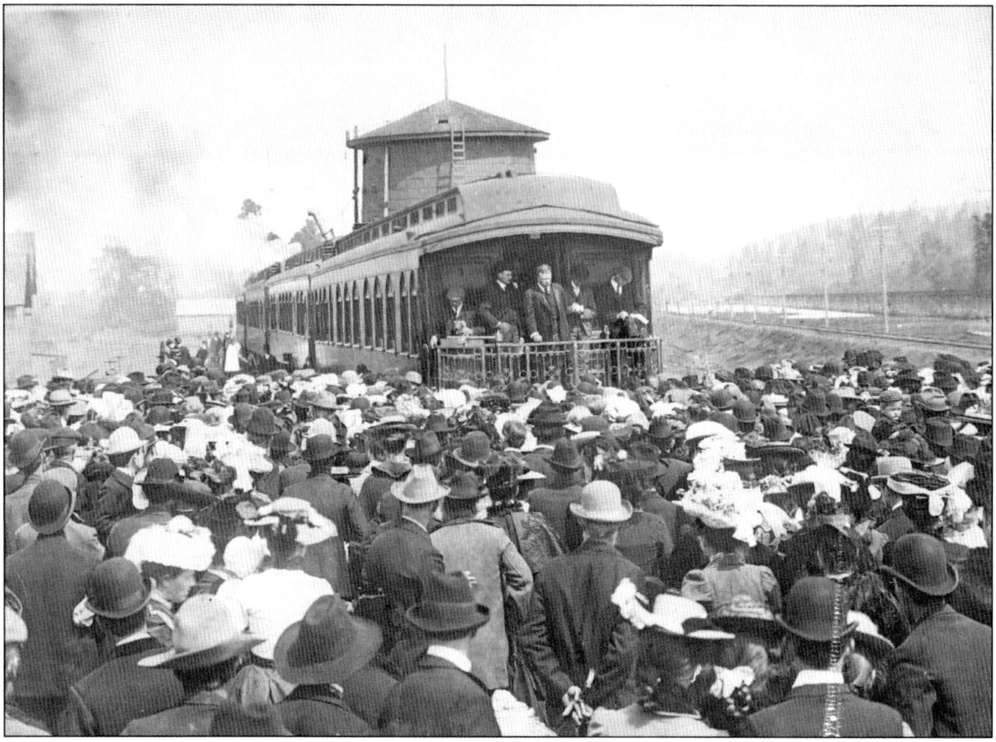

On May 22, 1903, Pres. Theodore Roosevelt crossed the Columbia River on the *Tacoma*. In Kalama, he spoke for 15 minutes to a crowd of 3,000. He was welcomed to the state of Washington by Governor McBride. (Courtesy of Joanna Boatman.)

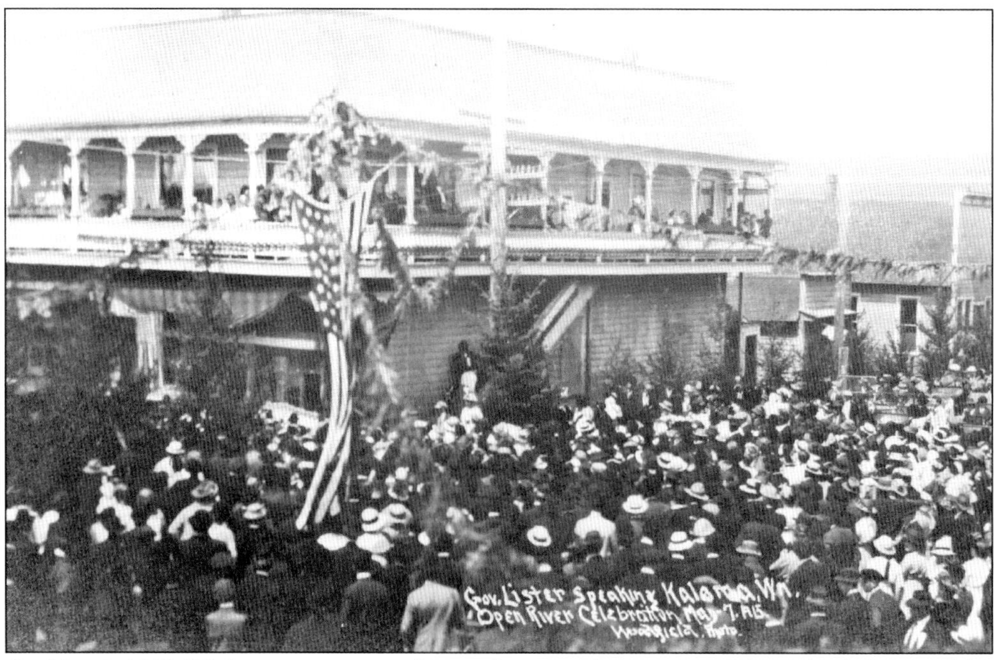

On May 7, 1915, Washington governor Ernest Lister spoke to a crowd from the balcony of the Fogerty Building. This building is now a grocery store. (Courtesy of Lee Bunn.)

Seven

FAITH AND FELLOWSHIP

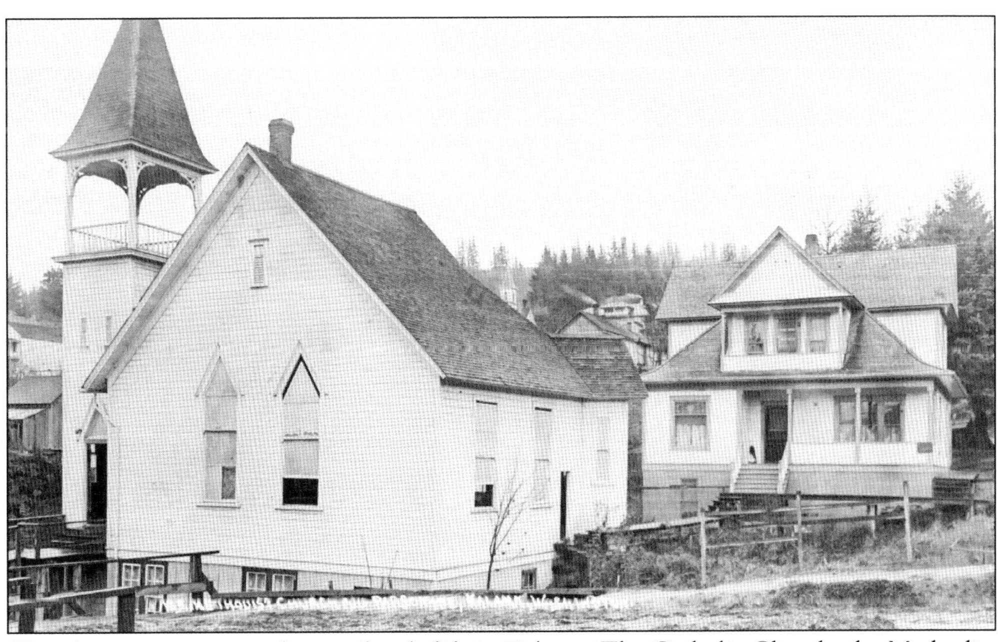

Churches were an integral part of early life in Kalama. The Catholic Church, the Methodist Church, and the Congregational Church all had congregations in the pioneer community. Pictured is the first Methodist church in Kalama. Later, this building was torn down, and a new church was built to replace it. The Methodist church today is a vital part of the Kalama community. (Author's collection.)

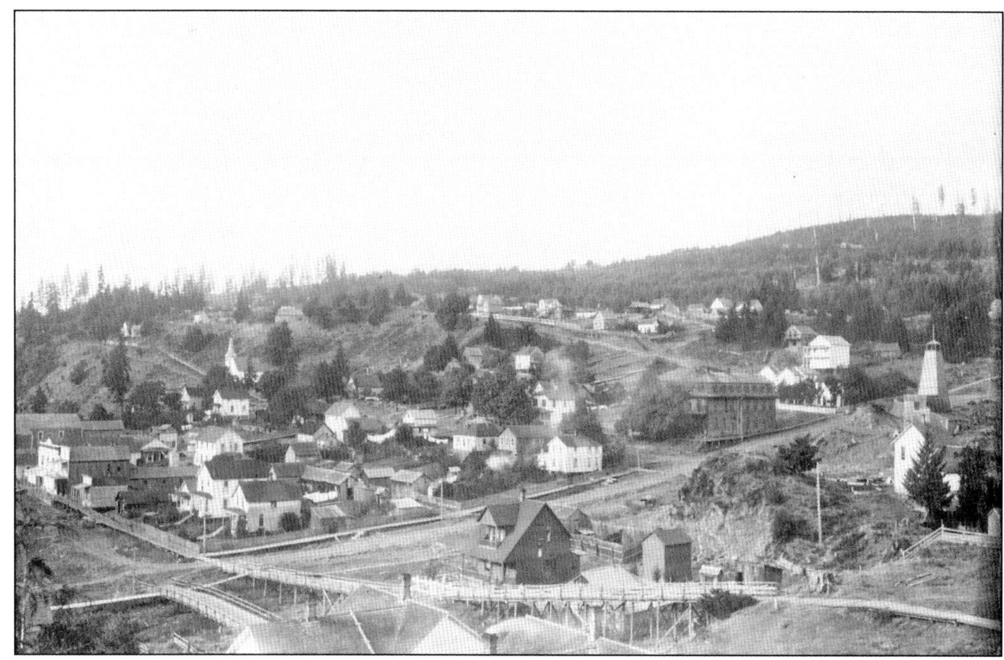
This view of early Kalama shows the Congregational church on the hill at the left in the picture. The church can be identified by its bell tower. To the right is the Kazano Hotel, and up the hill behind it is the fire tower. A rock quarry is located to the front of the hotel. The Congregational church no longer exists in Kalama.

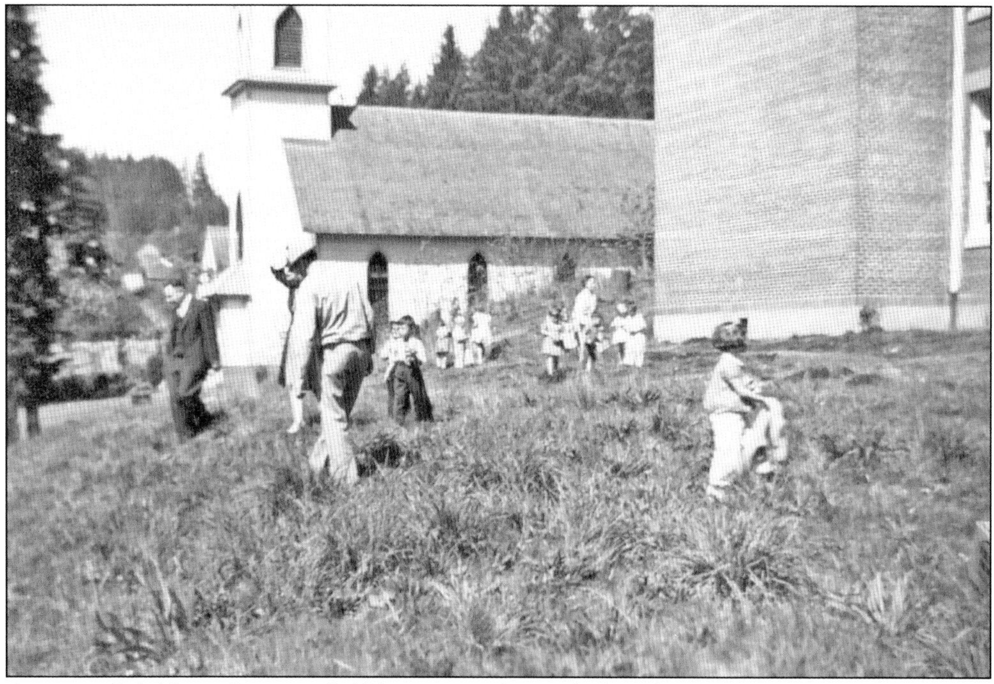
A group of children plays in a field by St. Joseph's Catholic Church. The kids are enjoying an Easter egg hunt. Kalama High School is the building to the right. (Courtesy of St. Joseph's Catholic Church.)

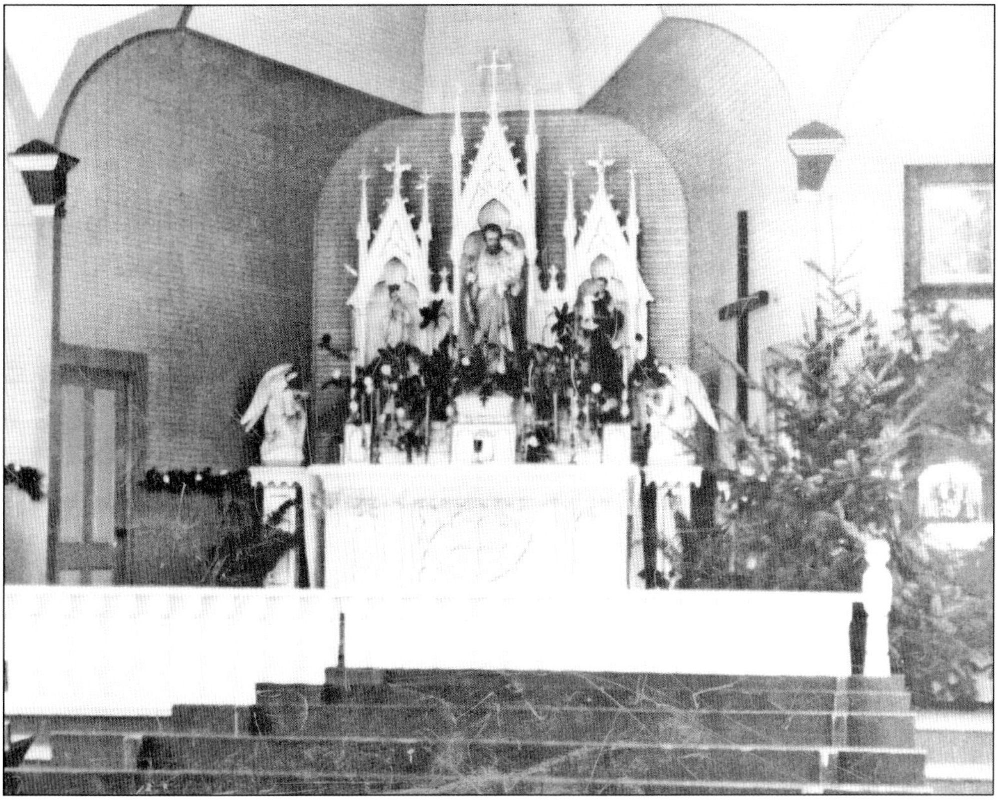

The first Mass was celebrated in 1874 in a private home. The first St. Joseph's was built in 1876, and the church was rebuilt in 1909. This is an interior view, showing the altar of the St. Joseph's Catholic Church built in 1909. The altar came from Italy by a ship that traveled around Cape Horn. (Courtesy of St. Joseph's Catholic Church.)

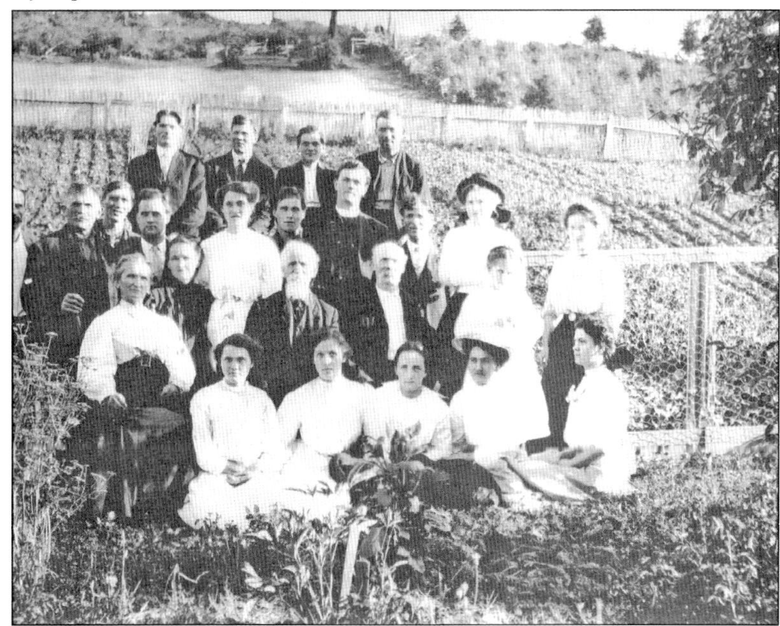

Members of St. Joseph's Catholic Church enjoy an outing around 1909. Father Capistran is pictured in the midst of the group. (Courtesy of St. Joseph's Catholic Church.)

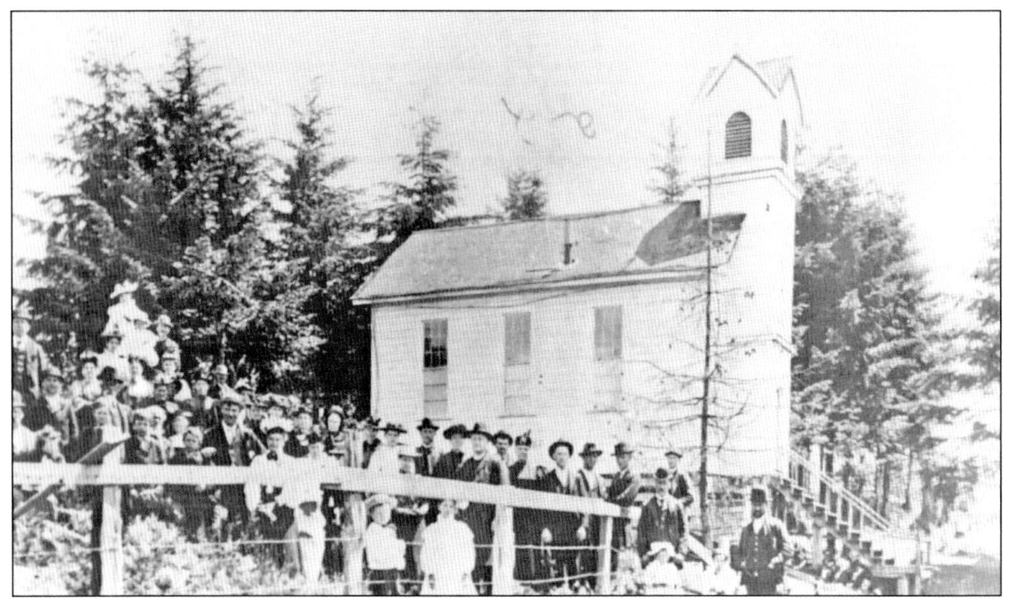

In 1881, the congregation of St. Joseph's Catholic Church is gathered for a group portrait at the old church that was built 1876. St. Joseph's Catholic Church was placed in the National Register of Historic Places in 1979. (Courtesy of St. Joseph's Catholic Church.)

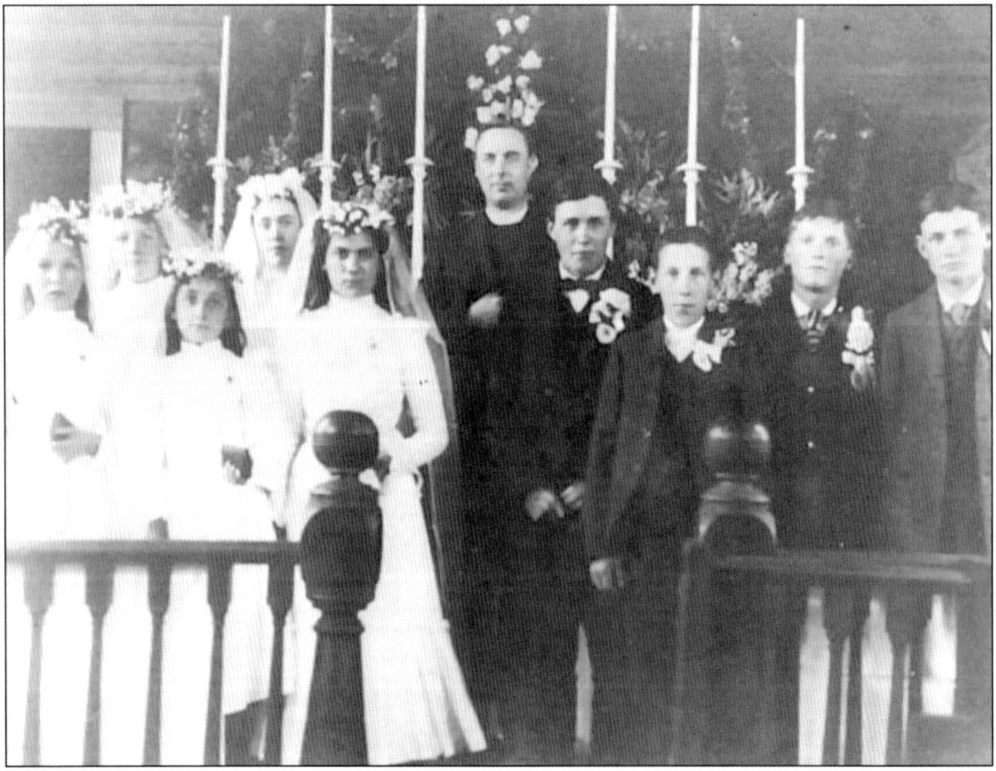

Rev. Fr. Ewald Soland, OFM, poses with a First Communion group in 1905. Father Soland once borrowed a horse and a canoe and traveled 33 miles from Cowlitz Prairie in the north to Kalama in order to say Mass on Sunday. (Courtesy of St. Joseph's Catholic Church.)

The exterior of St. Joseph's Catholic Church is seen in 1909. Father Blanchet had founded the mission St. Francis Xavier in 1838 at Cowlitz Prairie in Toledo. First built in 1876, St. Joseph was one of six churches belonging to the Cowlitz Prairie Missions. The steeple of St. Joseph's was used as a navigational marker in the late 1800s and early 1900s by mariners piloting ships on the Columbia River. (Courtesy of St. Joseph's Catholic Church.)

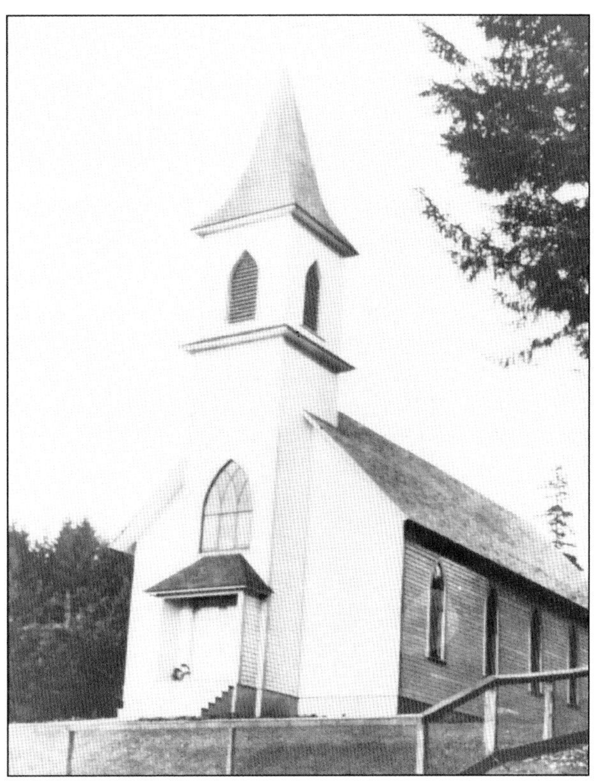

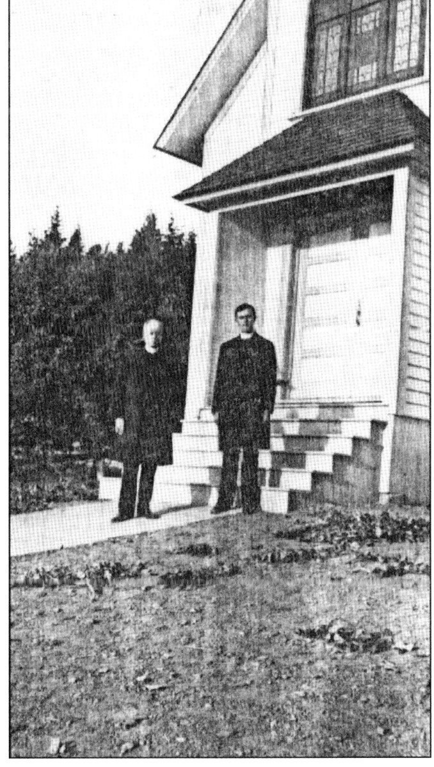

Pictured in front of the steps of St. Joseph's Catholic Church on October 10, 1909, are Bishop Edward O'Dea (left), who was the first bishop of Seattle, and Fr. John Capistran, OFM. They were there for the blessing of the new church. (Courtesy of St. Joseph's Catholic Church.)

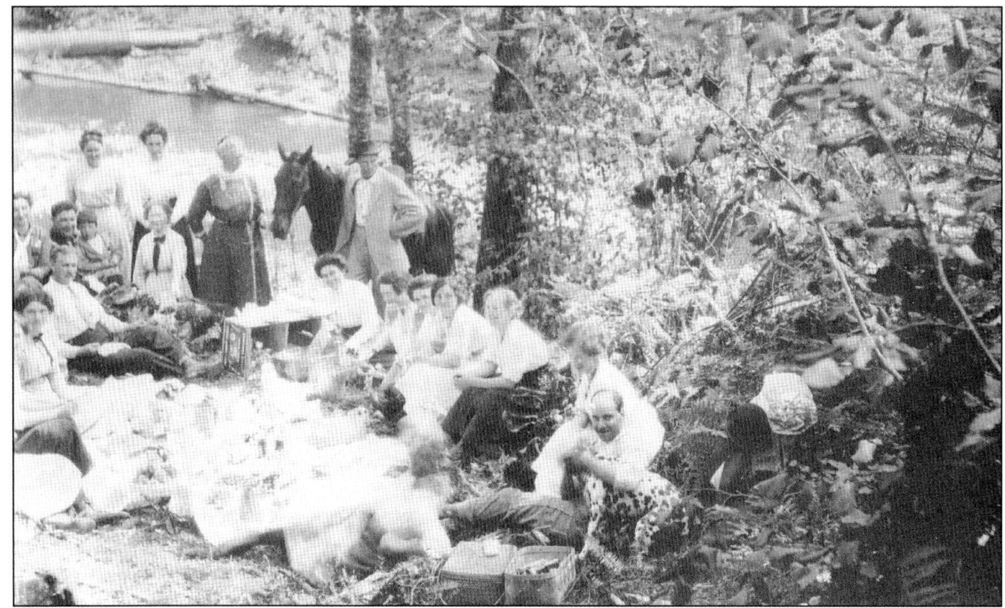

The Kalama River is flowing behind members of the St. Joseph's Catholic Church at a picnic on August 11, 1912. The parishioners of St. Joseph's have a long tradition of enjoying social activities with each other. (Courtesy of St. Joseph's Catholic Church.)

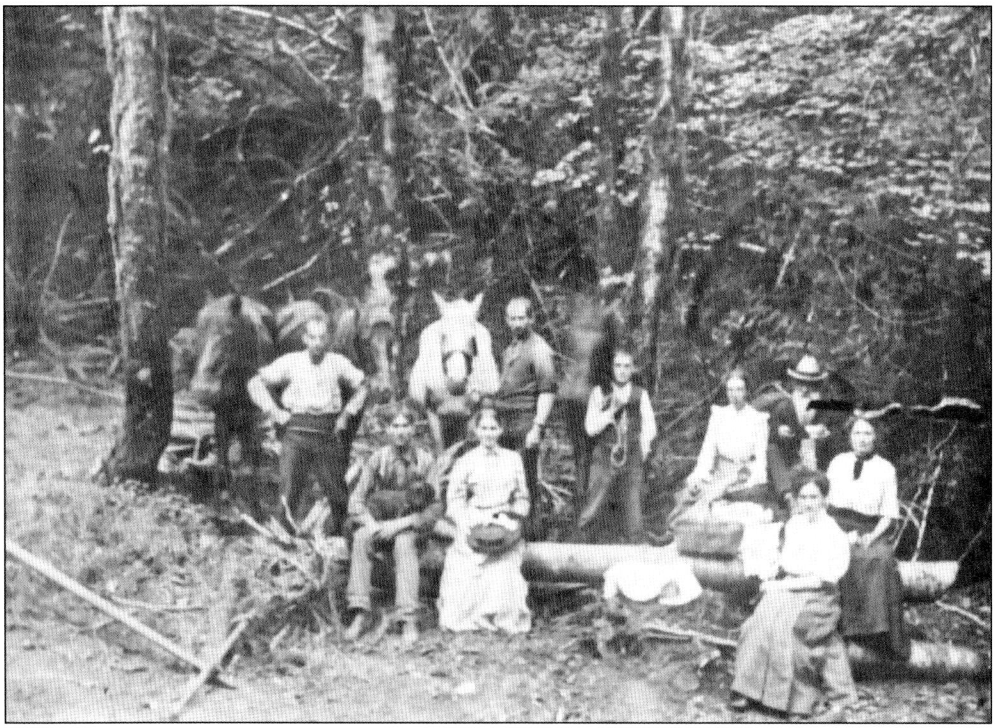

Picnics were a popular pastime in the early 1900s. Pictured at the Kalama River are, from left to right, (first row) William Modrow, Mrs. Dave Modrow Sr., Frances Schuable, and Mary Ahles; (second row) Lew Schauble, John Schmitt, Gilbert Schauble, Mary Lee Clark, and Charles Lee. (Courtesy of Joanna Boatman.)

Eight

School Days

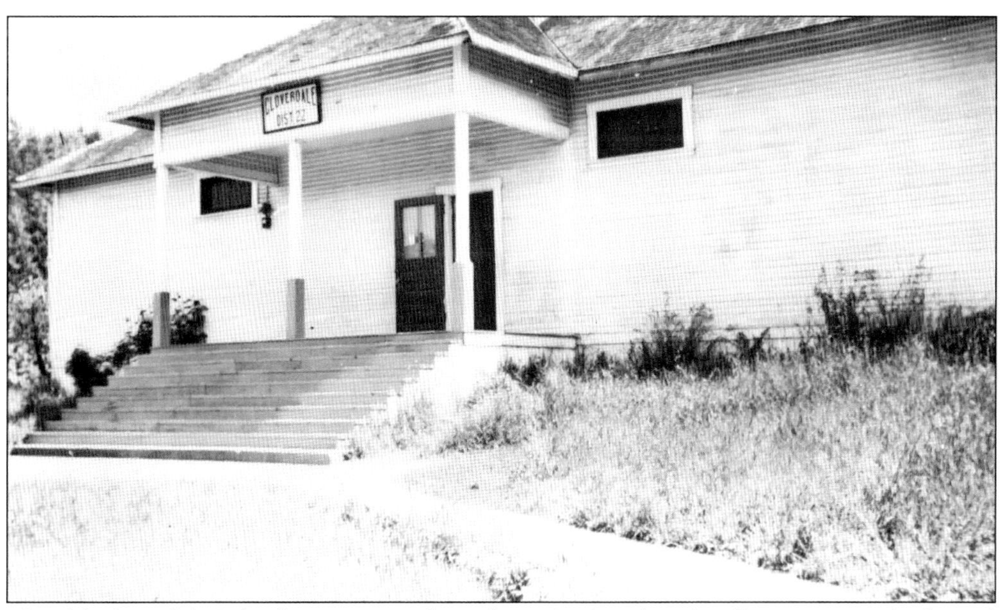

The old Cloverdale School District was formed in 1879, but the schoolhouse was not built until 1911. Prior to the construction of the Cloverdale School, children went to classes held at a local farm. The Cloverdale School District served the Cloverdale area until the 1920s. At that time, the Cloverdale School District merged with the Kalama School District, and children traveled into Kalama for classes.

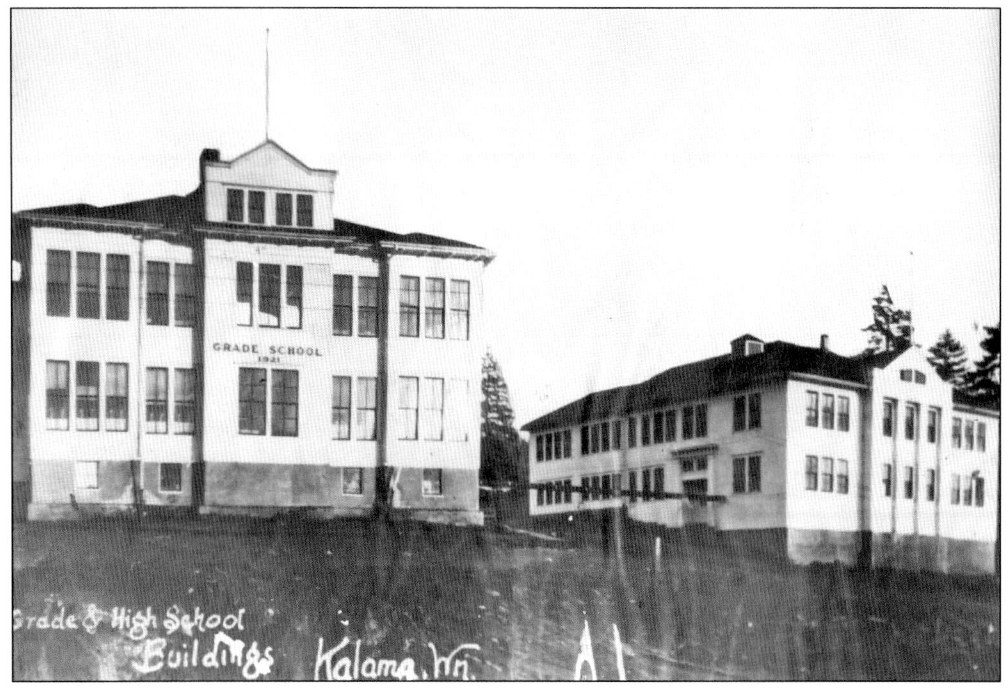

To the left is the Kalama Grade School, and to the right is the old high school. Each small community built its own schoolhouse, and children went to school for two to four months a year. Later, the school year was increased to six months. Attendance of students was irregular because of weather, illness, and work at home. (Courtesy of Joanna Boatman.)

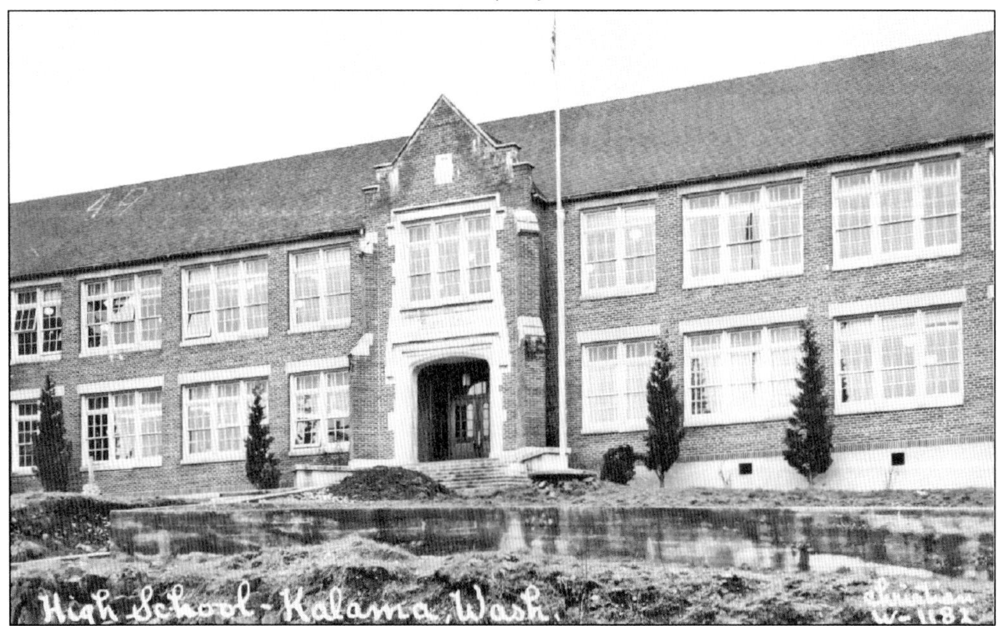

The Kalama High School presently in use was built in 1937. The school district was allotted $44,000 by the State of Washington for the destruction of the old school and the building of a new one. The Kalama High School was used as a location site for the filming of the movie *Twilight*. (Courtesy of Lee Bunn.)

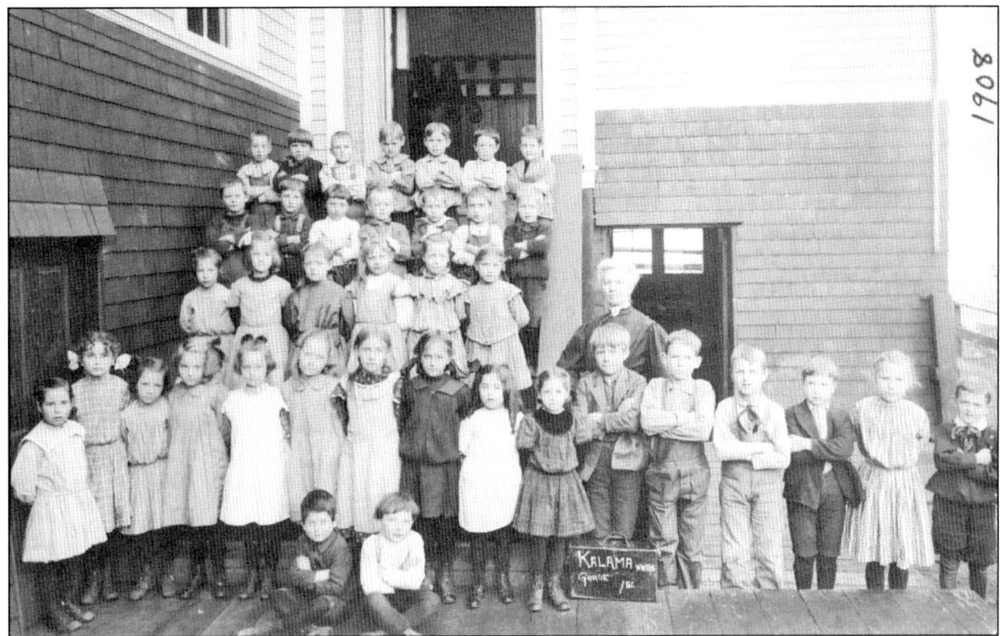

Pictured is a Kalama School first-grade class consisting of 38 children. A Mrs. Talbot is the teacher. In the 1800s, one became a schoolteacher by passing an examination given by the county superintendent. There were three levels of certifications, and after five years of experience, one could get a lifetime certification. (Courtesy of Catherine Applegate.)

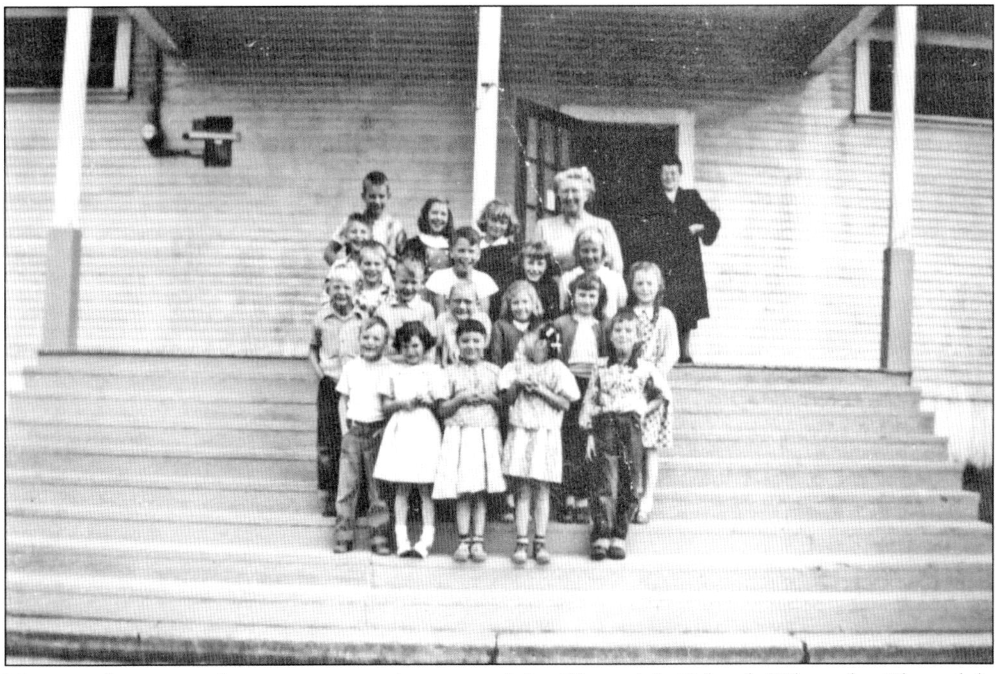

Here, students pose for a picture on the steps of the Cloverdale School. When the Cloverdale School District consolidated with the Kalama School District, children went to Kalama for classes. Today, the Cloverdale School is the location of a local organization, Helping Hands, which provides assistance for those in need.

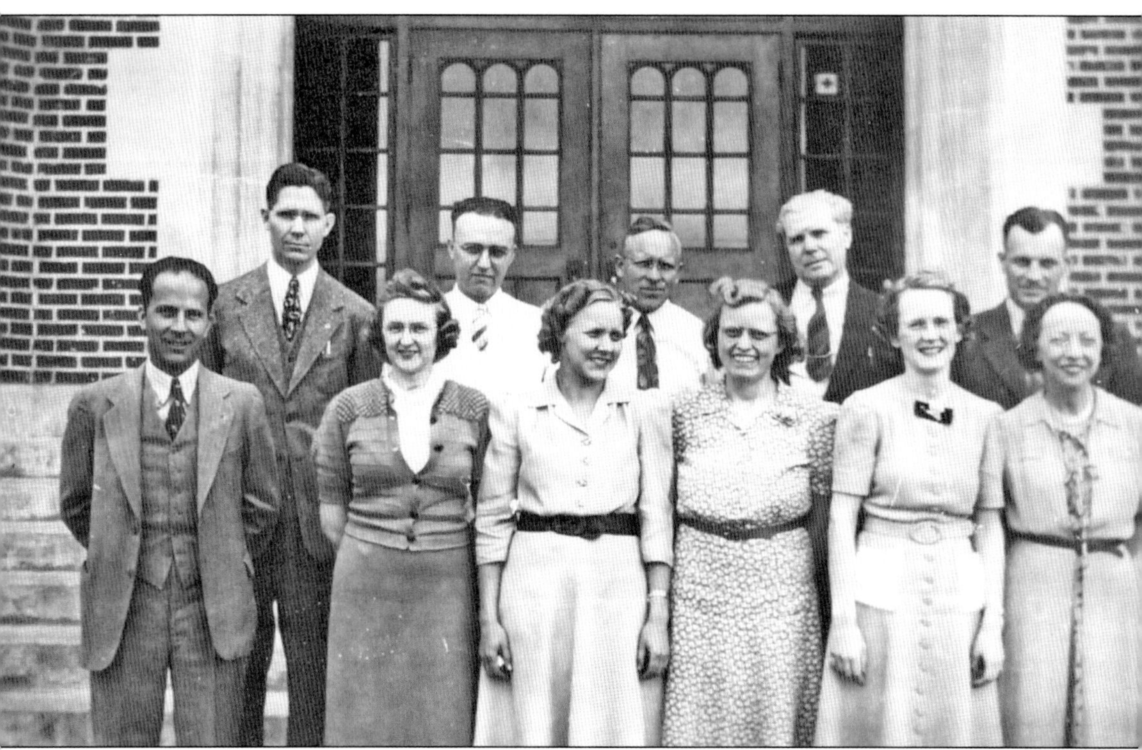

The 1941 faculty of Kalama High School and Junior High is seen here. High school teachers are Ida Granberg, Sally Spencer, Virgil Simmons, and Louis Poppe, and the junior high teachers are Inez Floren, Claude Wright, and Vernet Wahlgren.

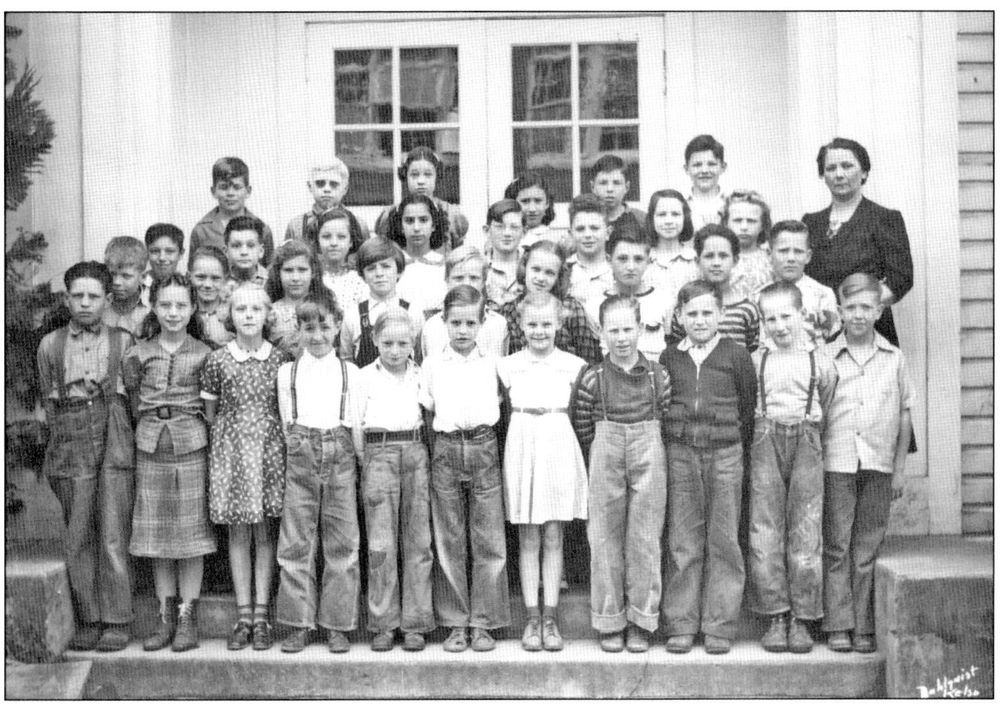

Taken in 1941, this picture is of a Kalama Grade School. The first school in Kalama was conducted in the Masonic hall. In 1874, construction began on the first schoolhouse.

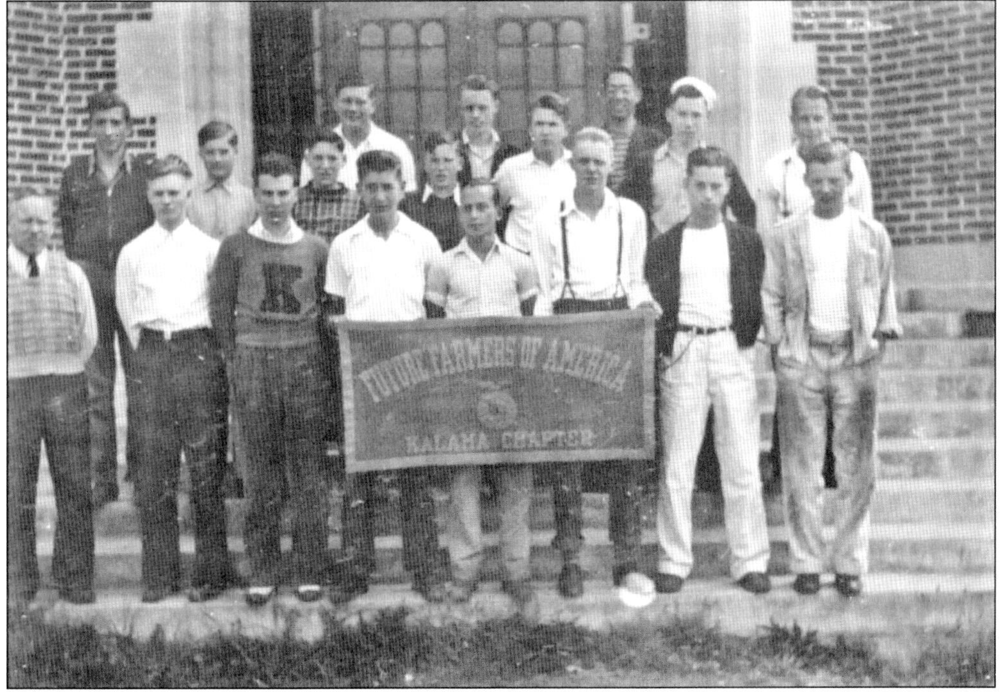

Family farms were common in the 1940s, and schools offered an organization for boys called Future Farmers of America, which prepared boys for careers in agriculture. Pictured is the club at Kalama High School in 1941. Louis Poppe, the teacher, is pictured at the far left.

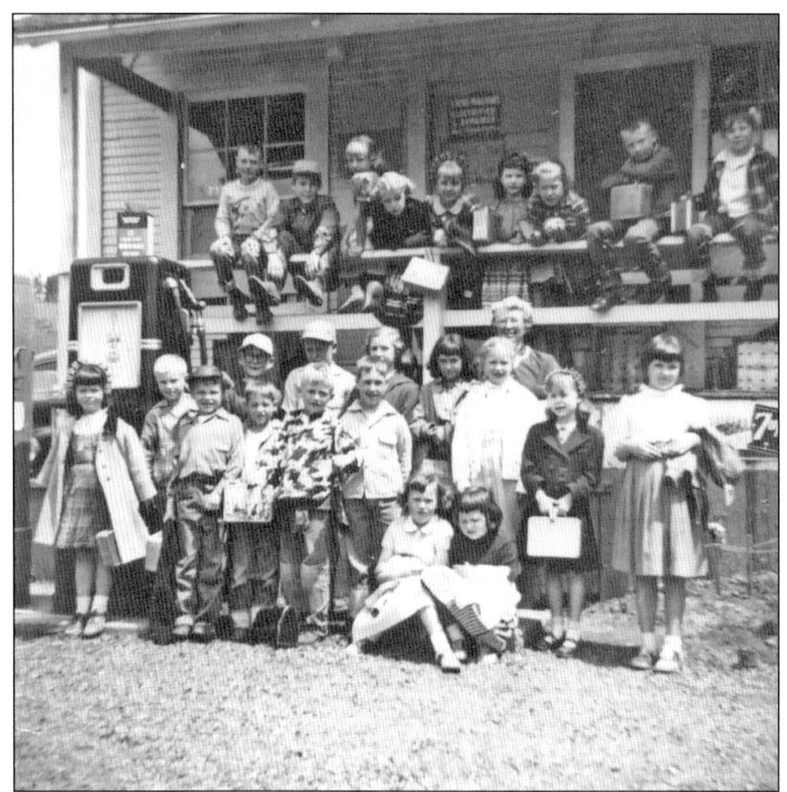

Pictured is a group of schoolchildren on an outing to the Cloverdale Store. The teacher is Minnie Kane. A gas pump is located right by the steps, and many of the children are holding their metal lunch boxes.

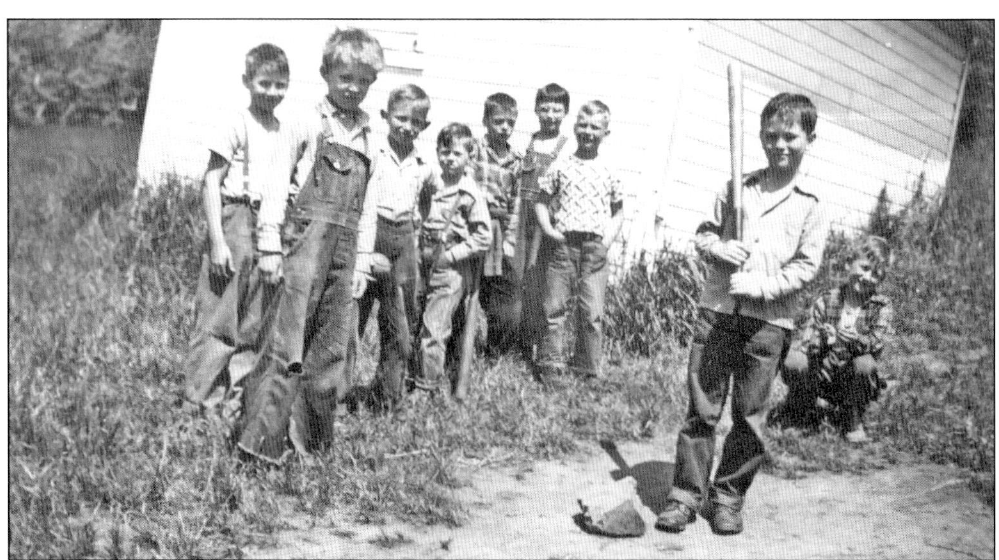

A group of boys is playing baseball and using a large rock as home plate. In the mid-1940s, children played a variety of games. Most boys played marbles and town ball (similar to baseball), and most girls played drop the handkerchief and ring-around-the-rosy.

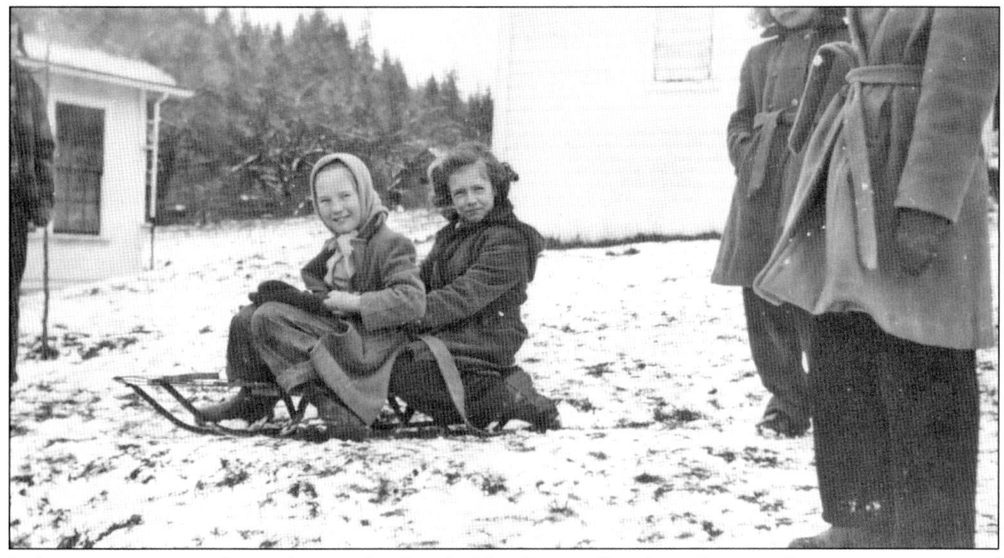

It does not snow much or often in the Pacific Northwest. So when the area does get snow, even if it is just a dusting of snowflakes, kids rush outdoors to play in it. These two young girls are going for a sled ride even though grass is poking through the thin layer of snow.

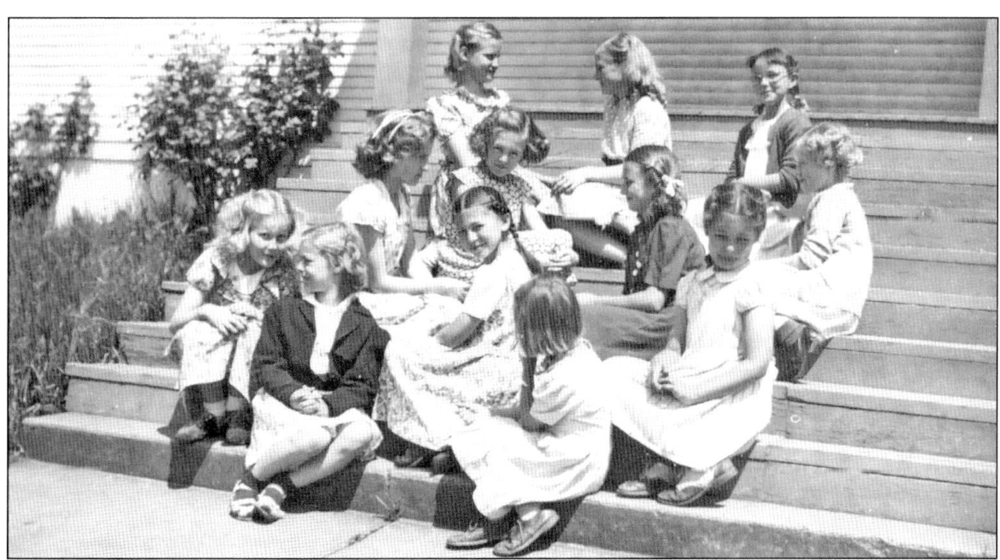

A group of vivacious young girls sits on the steps of the Cloverdale School. They are probably enjoying recess or lunchtime. Young ladies in the late 1940s were required to wear dresses to school. The dress code did not allow girls to wear jeans or pants.

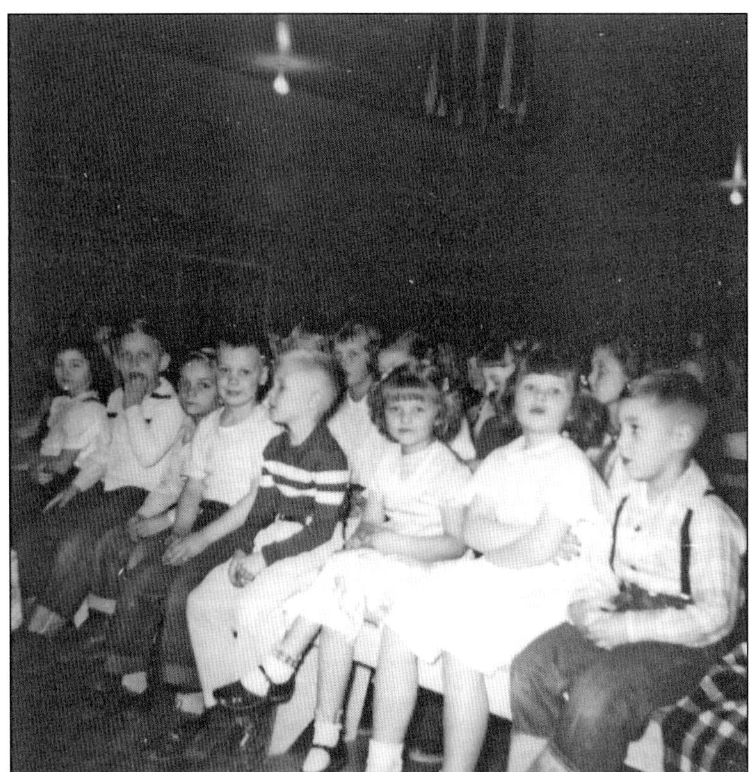

Elementary school kids are sitting in the gym of the Kalama School anticipating the program to be presented. Assemblies were commonly held for the entire student body.

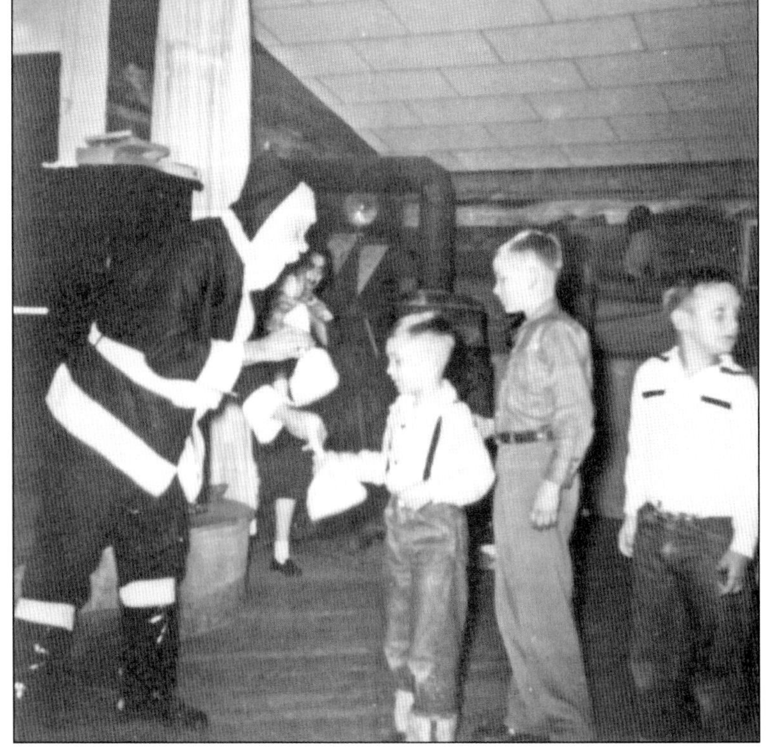

Santa Claus is seen visiting children from the Kalama Elementary School; he is handing out bags of treats to boys waiting patiently in line. Children attending school after World War II anticipated a visit by Santa Claus and receiving modest gifts at the annual school Christmas party.

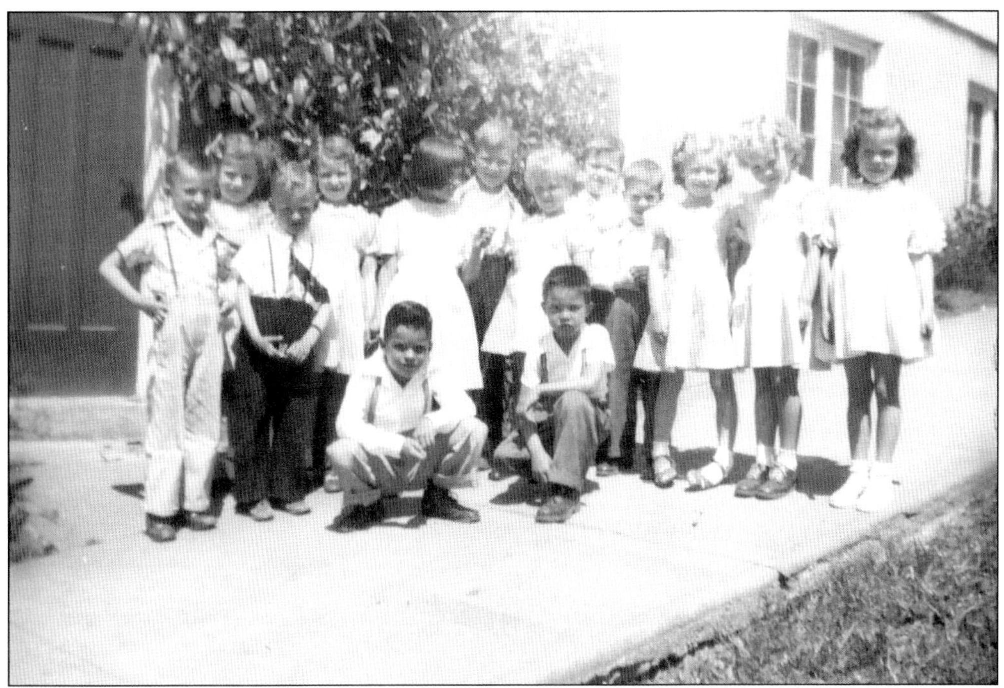

These are students in the first kindergarten class held in Kalama. (Courtesy of Brian LaRoy.)

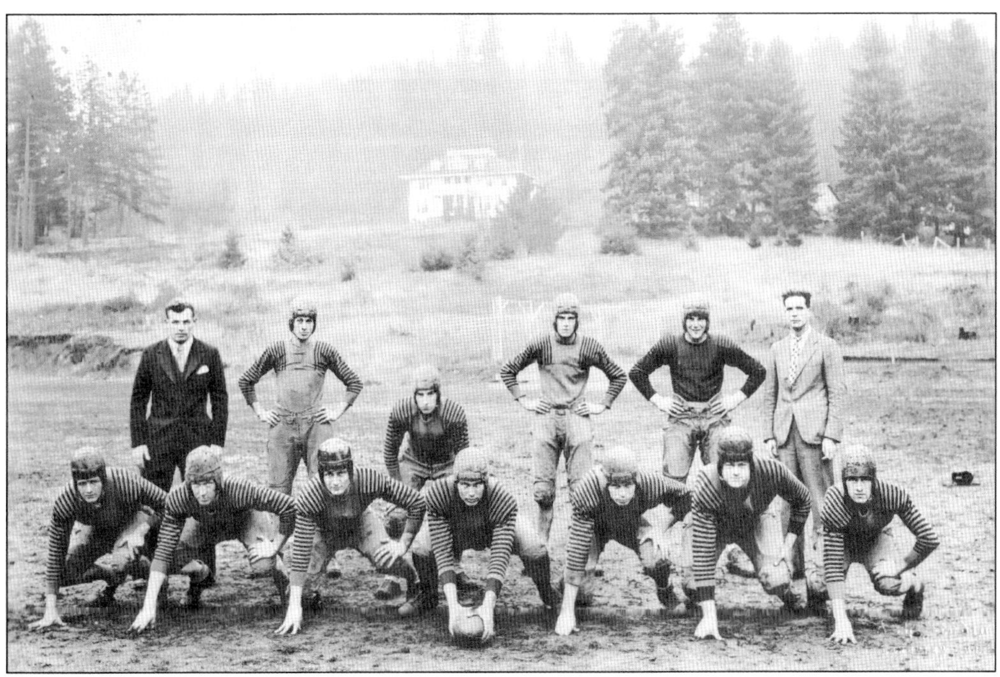

The 1930 Kalama High School football team and coach are shown here. Pictured are, from left to right, (first row) Johss, Stehman, Wood, LaRoy, Schoonover, Howe, and Blye; (second row) coach Virg Simmons, Geo, John Hart, Vick, unidentified, and unidentified. (Courtesy of Brian LaRoy.)

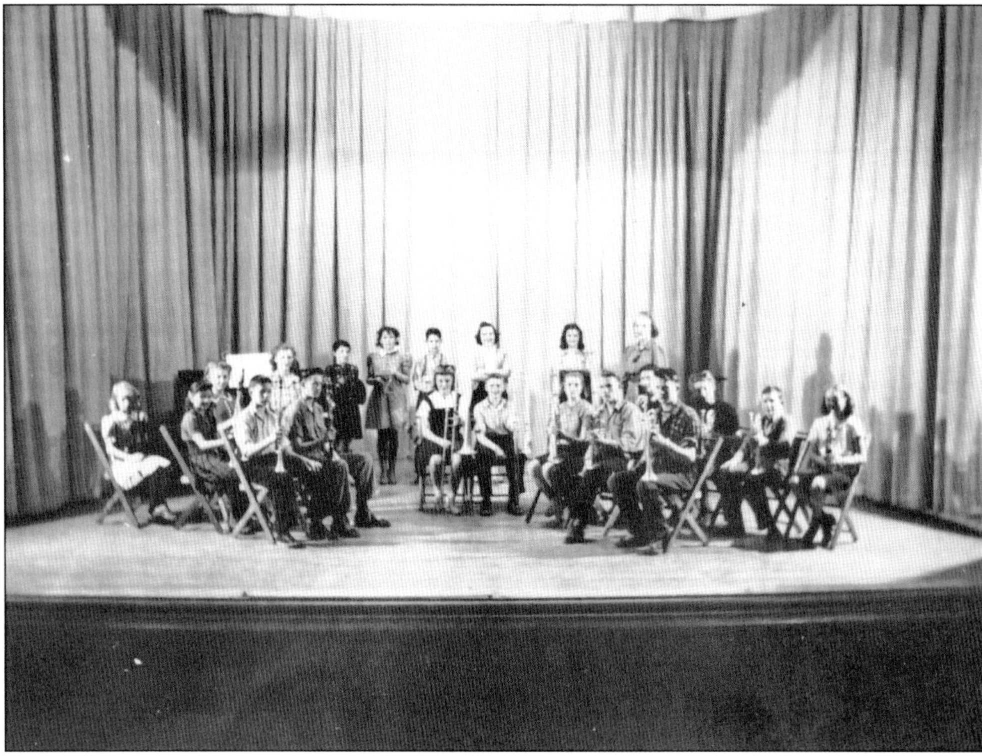

This orchestra, pictured in 1941, was comprised of Kalama students from the grade school, junior high school, and high school. They performed at Parent-Teacher Association (PTA) meetings, assemblies, and a spring concert. Their director was Vernet Wahlgren.

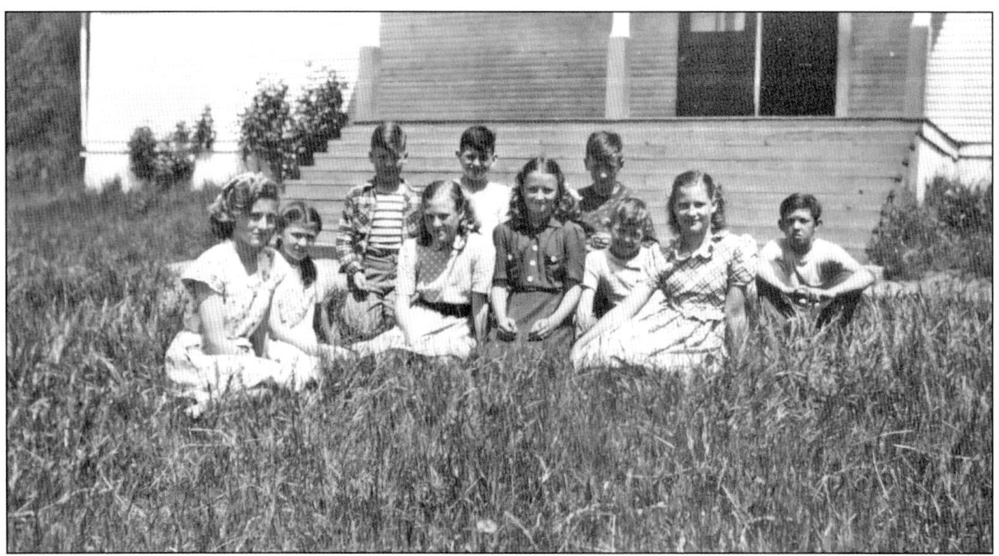

While taking a break from the classroom, children squint in the sunlight as they pose for their picture sitting on the lawn in front of the Cloverdale School.

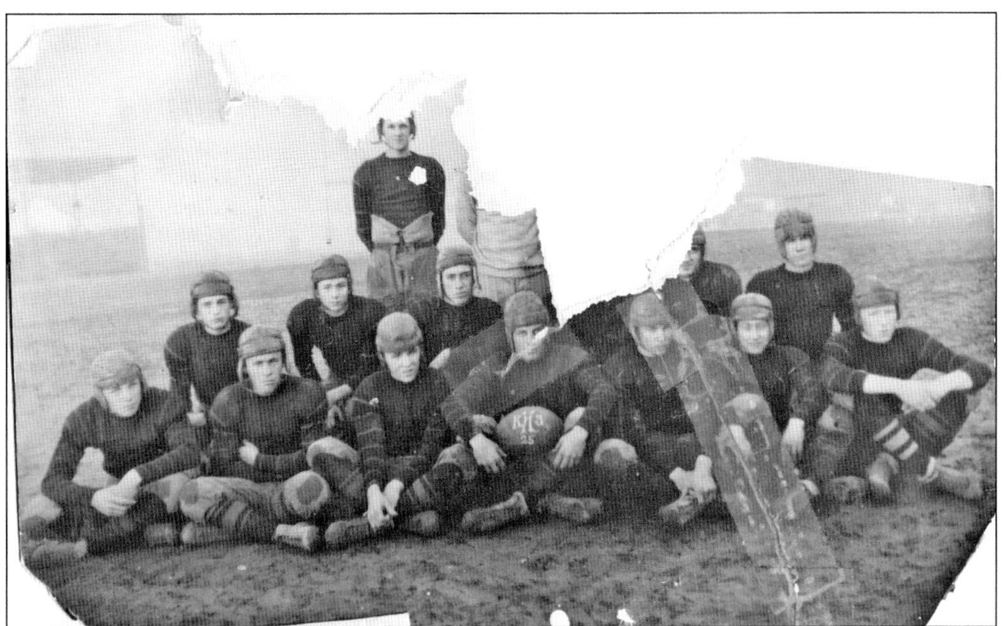

The 1925 Kalama High School football players are wearing leather helmets. The team, the Chinooks, is named after local Native Americans. Football has always been much loved and avidly supported by Kalama residents.

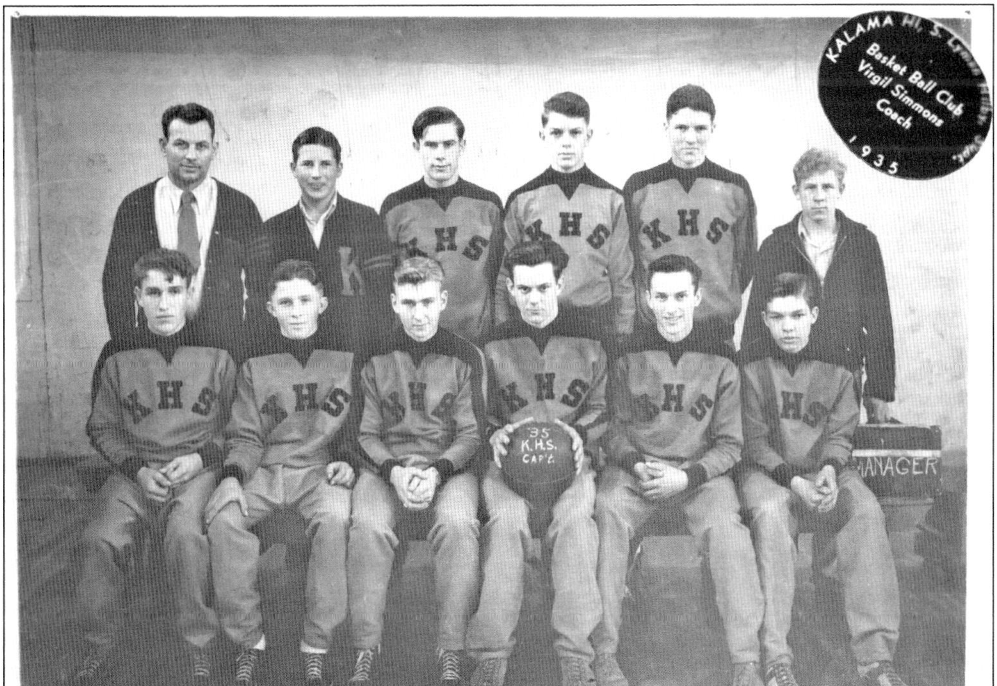

Coach Virgil Simmons poses with his 1935 Kalama High School basketball team. A Kalama schoolteacher, Simmons coached both the Kalama football team and the Kalama basketball team for many years.

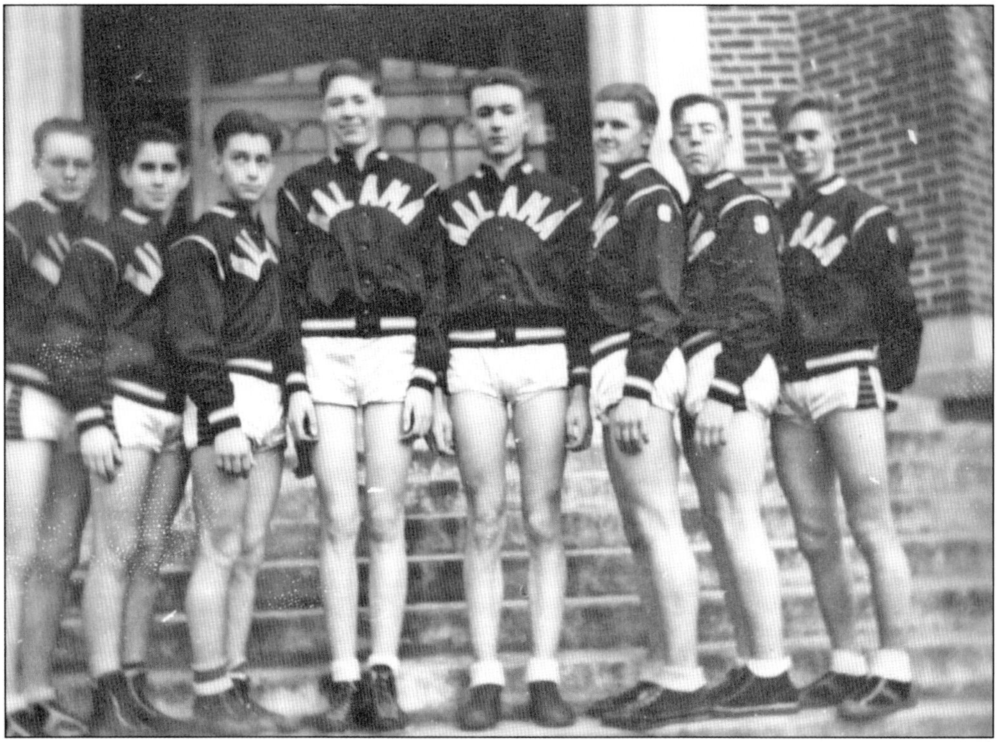

The first-string basketball team of 1941 is pictured. Players are, from left to right, Tony Johnson, Bob Cramer, Tom Cooper, Arne Ranta, Vernon Magus, James Toteff, Leonard Thorne, and Ralph Tidrick.

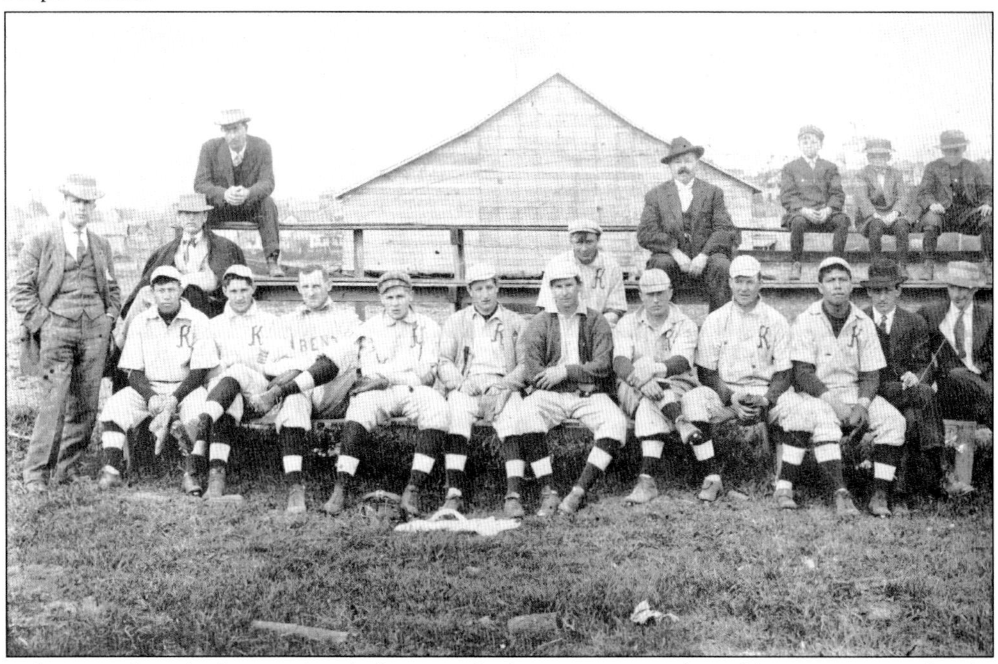

Kalama residents had a town baseball team, which was active until World War II. Pictured is the Kalama baseball team in the 1920s.

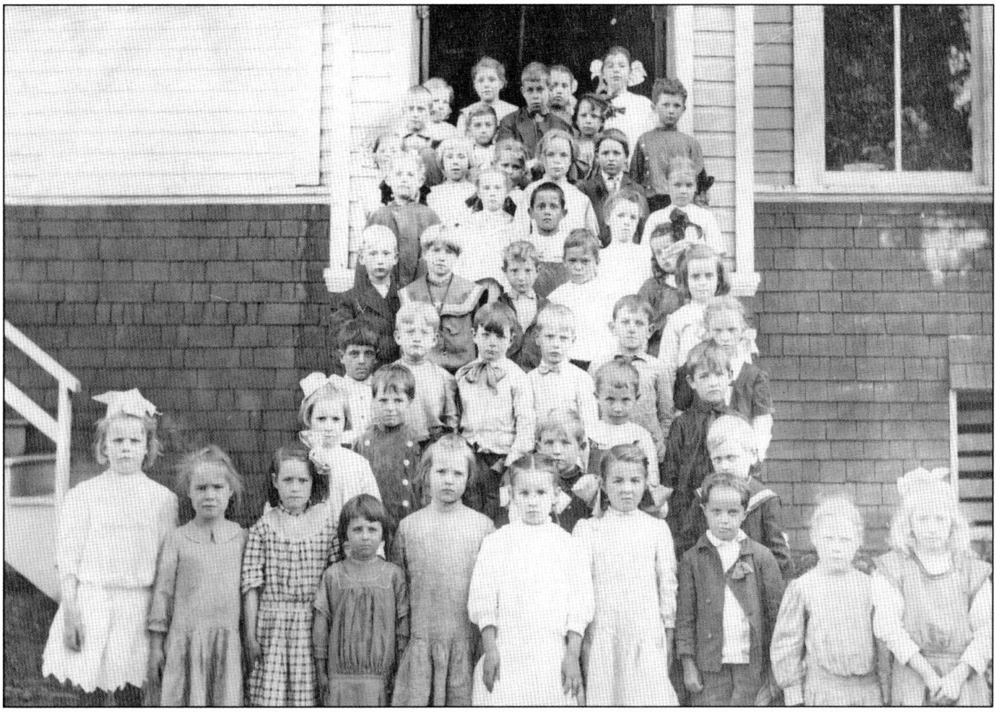

Kalama Grade School students pose on the steps of their school in the early 1900s. Before school districts consolidated, each district would have several independent schools. In the late 1800s and early 1900s, there were schools at Kalama, Kenyon (Cloverdale), Little Kalama, Kalama River, and Carrollton (Carrolls). (Courtesy of Art Godfrey.)

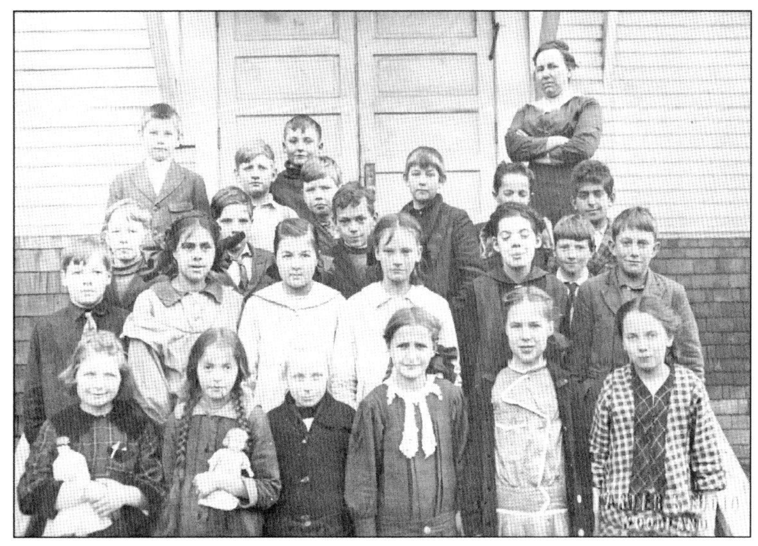

On the steps of the Cloverdale School, a class poses for its picture. Cloverdale was the location of many family farms that specialized in growing strawberries. Strawberry picking in the summer provided students a way of making spending money. (Courtesy of Art Godfrey.)

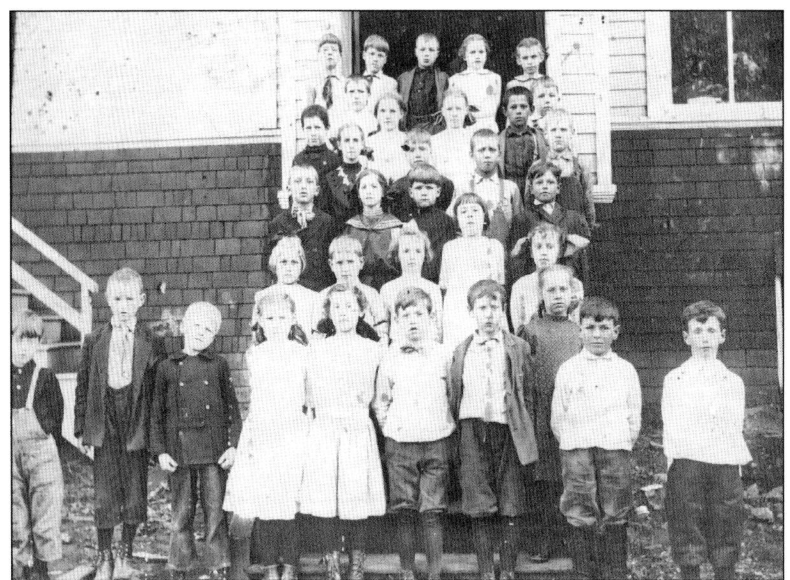

Prior to 1871, all schools between the Kalama River and the Lewis River to the south were under the jurisdiction of Clark County. In 1891, the schools came under the jurisdiction of Cowlitz County. (Courtesy of Joanna Boatman.)

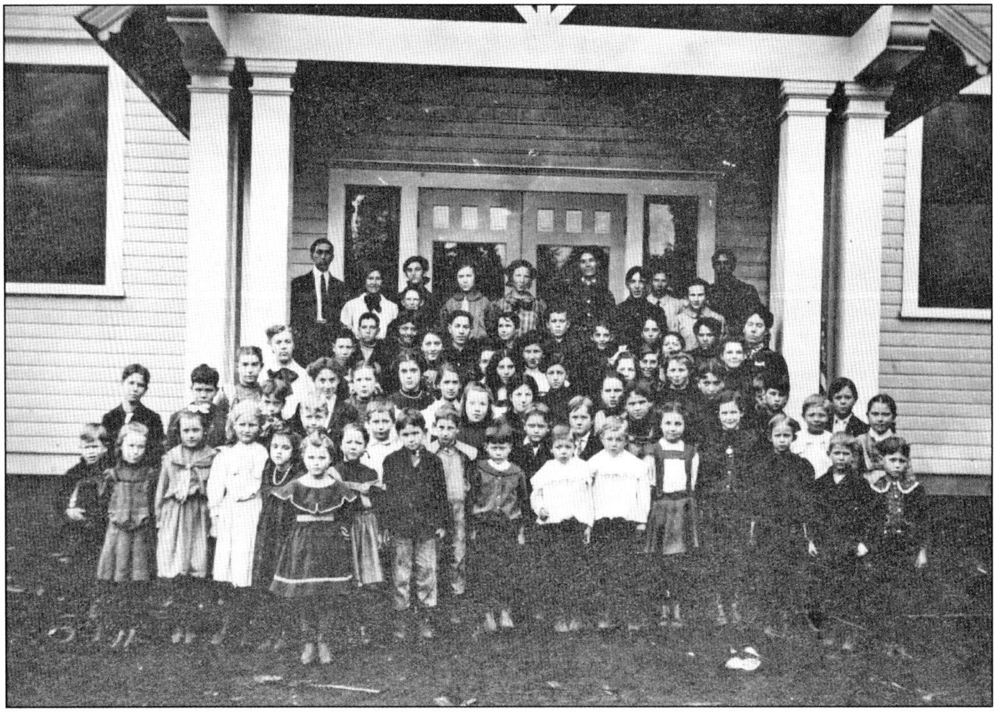

The Cloverdale School District was formed in 1879, and school was held at a private farm for three months of the year. In 1911, a two-room schoolhouse was built, and four grades were taught in each room. High school–age children either walked or rode horses to Kalama High School for class. (Courtesy of John Norton.)

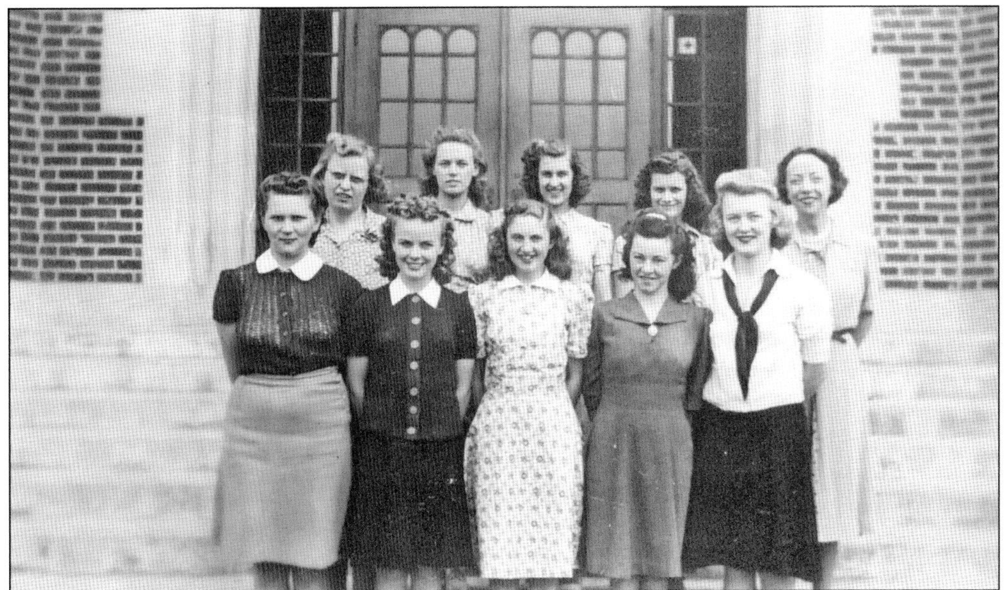

Pictured is the Kalama Girls League of 1941. Members include Clista Dickey, Helen Williams, Celeste Tohill, Kallie Kockritz, Nancy Ann Finke, Mae Harmon, Joyce Ruth, and Eva Watson. (Courtesy of Joanna Boatman.)

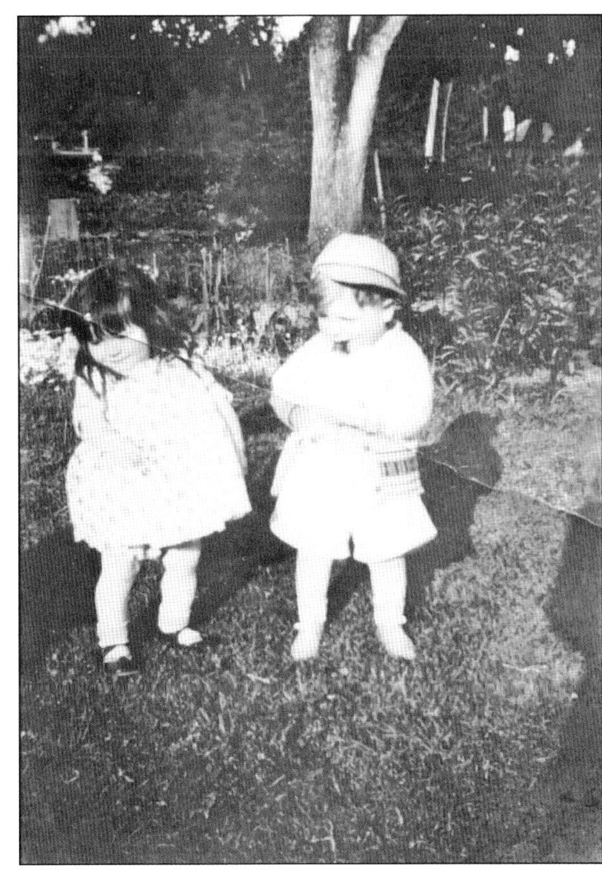

In 1930, Vira and Bill Boatman are pictured playing in their yard and are enjoying the freedom of childhood before it is their time to go to school. Tragically, Vira died from injuries received in an accident shortly after this photograph was taken. (Courtesy of Joanna Boatman.)

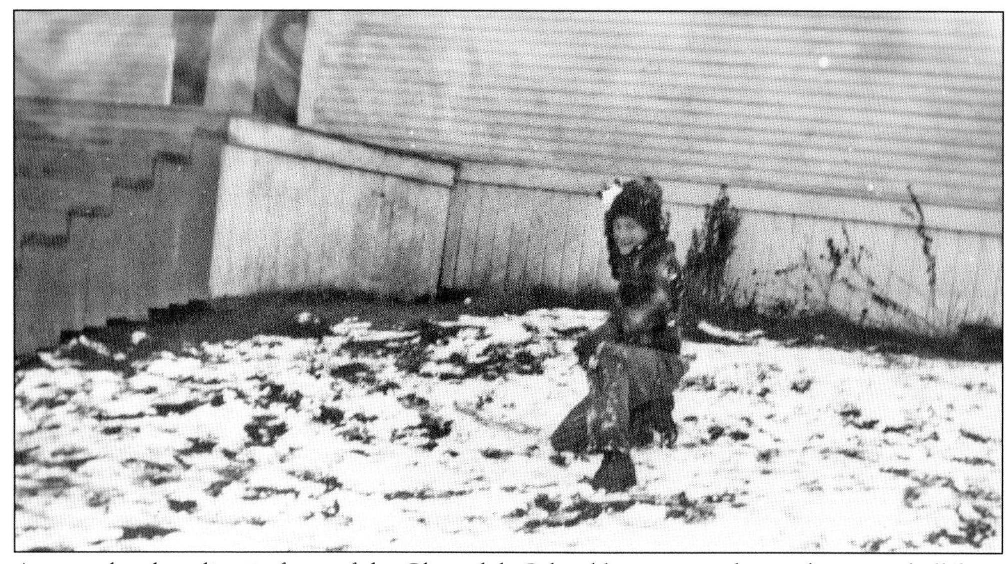

A young boy kneeling in front of the Cloverdale School has managed to make a snowball from the scant amount of snow on the ground. Snow on the west side of the Cascade Mountains is very wet, and anyone hit with a snowball is going to get soaked.

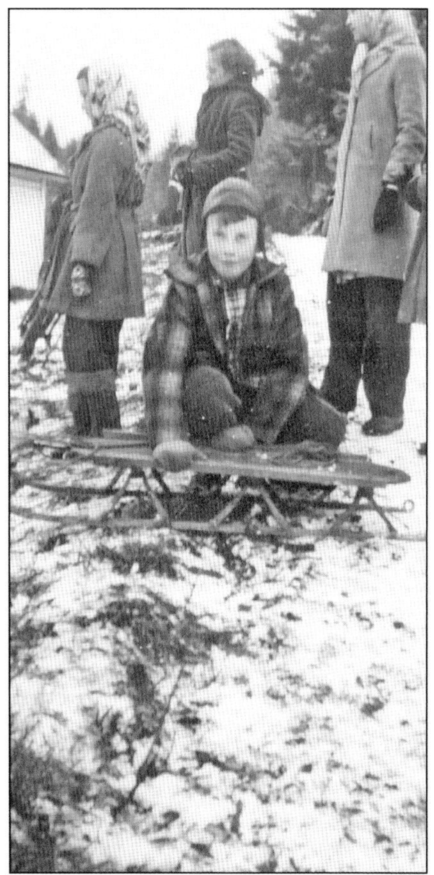

Even though there is very little snow on the ground, this boy and the girls behind him are determined to ride their sleds and to enjoy what small amount of winter they have. Snowfall is rare in Kalama and seldom lasts more than a day. Children are quick to take advantage of any snowy day.

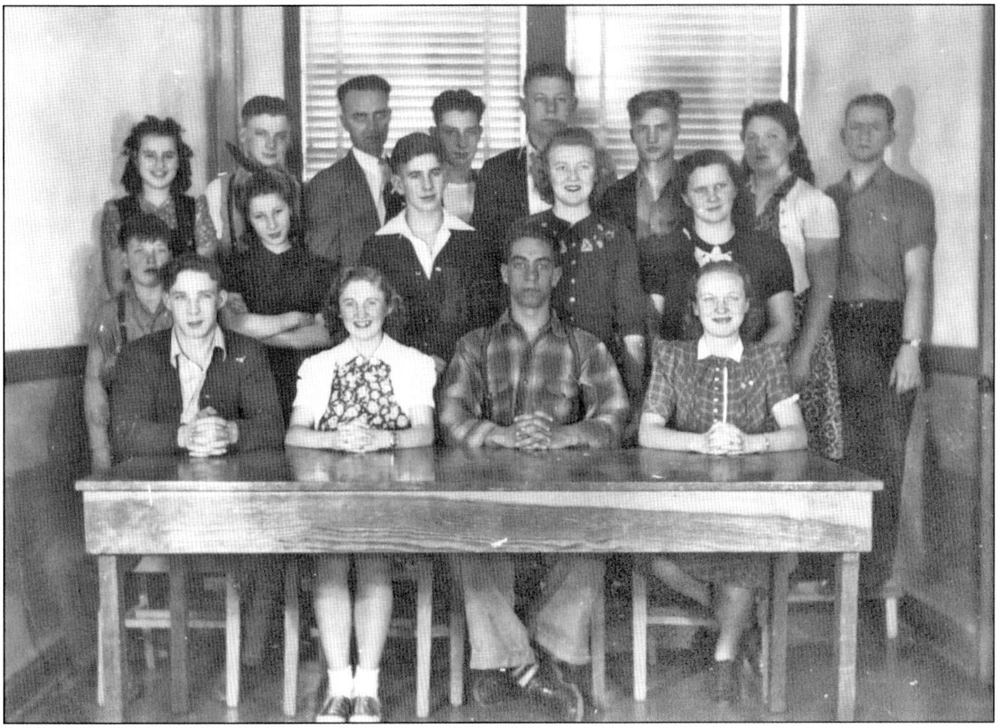

Pictured is the 1941 Kalama High School Student Council. Shown are advisor Mr. Frost and students Rupert Lusk, Bernard Hoggatt, Clista Dickey, Jean Williams, Gloretta White, Daisy Pitkonen, Harold Whetstine, Vernon Morgus, Vera Ruth, Dolores Vivian, Darrel Nixon, Joe Nelson, Kallie Kockritz, Bob Cramer, Nancy Finke, Ralph Tidrick, and Irvine Hunington.

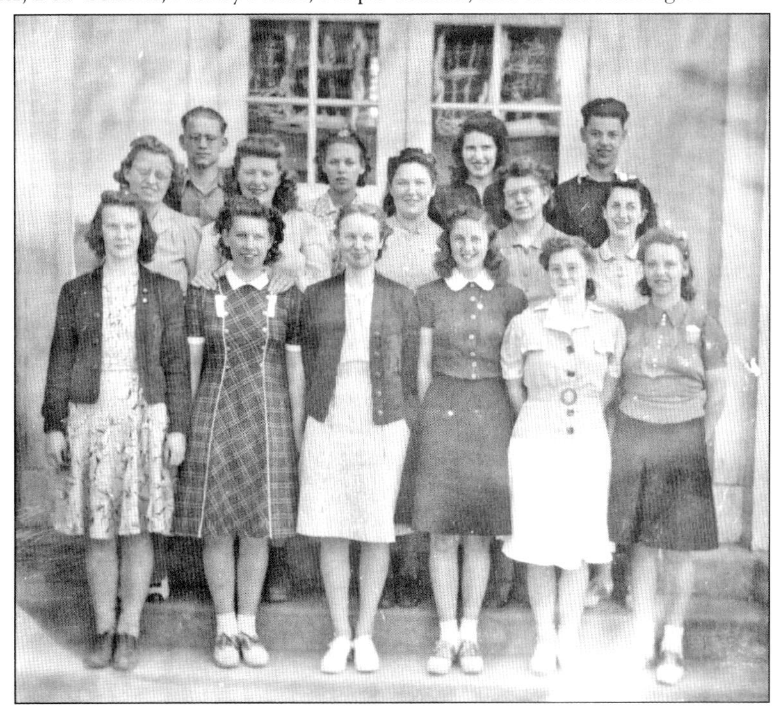

Kalama High School's yearbook committee poses for a photograph in 1941. The yearbook was called the *Kawaco*. The 1941 yearbook included actual photographs of each group represented. The photographs of students and class activities were glued, by hand, into the yearbook.

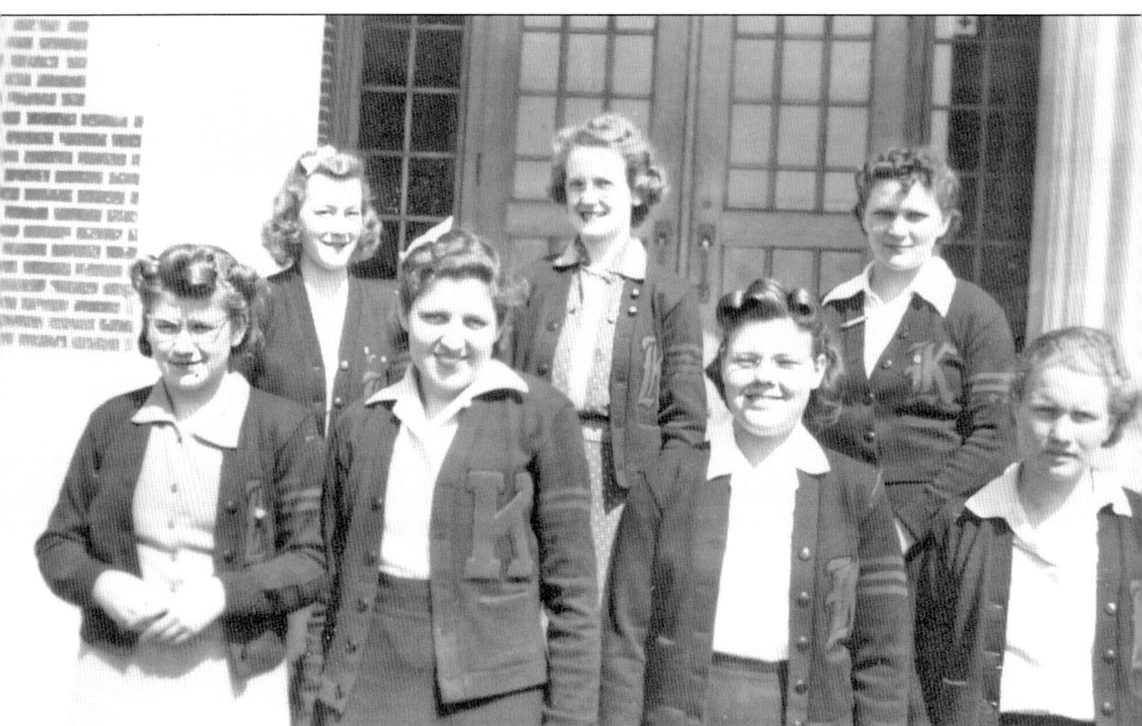

This Girls' Athletic Association (GAA) photograph includes, from left to right, (first row) Kallie Kockritz, Pat Lamb, Alice Grey, and Laura "Sutler" Rowland; (second row) Flora Hunington, Ileen Littlefield, and unidentified. Each girl had earned a varsity letter for participating in a sport. The letter is sewn onto the girl's sweater.

Nine

Celebrations

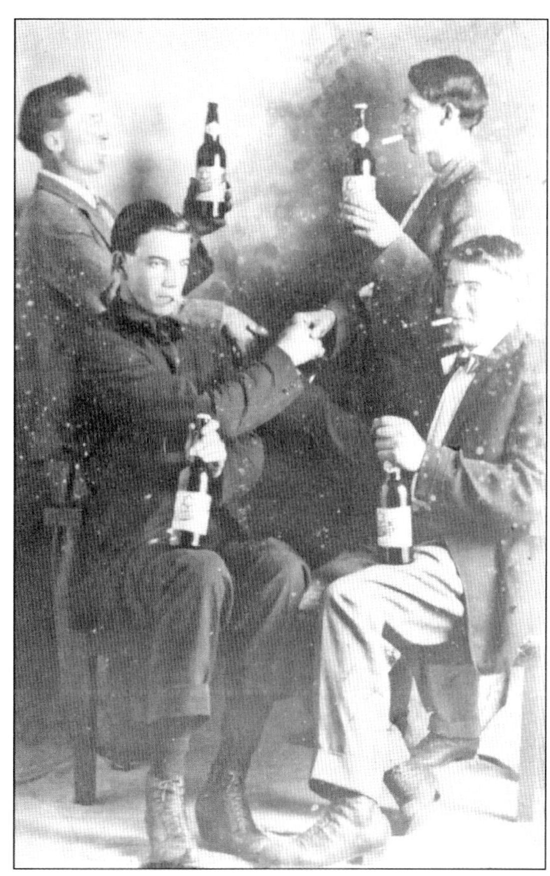

Four unidentified young men pose for the camera, cigarettes in their mouths and bottles of beer in their hands. Doubtlessly, they are trying to convince the viewer of their worldly sophistication. (Courtesy of Cleone Kockritz.)

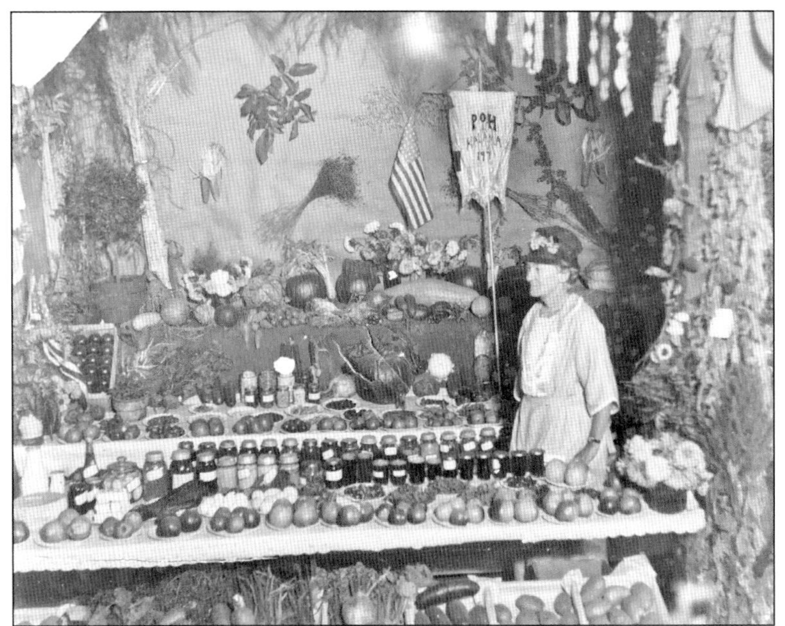

A woman is standing in a Grange booth at a Kalama Fair. With its rows of canned goods and fruits and vegetables artfully displayed, the booth is designed to show off the bounty of local farms and personal gardens.

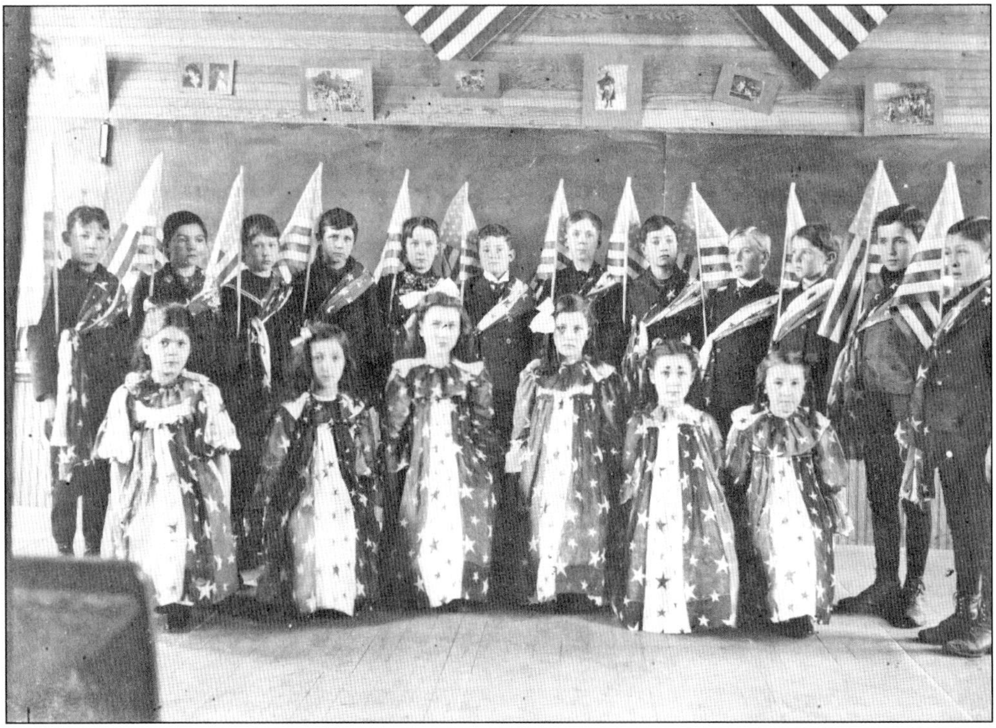

The children are seen wearing patriotic attire to celebrate the Fourth of July. The boys are holding flags, and the girls are wearing dresses featuring the stars and stripes associated with the holiday. (Courtesy of Joanna Boatman.)

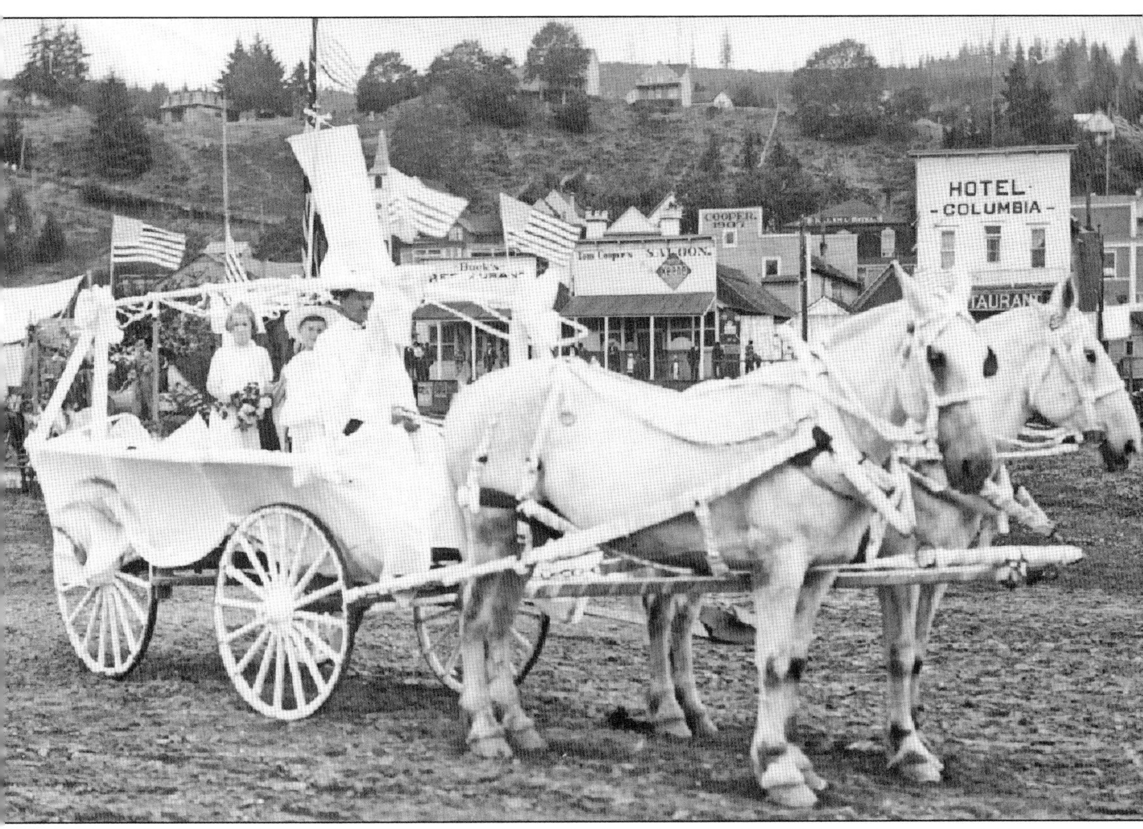

In the background are Tom Cooper's Saloon, the Hotel Columbia, Kalama Hotel, and Buck's Restaurant. The photograph was taken in the early 1900s, and the people in the buggy are ready to participate in a Fourth of July parade. (Courtesy of Lee Bunn.)

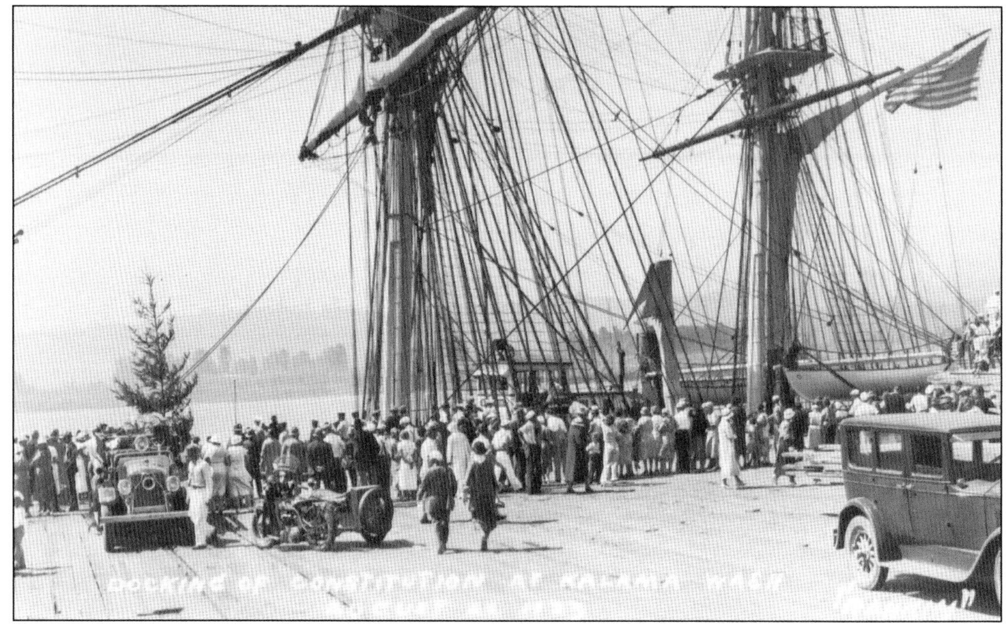

On August 22, 1933, the sailing ship USS *Constitution* docked at the port of Kalama. The visit of "Old Ironsides" was an important cultural event for the city, and residents crowded the dock to tour this historic ship.

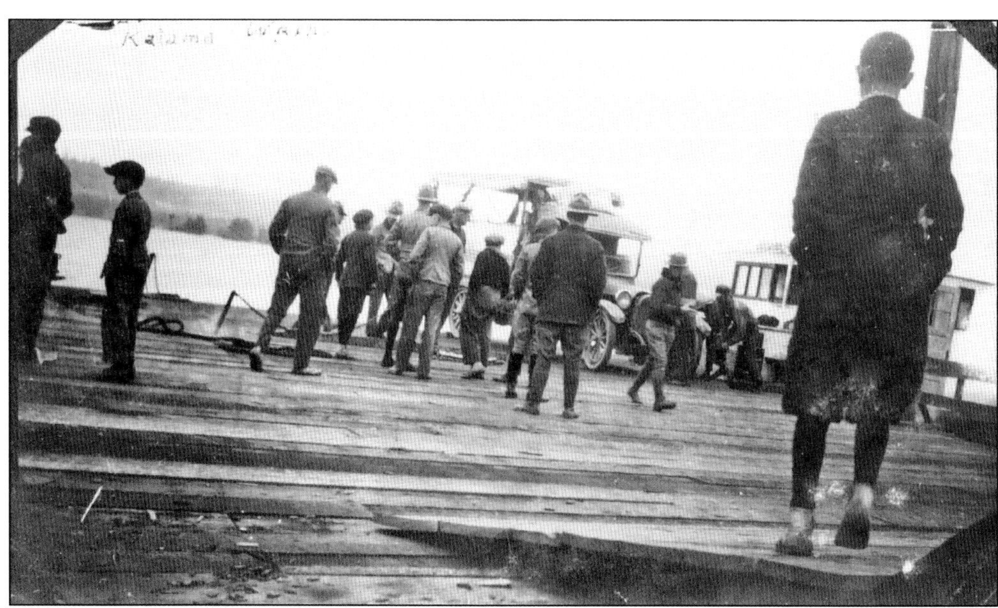

A troop of Boy Scouts, perhaps Sea Scouts, participates in an unidentified event on the docks of the Kalama waterfront. (Courtesy of Lee Bunn.)

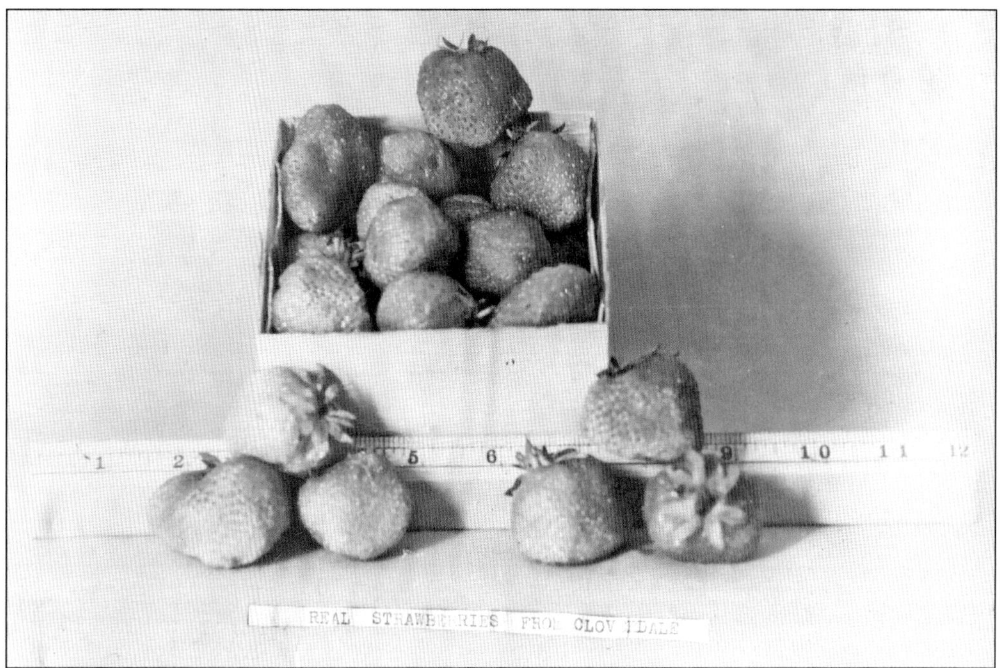

Pictured are the strawberries from the farms located in Cloverdale. They have been photographed with a ruler to show how big and luscious they are. Strawberries thrived in Cloverdale because of the temperate climate. The crop had the advantage of being low maintenance and high in yield.

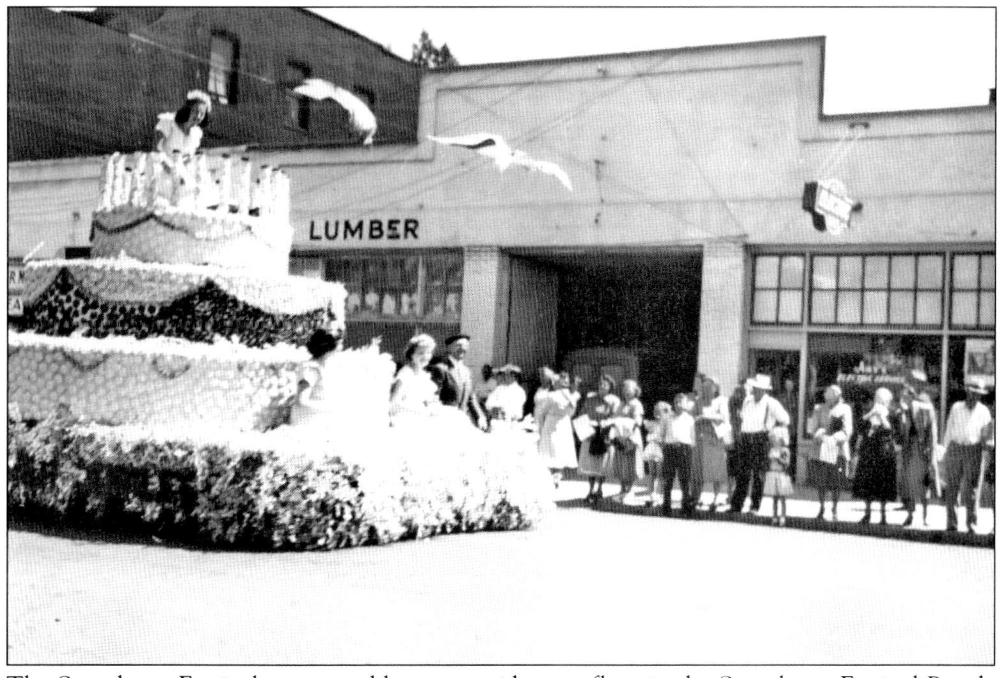

The Strawberry Festival queen and her court ride on a float in the Strawberry Festival Parade on the main street of Kalama. The Strawberry Festival was held in late July from 1939 through 1951—except during World War II.

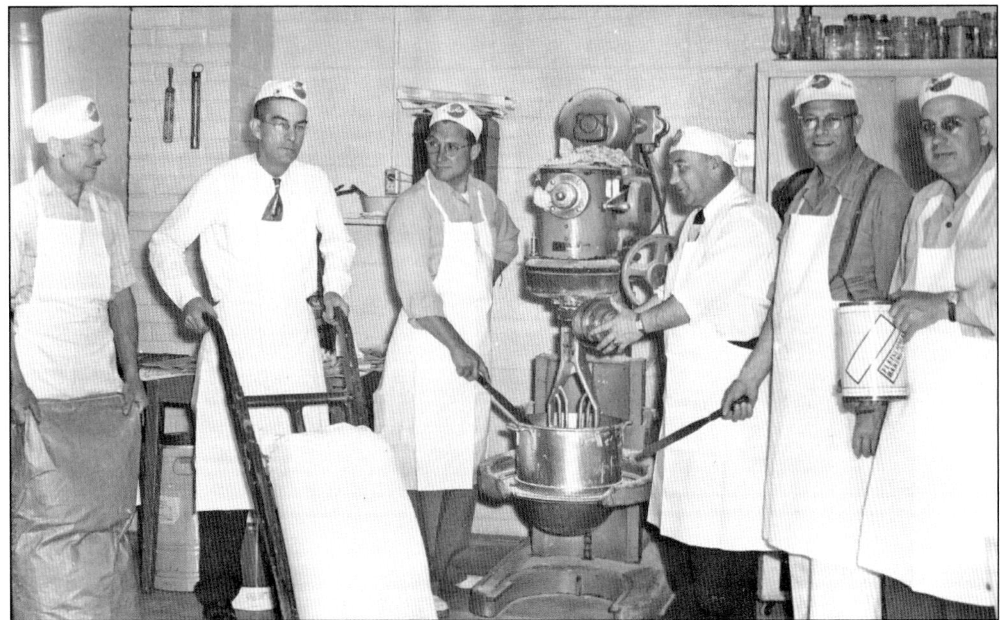

Kalama men are mixing up shortbread batter to make shortbread for the world's largest strawberry shortcake for the annual Strawberry Festival. The 1951 shortcake was 35 feet long. Pictured are, from left to right, Louis Zigler, Lawrence Ruth, R. VanBeavers, Frank Jaeger, Otto Englemann, and Don McLucas.

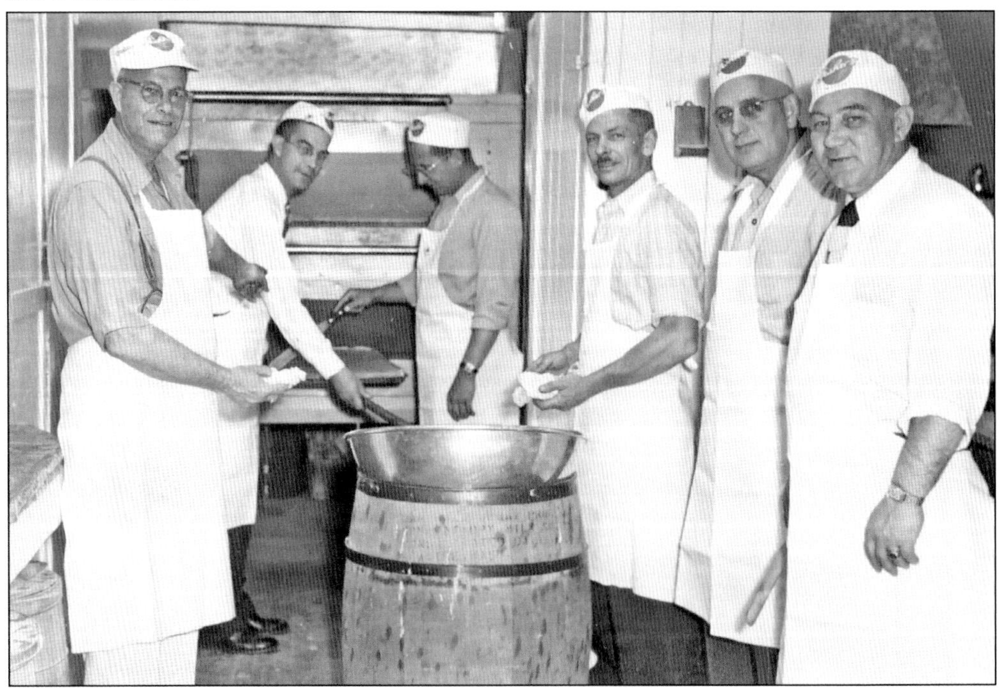

Here, the shortbread batter has been made and is going into the oven to be baked for the Strawberry Festival. Ghanks to the festival, Kalama was known as the "Strawberry Capital of the World." Pictured are, from left to right, Otto Englemann, Lawrence Ruth, R. VanBeavers, Louis Zigler, Don McLucas, and Frank Jaeger.

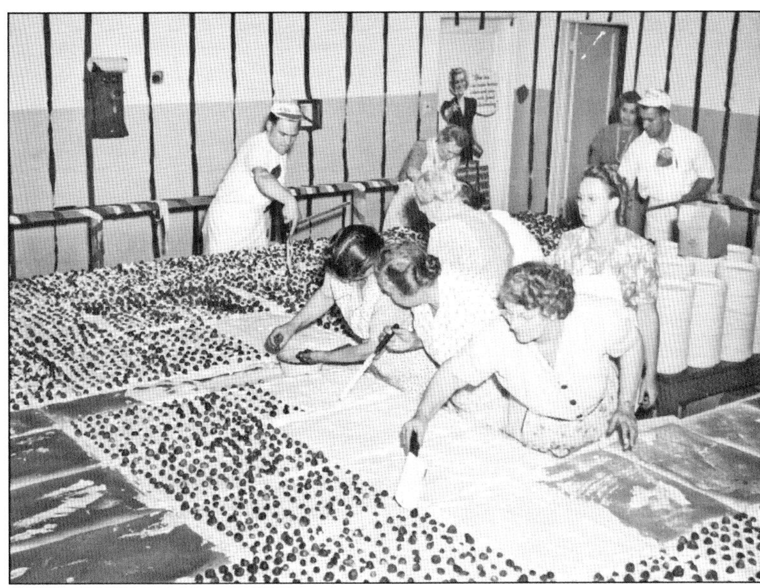

Three women work diligently to put strawberries on the world's largest strawberry shortcake. The shortcake was made every year that Kalama celebrated the Strawberry Festival. The strawberry harvest was picked primarily in May and June, making July the perfect month to celebrate the harvest.

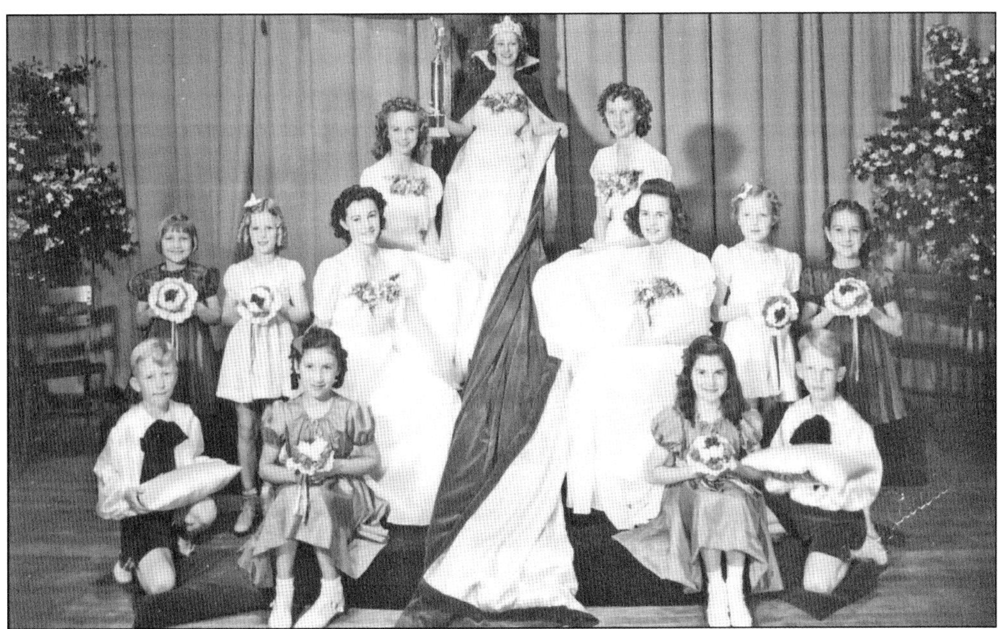

A Strawberry Festival queen is pictured with her court. The queen's coronation was held at the school gymnasium on a Friday night. It was followed by the Queen's Ball, which was the social event of the year in Kalama. Pictured are Strawberry Festival queen Darlene Hoggatt and, in no particular order, princesses Celeste Tohill, Betty Victor, Helen Williams, and Bonnie Nicholson. The children are, from left to right, (first row) page Dennis Dunn, flower girls Beverly Henshaw and Illeanna Boatman, and page Ronnie Modrow; (second row) flower girls Willavere McKinney, Leona Rae Cliff, Patricia Thorne, and Sally Kane.

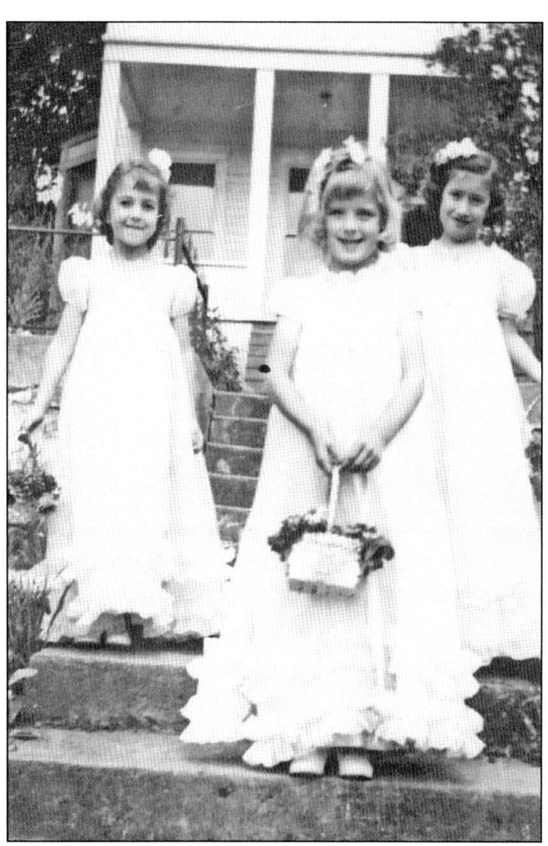

Three little girls are all dressed up to be a part of the queen's court for the Strawberry Festival. They are the flower girls for the court, and they also danced around the maypole. Young boys participated in the court and acted as pages.

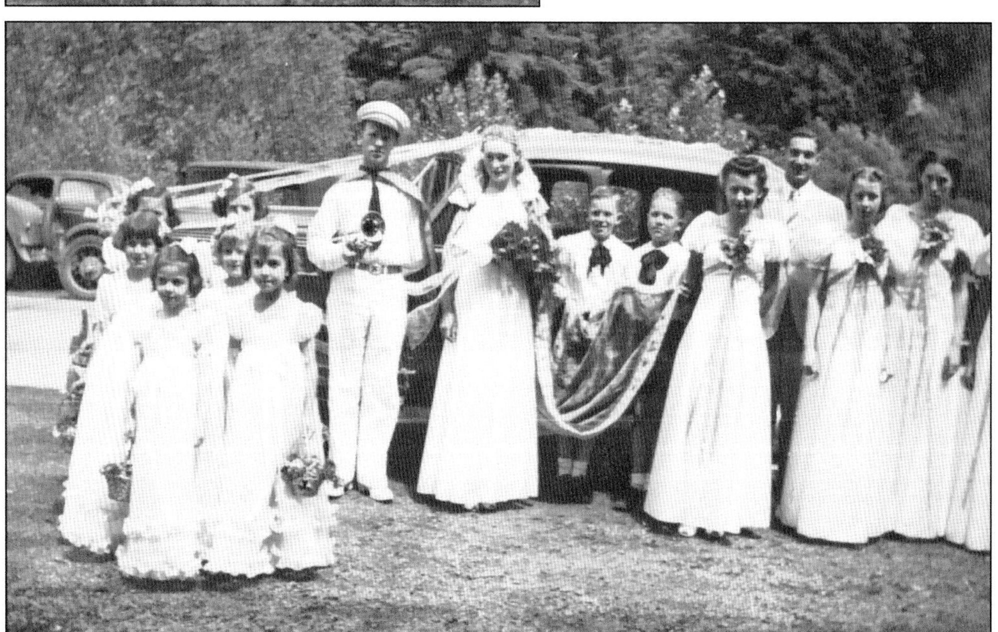

Strawberry Festival queen Elsie Heuchert poses in front of a decorated car with her court. The first Strawberry Festival was held June 23–24, 1939. A total of 16 businesses and organizations and 150 people planned and presented the annual Strawberry Festival.

The Strawberry Festival was celebrated for two days. Events included outboard motor races, a fat man race, and water fights. A carnival was set up between the main street and the railroad depot. The festival was well attended by not only Kalama residents but also by people throughout the surrounding region. Pictured in 1939 is Queen Elsie Heuchert. To the immediate right of the queen are Fred Turner and Abe Moawad, and the flower girls are Nancy Hatt, Sally Kane, Leona Rae Clift, Illeanna Boatman, Joanna Boatman, and Beverly Henshaw.

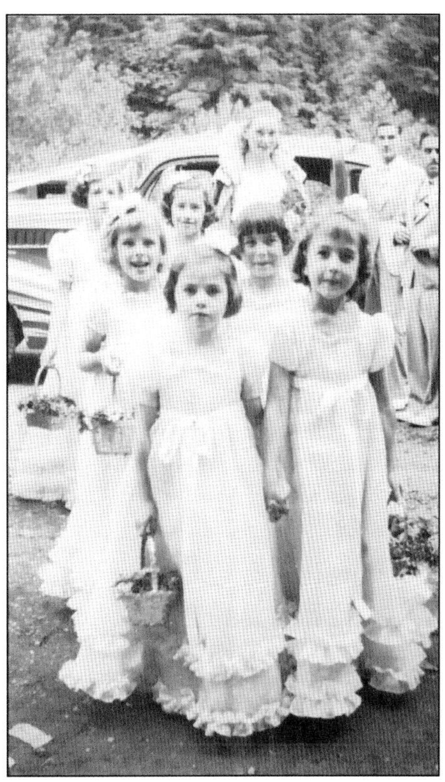

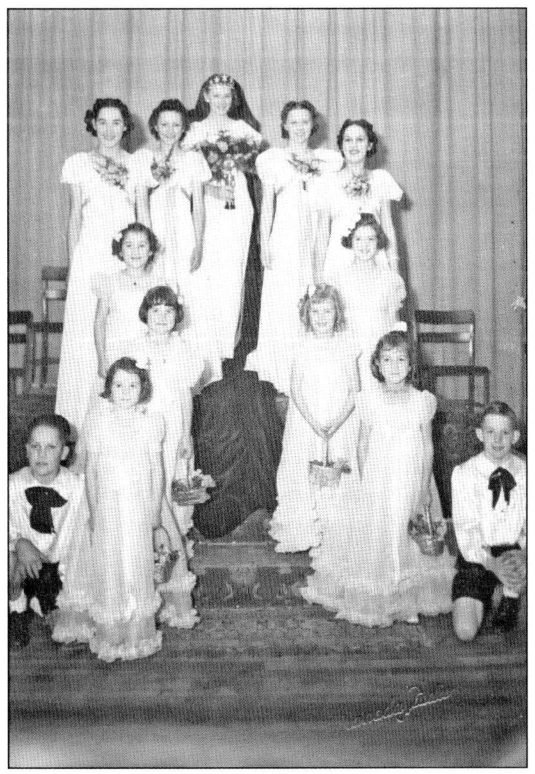

In 1939, Elsie Heuchert was the queen of the first Strawberry Festival court. During the weeks prior to the event, five princesses, chosen by their classmates at Kalama High School, conducted a button-selling campaign to elect one queen. The winner was a closely held secret until the queen was announced and crowned at the coronation celebration.

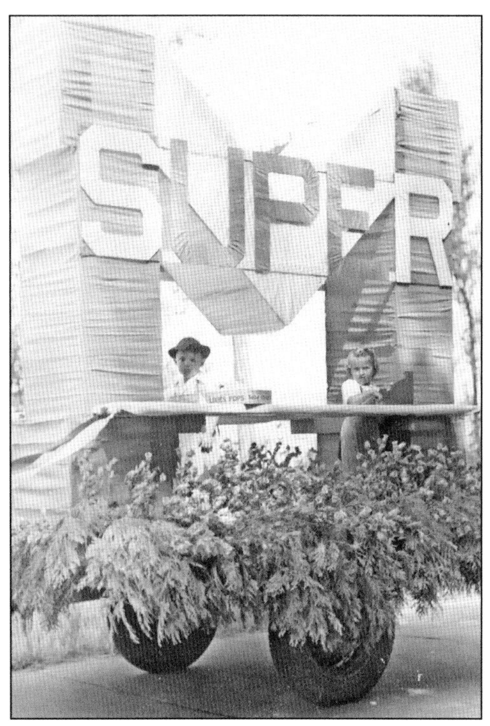

Mick Moses and his cousin Rita Mason ride in a float entered in the last Strawberry Festival Parade. The float was entered by the Super M Store. The Super M Store was owned by Mansur Moses, and the building it occupied is still a grocery store. The last Strawberry Festival was held in 1951. (Courtesy of Cleone Kockritz.)

Frank Boatman was the marshal for the city of Kalama and the only law enforcement officer at that time. He was on call 24/7. An avid horseman, he is pictured doing tricks with his horse Killer during an annual Strawberry Festival Parade held after World War II. (Courtesy of Cleone Kockritz.)

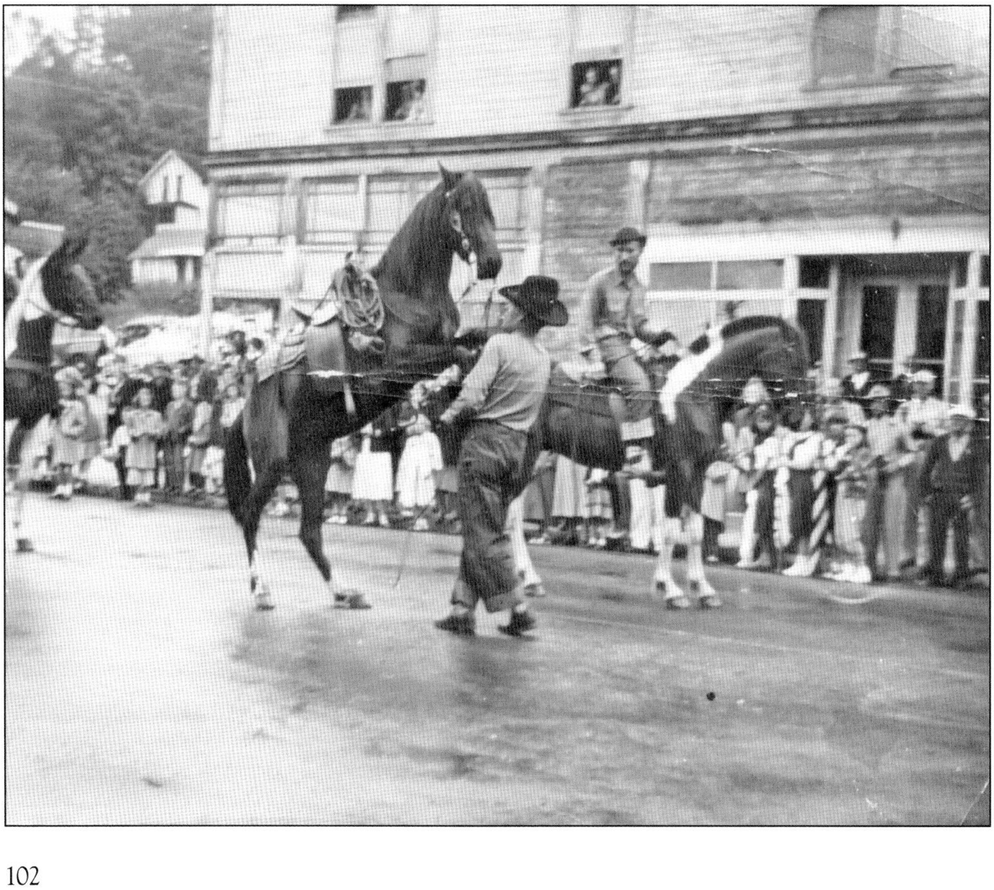

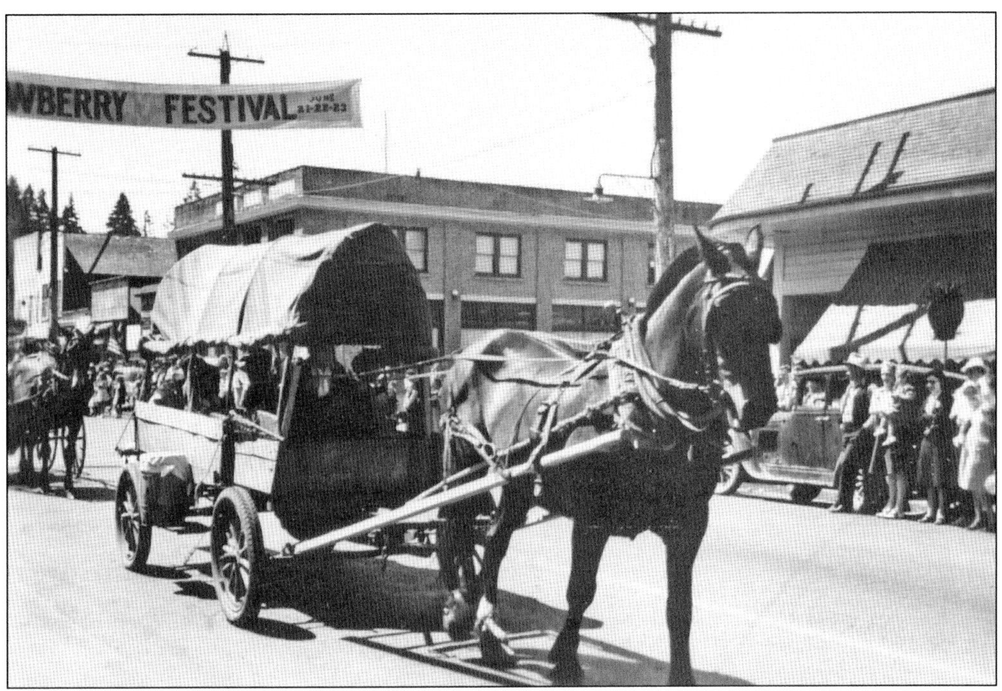

The Strawberry Festival Parade was an important part of the Strawberry Festival. Frank and Elizabeth Boatman, active community members, built this covered wagon. The Boatman family's wagon is being driven in an annual Strawberry Festival Parade. (Courtesy of Joanna Boatman.)

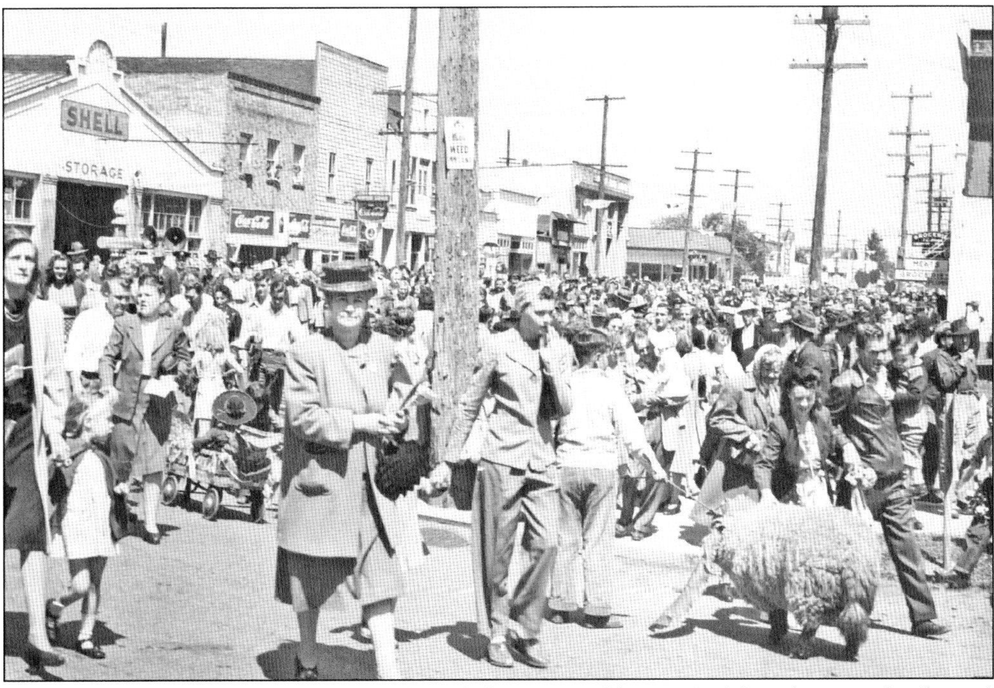

The Strawberry Festival was not celebrated during World War II. After the war, the festival returned. The streets of Kalama are filled with citizens enjoying the opportunity to enjoy the Strawberry Festival. The Shell Storage is now the location of an antique store.

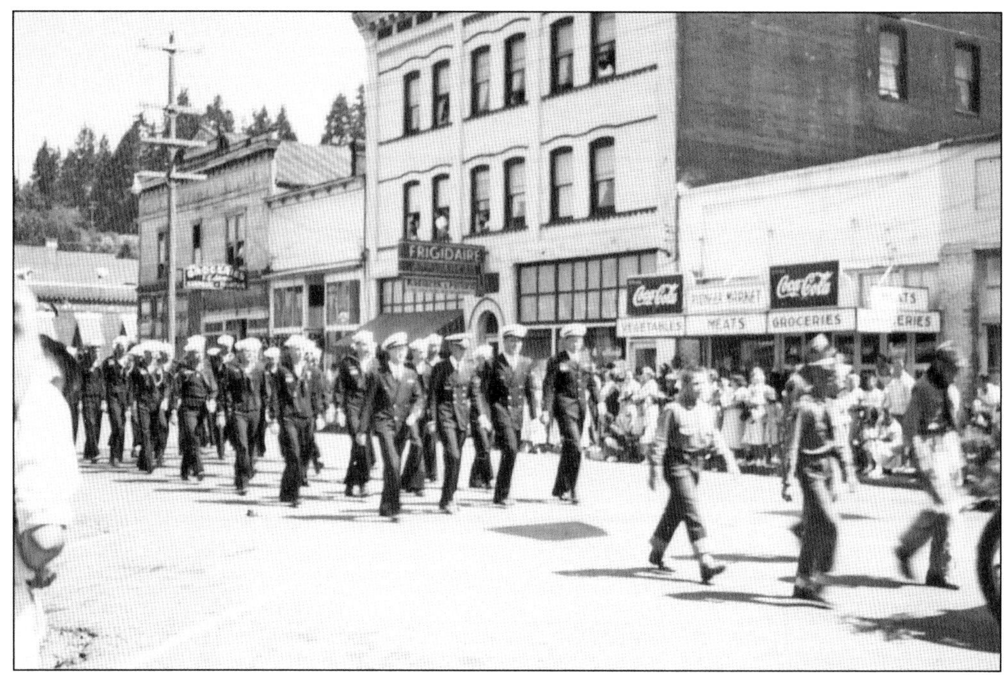

Here, World War II soldiers and sailors march in a Strawberry Festival Parade held after the end of the war. (Courtesy of Janice Whiteaker.)

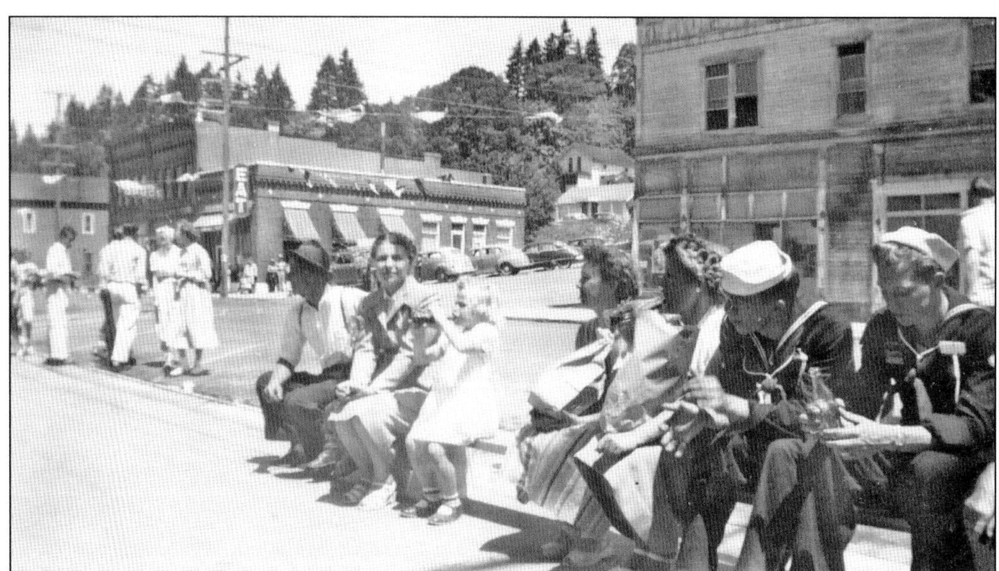

A group of Kalama residents is seen on benches at the corner of First and Fir Streets to view the festivities. The Cloverdale Berry Association closed in the 1950s, and on August 15, 1963, the co-op building was destroyed by fire. (Courtesy of Janice Whiteaker.)

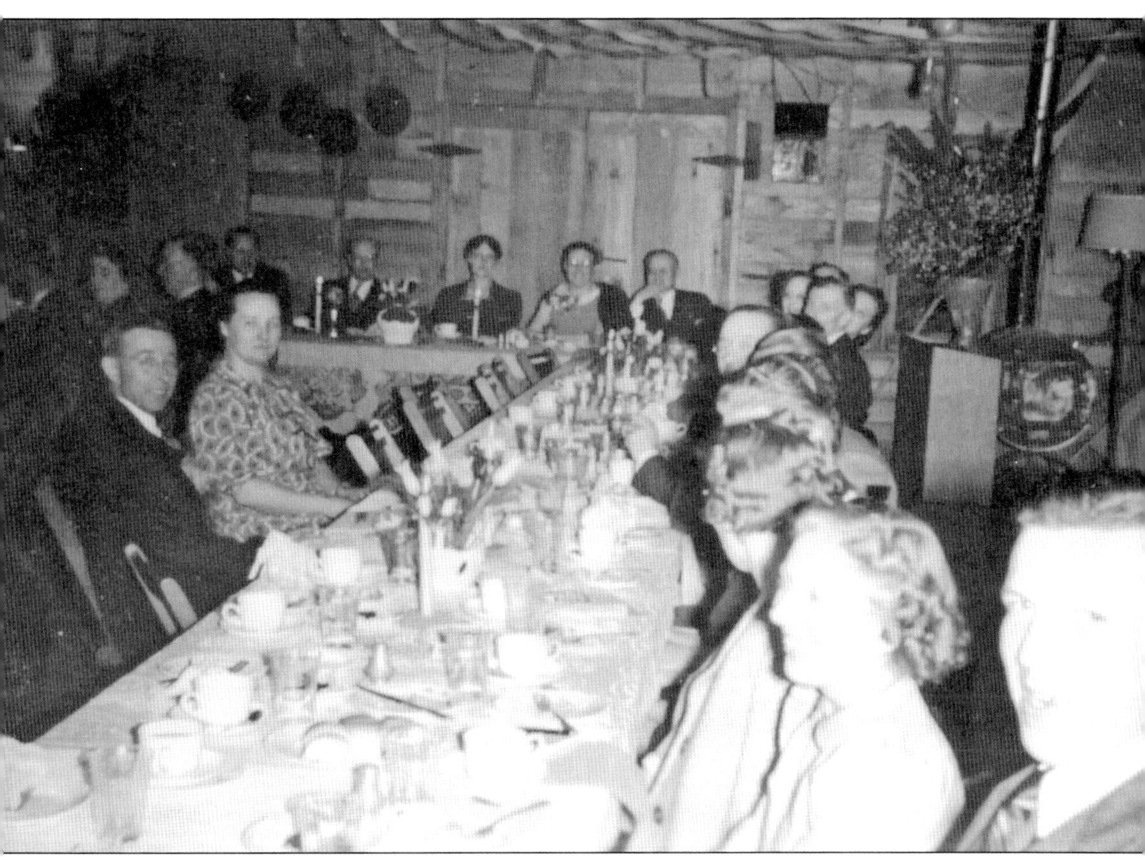

A group of Kalama residents enjoys a community meal for an unidentified event. At the end of the table, Clyde Wright leans his chin on his hand. Seated on the left side of table is Ellen Englemann.

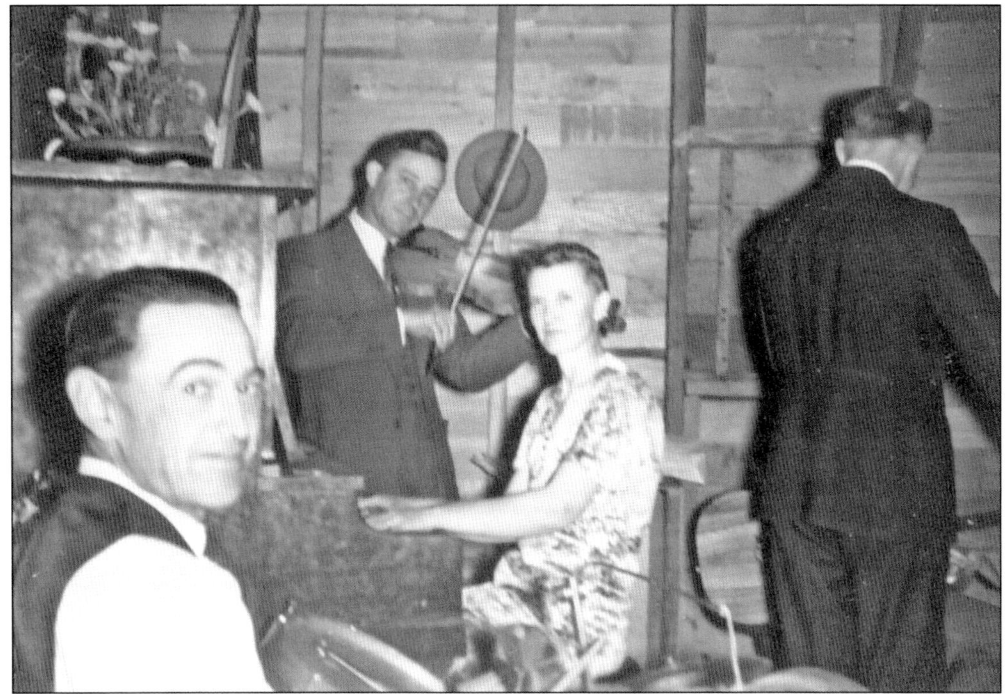

Neimi's Band played at events in Kalama for many years; band members are pictured entertaining at a Friday-night dance in the community building. Eva Pakala is playing the piano, and Darrell Coffey is in the foreground.

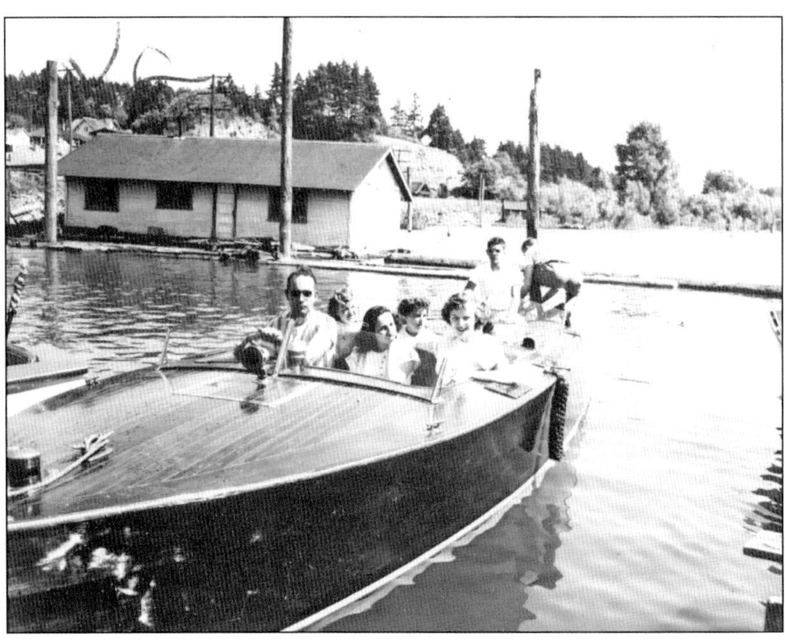

Don Merz is piloting his boat during the 1948 flood. He is transporting people through the floodwaters.

Ten

Meeting Challenges

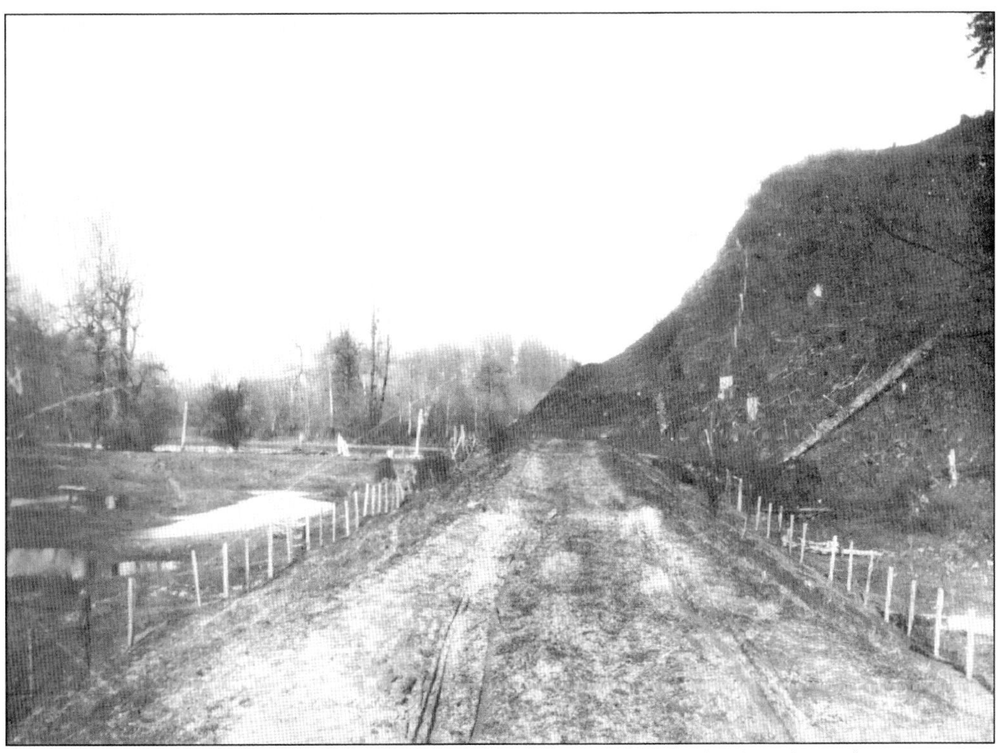

One of the greatest obstacles facing the city of Kalama was the lack of roads, and constructing roadways was a major challenge. The road being built here led to the Kalama River. Road building was forbidding because on the north side sheer cliffs left little space for road construction. It was easier to walk or ride a horse to get to one's destination. (Courtesy of Joanna Boatman.)

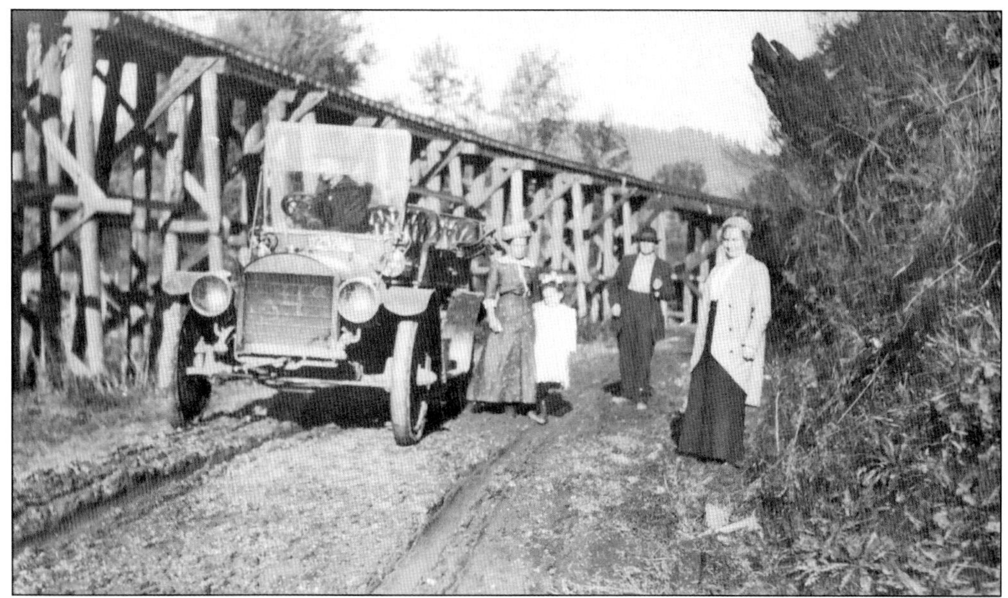

A family poses beside their automobile on the unpaved Old Pacific Highway (Highway 99) at the Kalama River. In the background is the Mountain Timber Railroad trestle. One of the women is identified as Clara Miller. (Author's collection.)

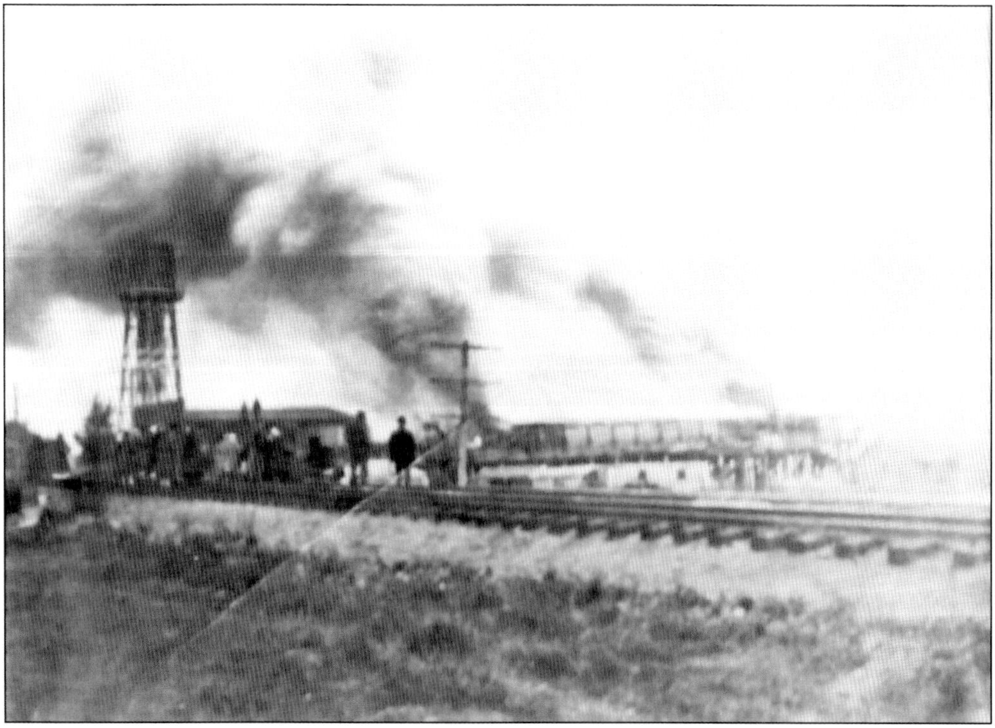

The fire pictured is at the Columbia Shingle Company's mill in Kalama on May 23, 1922. The fire destroyed the dry kilns as well as three million shingles. (Courtesy of Joanna Boatman.)

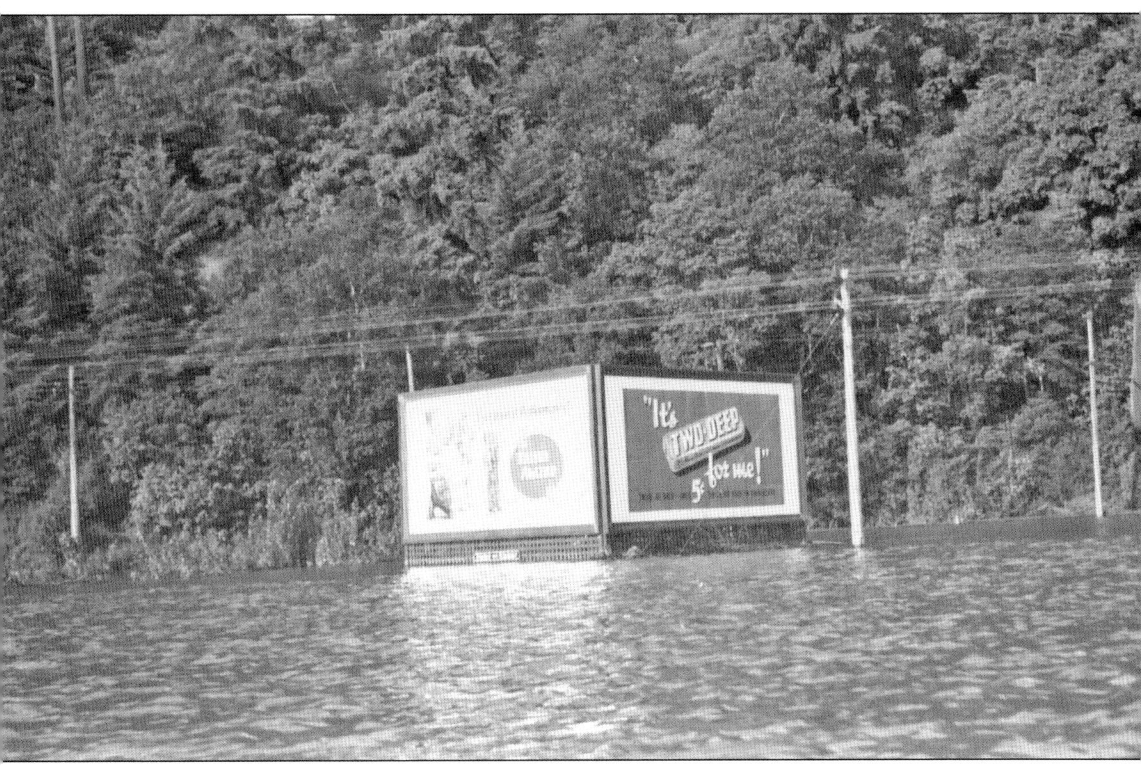

The billboard advertising a candy bar expresses what Kalama residents felt during the 1948 flood: "It's two-deep for me!" The greatest spring melt recorded on the Columbia River caused significant flooding to communities along its course.

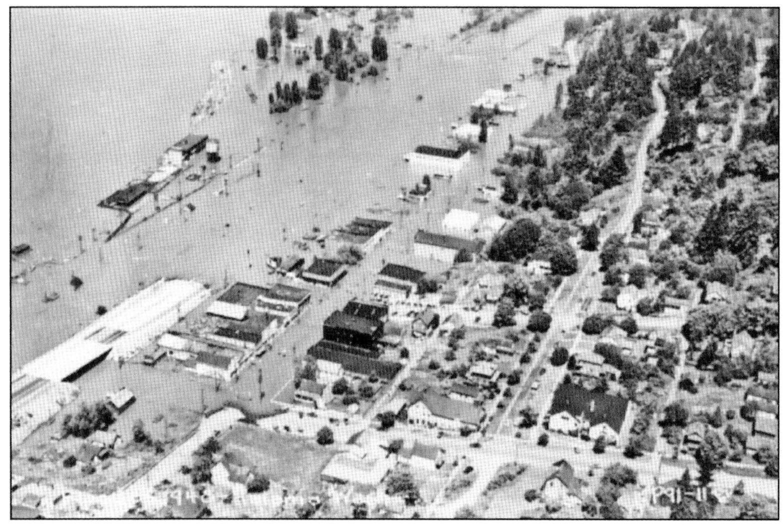

This aerial view of Kalama during the 1948 freshet depicts the extent of the flooding. The houses on the hill are up high enough to stay dry, but structures built on the flats are underwater. (Courtesy of Lee Bunn.)

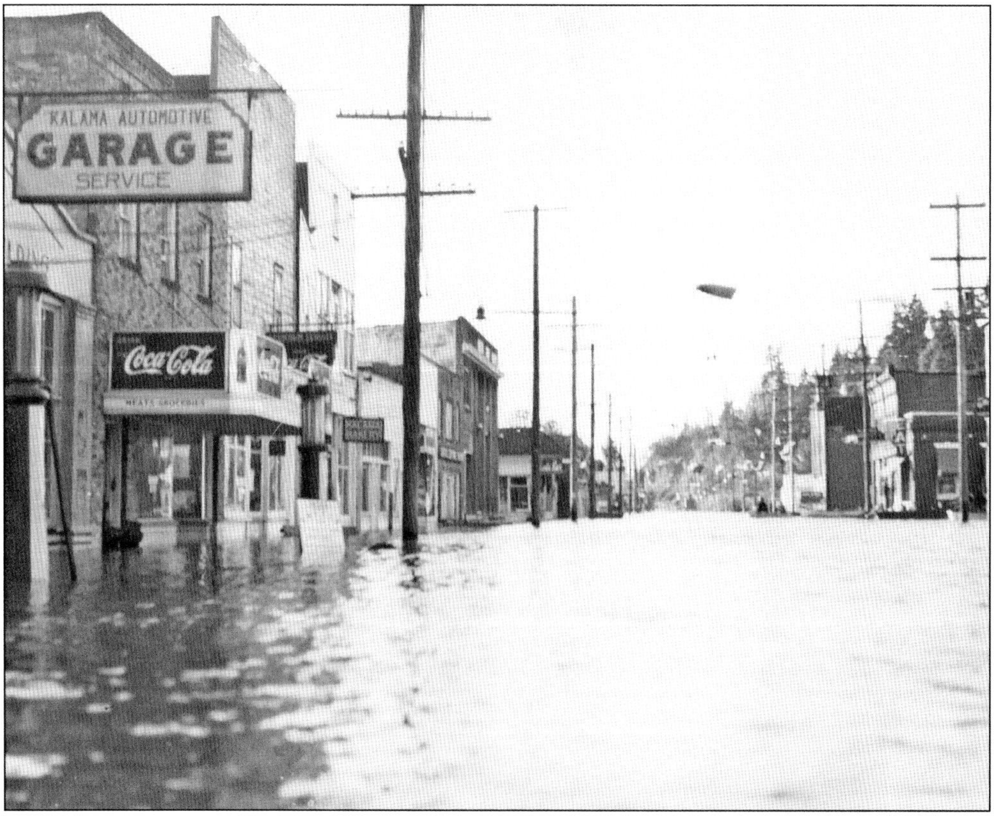

In this view looking north on First Street, the main street of Kalama's business district is underwater. The 1948 flood destroyed many communities along the Columbia River, and some were destined to be gone forever, but Kalama survived and rebuilt.

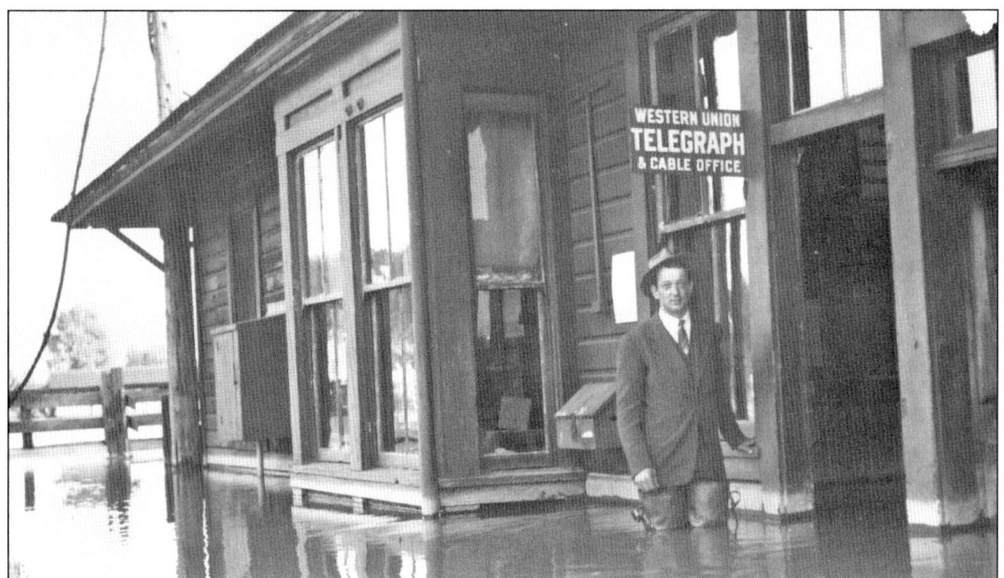

Wearing his hip waders to keep dry, the unidentified man stands by the flooded Kalama train depot located near the Columbia River waterfront. (Courtesy of John Norton.)

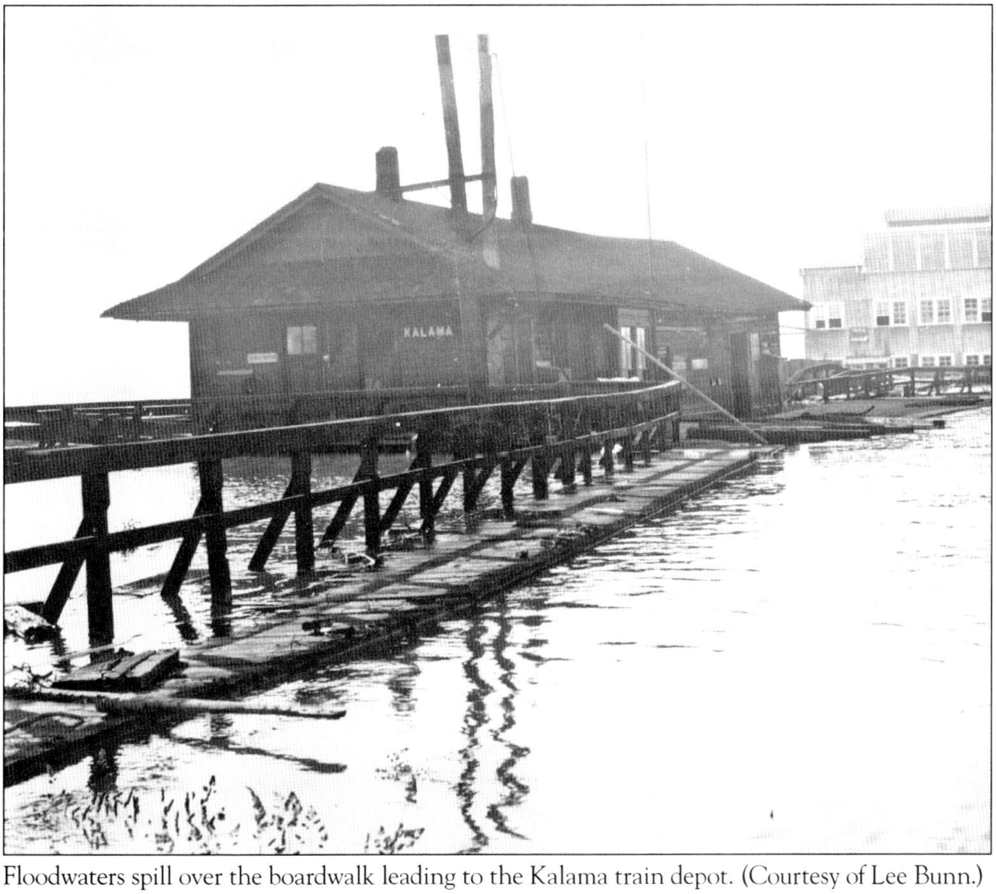

Floodwaters spill over the boardwalk leading to the Kalama train depot. (Courtesy of Lee Bunn.)

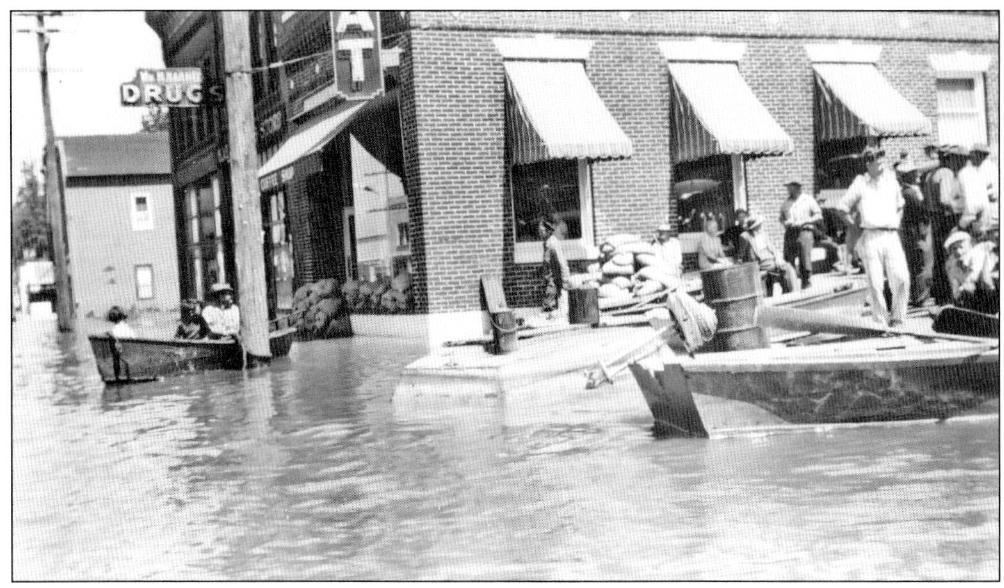

Boats are pictured navigating the floodwaters and being docked by Lang's Café, located beside Harned's Drugstore on First Street. Sandbags are piled beside the building.

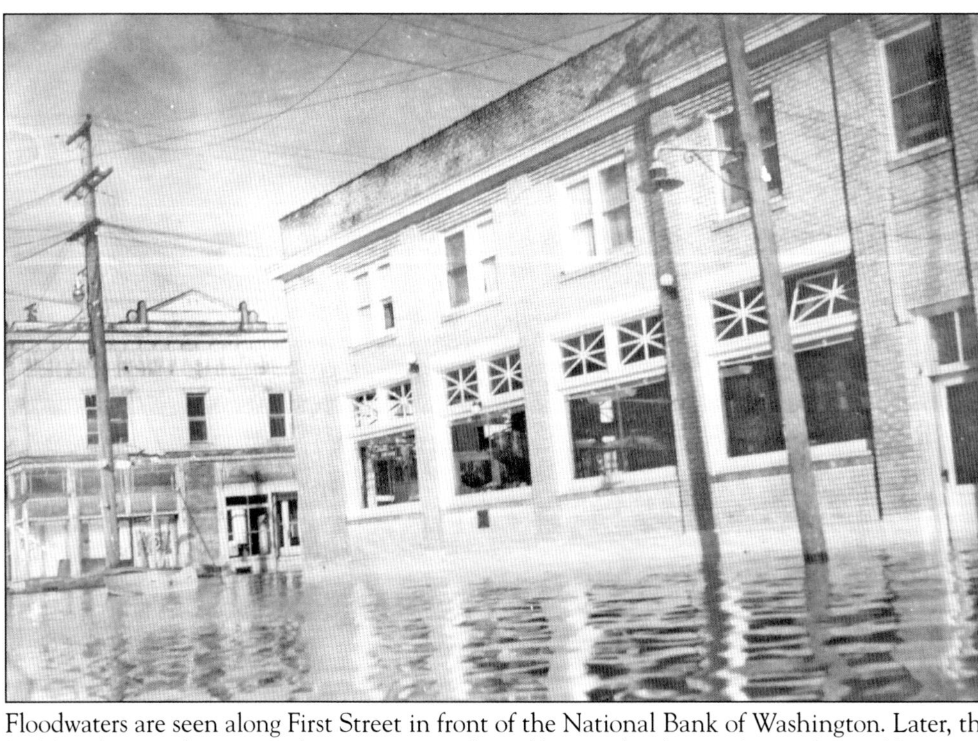

Floodwaters are seen along First Street in front of the National Bank of Washington. Later, the building became known as the Heritage Bank Building. A bank is no longer located here, and the structure, which survived the flood, is now occupied by offices for the City of Kalama.

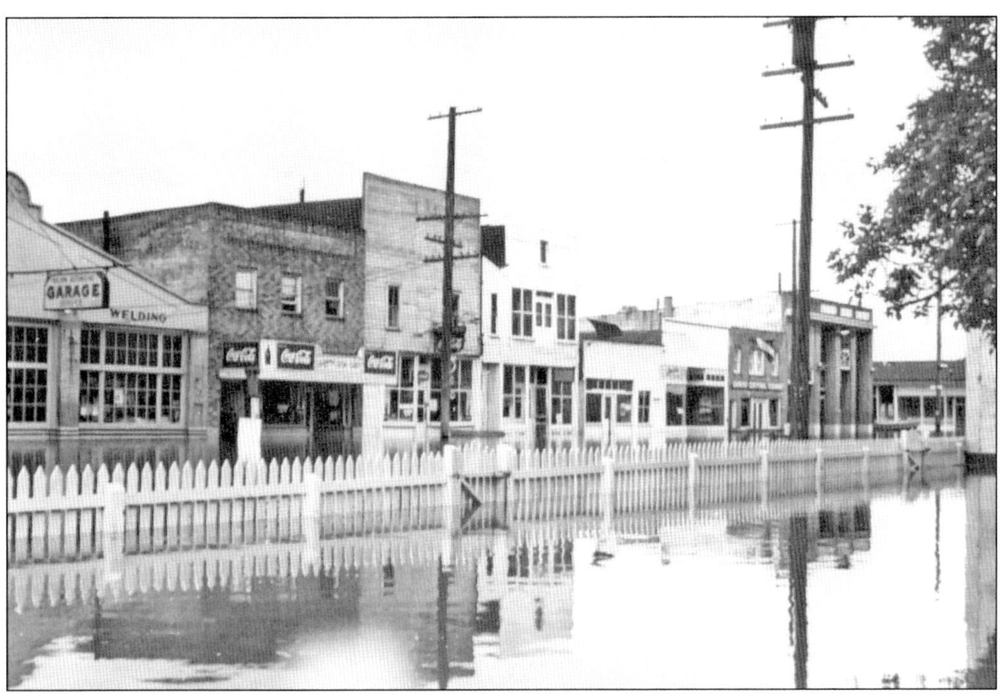

This photograph of the 1948 flood shows the business district underwater. Old-timers recount how they could row boats up and down Main Street.

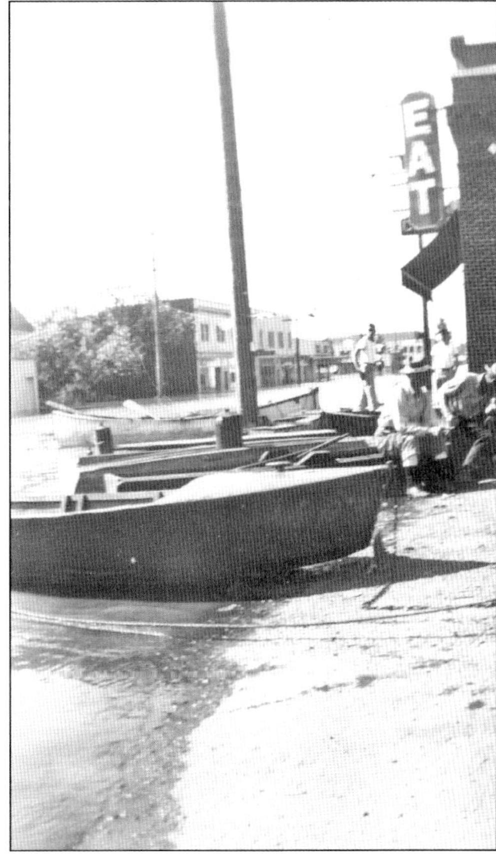

A small flotilla of boats is beached at the corner of First and Fir Streets. Boats were the preferred and only method of transportation through the business district of Kalama during the flood of 1948. (Courtesy of Janice Whiteaker.)

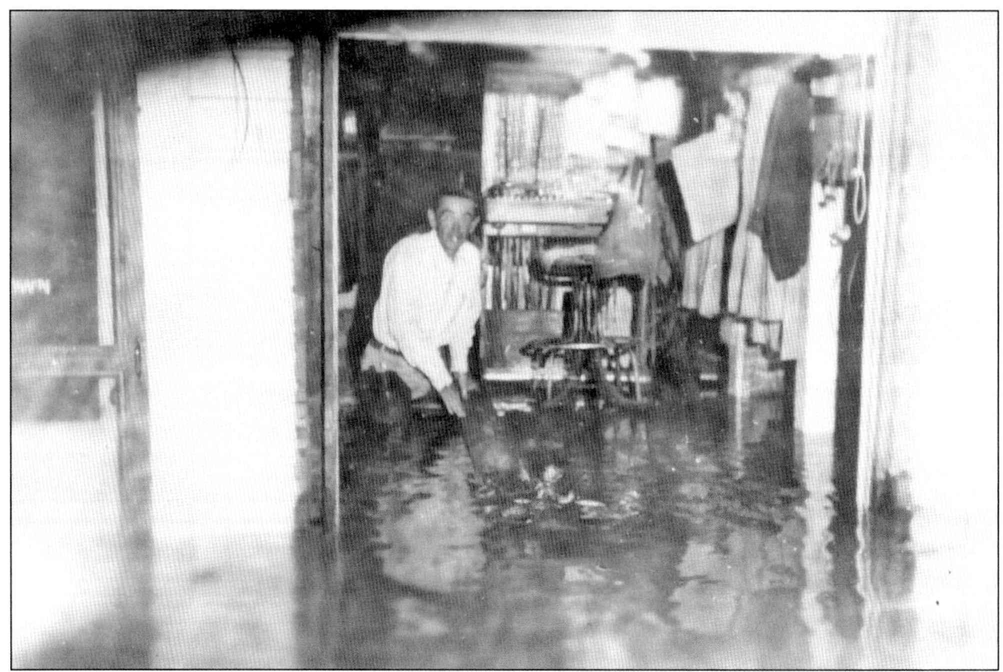

Darrell Coffey wades inside the Kalama Phone Company. The company continued to provide phone service to Kalama residents during the flood. (Courtesy of Art Godfrey.)

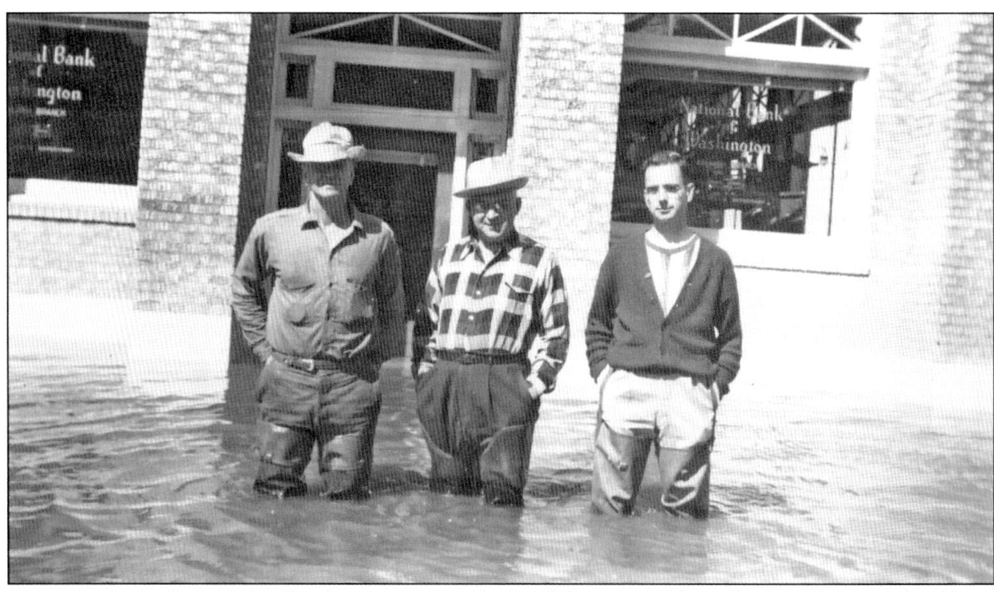

Three men standing in the floodwaters pose in front of the National Bank of Washington building. They are, from left to right, Page Stewart, bank manager Gus Jaeger, and Bill Merrill.

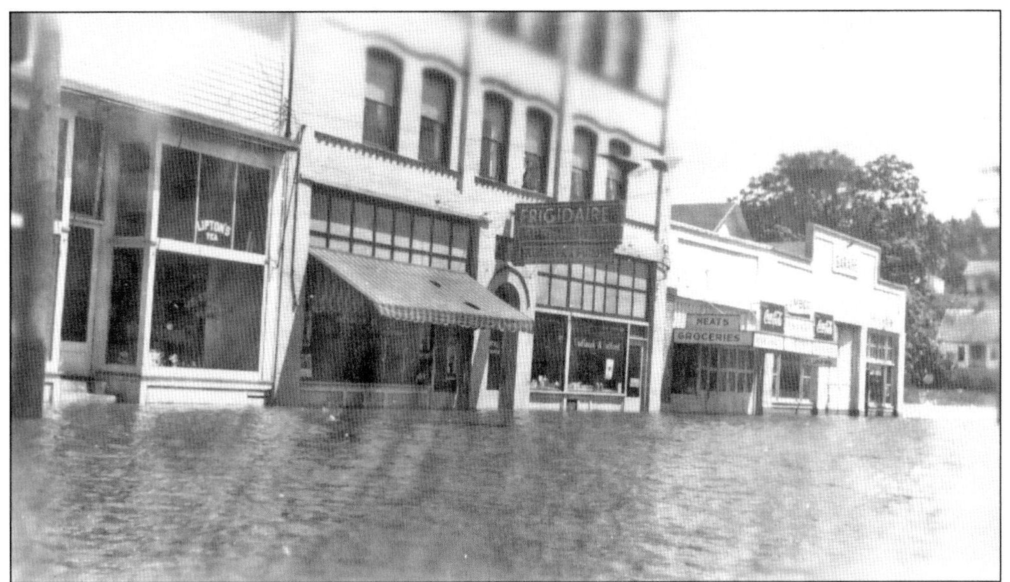

A warm May in 1948 resulted in rapid snowmelt in the Cascades. By May 25, 1948, the Columbia River was eight feet over flood stage. Built on the flats by the Columbia, Kalama was especially vulnerable to flooding. (Courtesy of Art Godfrey.)

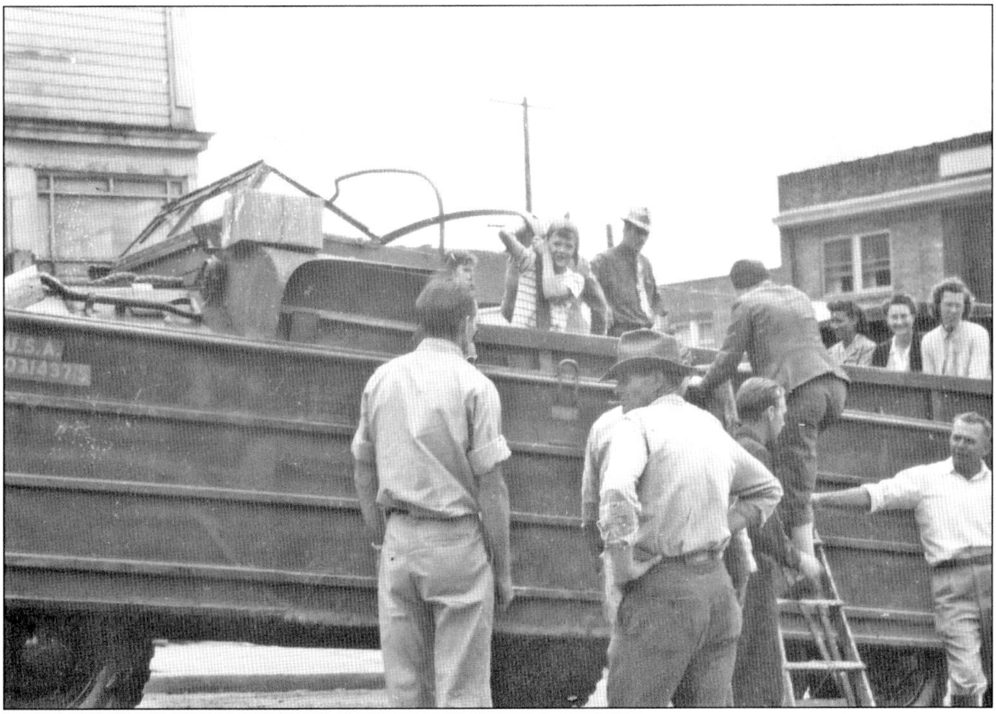

Kalama residents climb a ladder to get into an Army Duck. The Army Duck is capable of traveling on dry land and in water. The people in the Duck are getting ready for a tour of the flooded streets of Kalama.

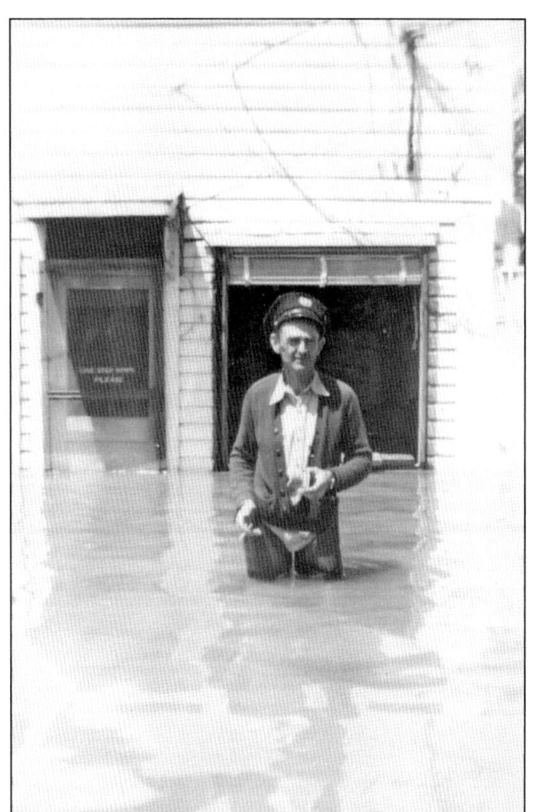

Darrell Coffey stands by the offices of the Kalama Phone Company. A boat is tied to the building, and it was used to help phone company employees to get in and out of the office, as they kept the phone company operating during the flood. (Courtesy of Catherine Applegate.)

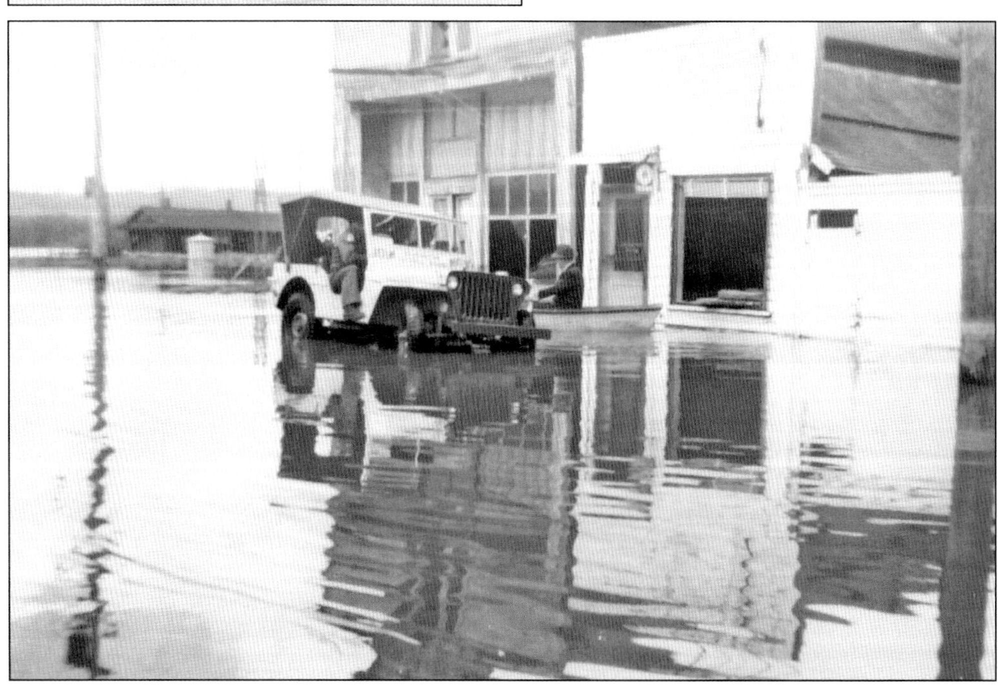

The governor of Washington State is in a rowboat taking a firsthand look at the devastation caused to Kalama by the flood of 1948. (Courtesy of Catherine Applegate.)

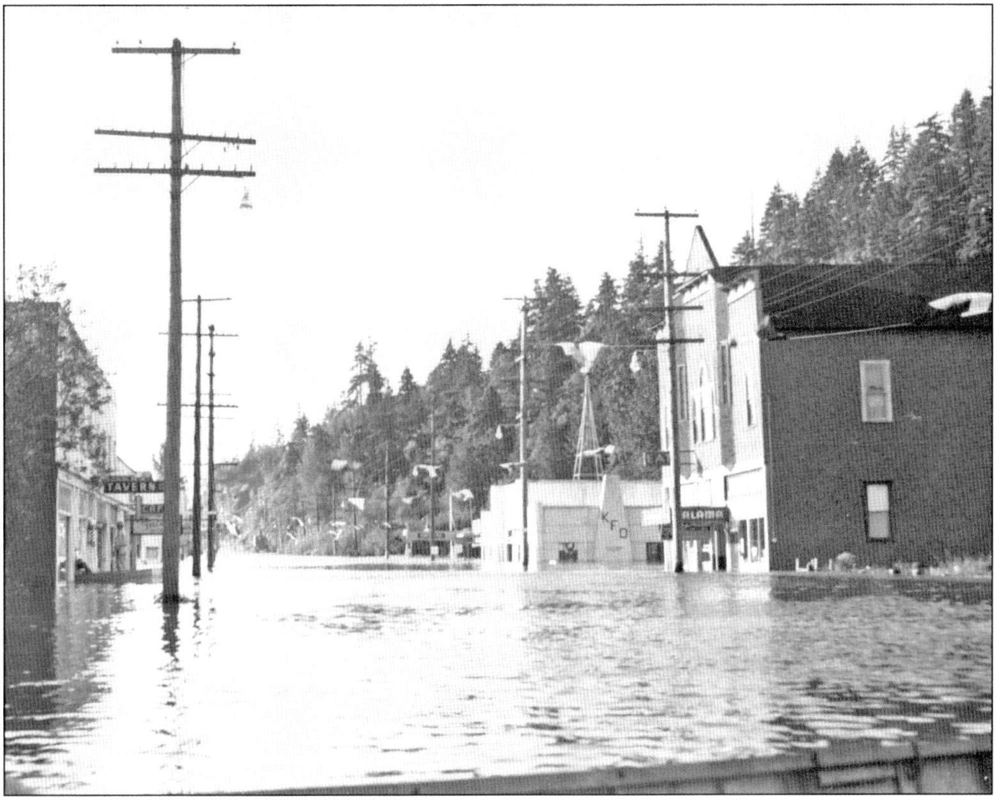

A radio alert was issued the night before the flood, and some residents moved their belongings into attics and upper floors, but few imagined how quickly the water levels would rise or how high the water levels would be. (Courtesy of Lee Bunn.)

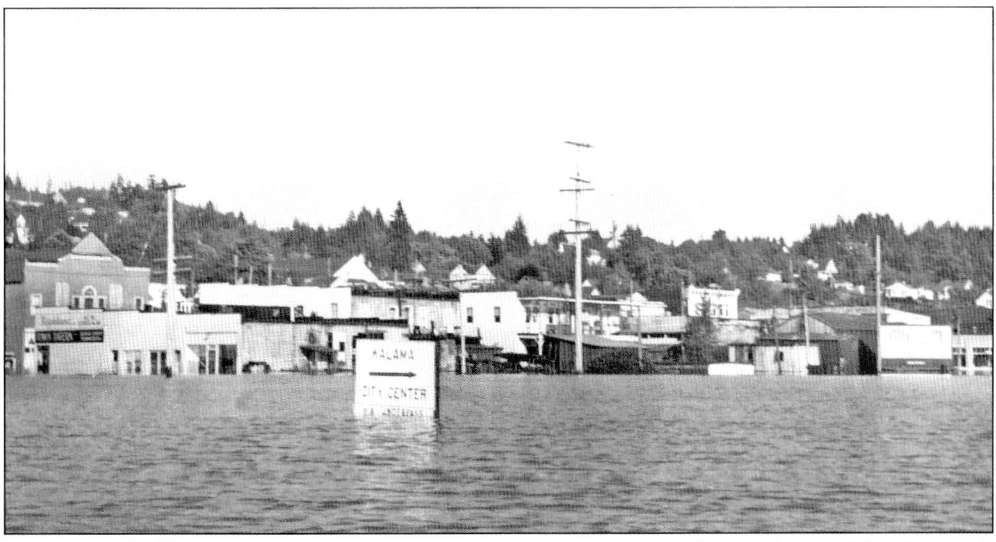

The region had two major rainstorms—one on May 19, 1948, and the other on May 23, 1948. The rainfall combined with the melted snow swelled the many tributaries feeding the Columbia River, adding to the floodwaters. This photograph with a view looking east from the Old Pacific Highway shows the extent of the floodwaters in Kalama. (Courtesy of John Norton.)

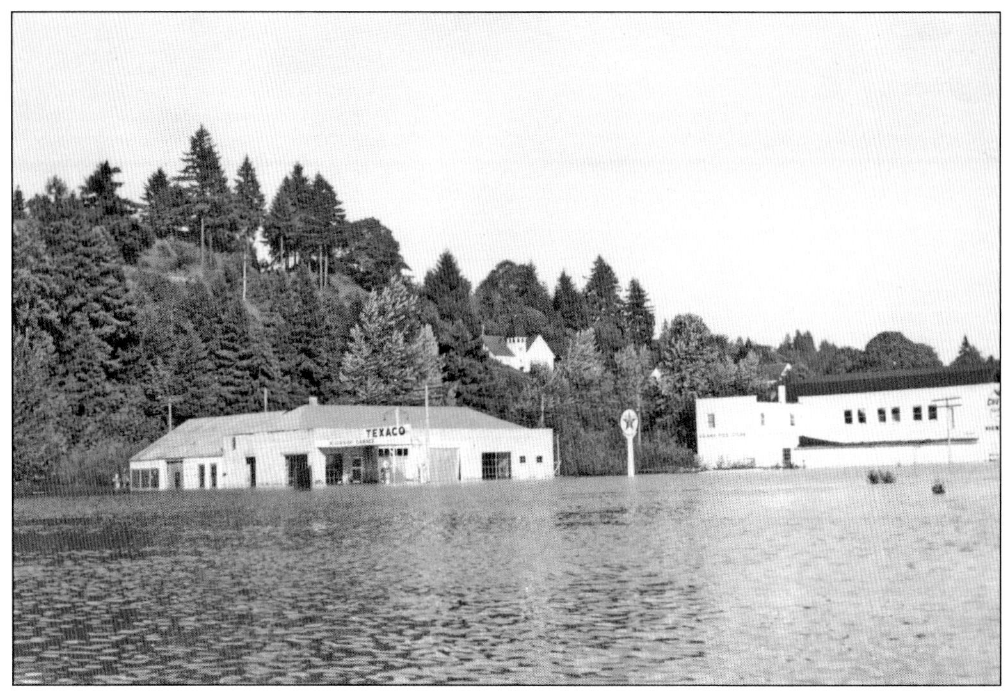

The Kalama Texaco gas station is underwater, but the quick rise in land elevation has made the houses and church built behind the service station free from the floodwaters. (Courtesy of John Norton.)

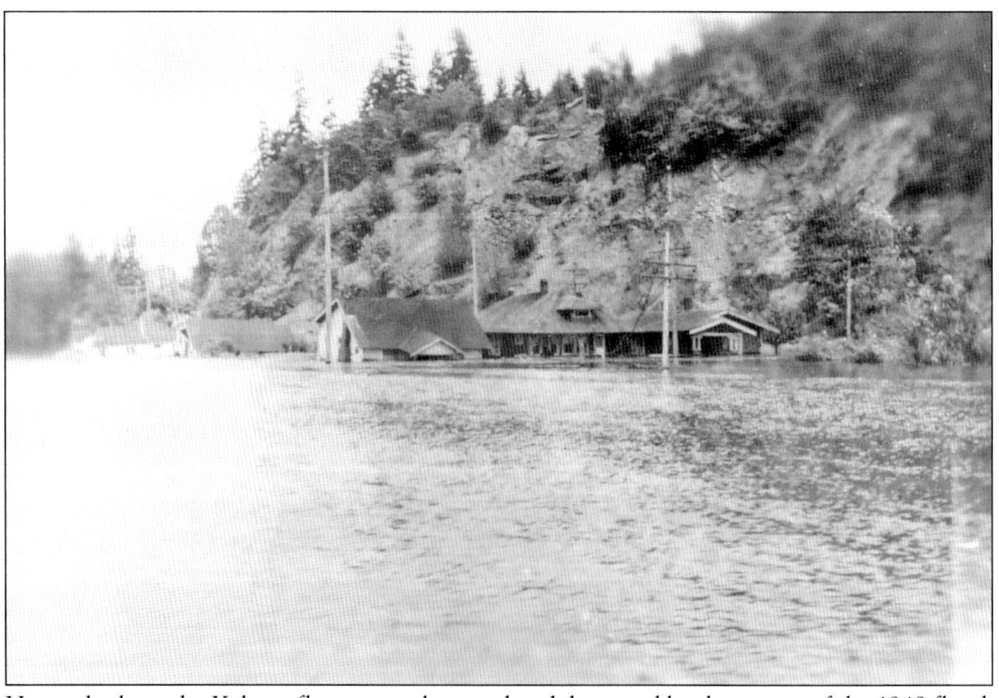

Houses built on the Kalama flats were submerged and destroyed by the waters of the 1948 flood. (Courtesy of Art Godfrey.)

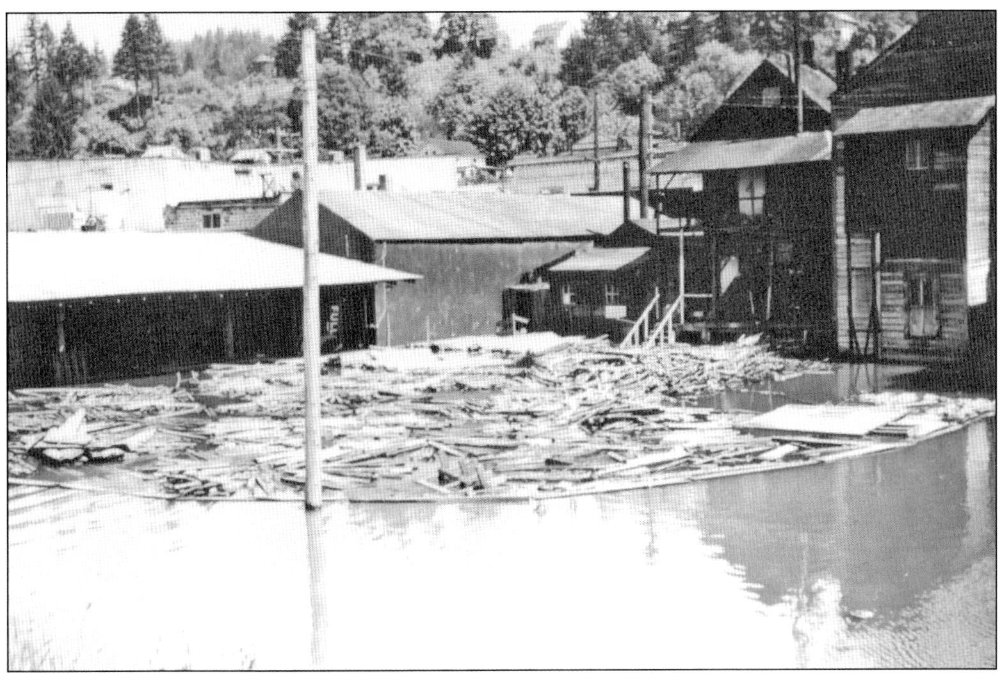

Here, debris washed in by the floodwaters piles up against houses in Kalama during the 1948 flood. Such debris caused severe damage to buildings and required extensive cleanup.

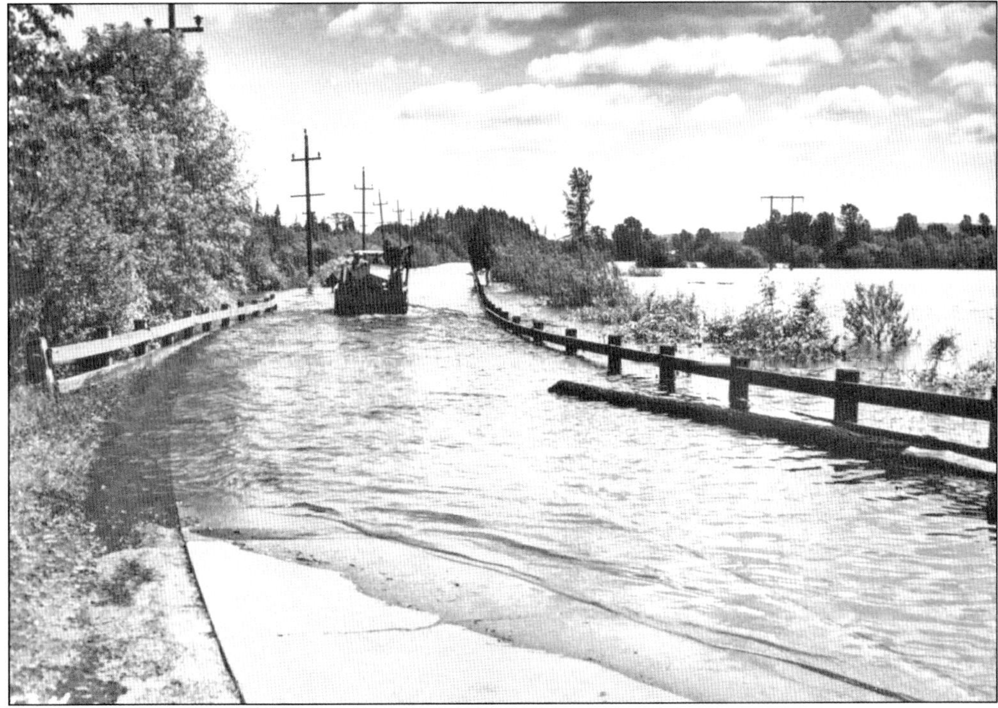

The floodwaters of 1948 covered part of the Old Pacific Highway (Highway 99). Boats were able to navigate along stretches of the highway. This Army Duck was used to transport workers through the flooded areas so they could get to their jobs. (Courtesy of Cleone Kockritz.)

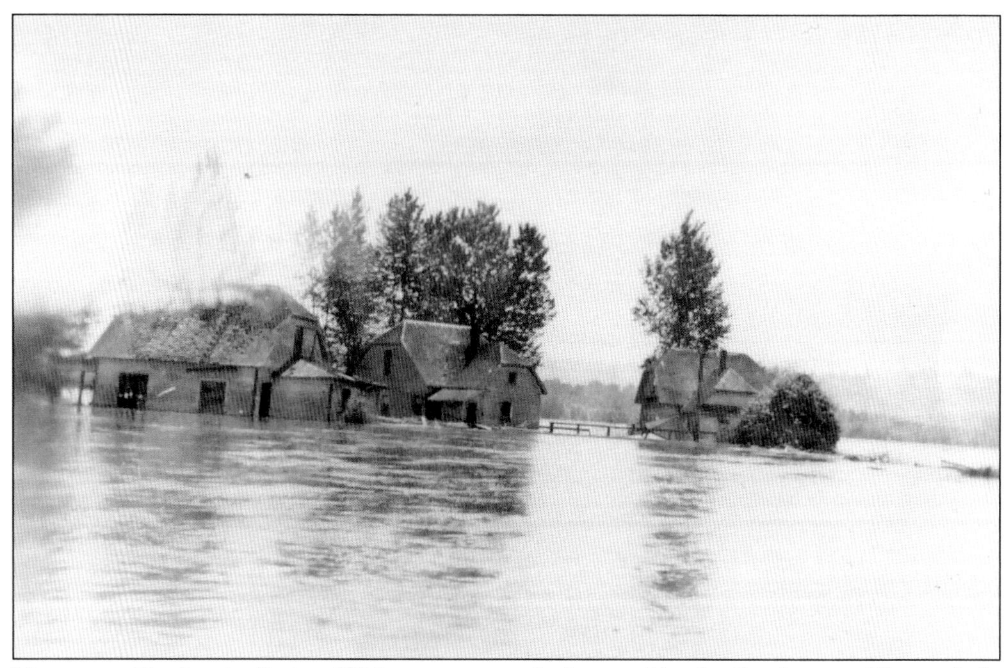

Houses outside the city limits of Kalama are severely damaged by the floodwaters. The roof of a gazebo on the right can be seen tilting from the effects of the force of the floodwaters. (Courtesy of Art Godfrey.)

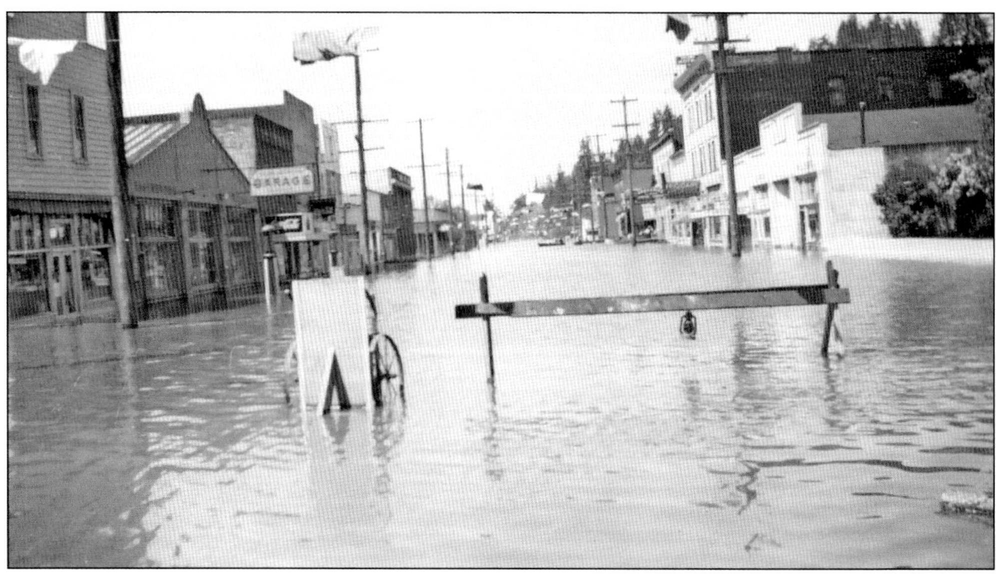

At the height of the flood, boats were the only method of transportation able to get down the main street of Kalama. The flood lasted for two weeks. (Courtesy of Cleone Kockritz.)

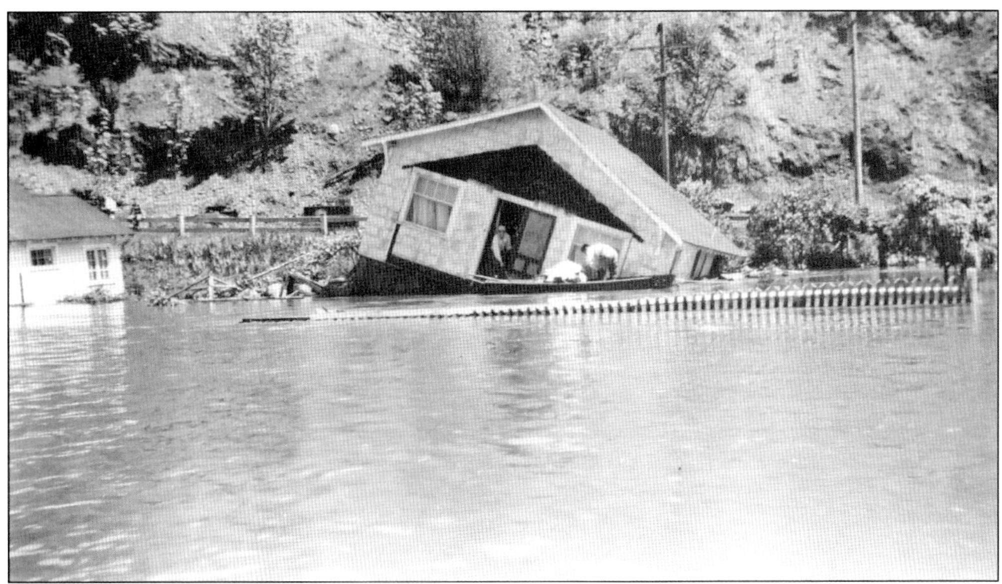

The force of the floodwaters has knocked this house off its foundation. Men are using a boat in an effort to salvage belongings from the destroyed home.

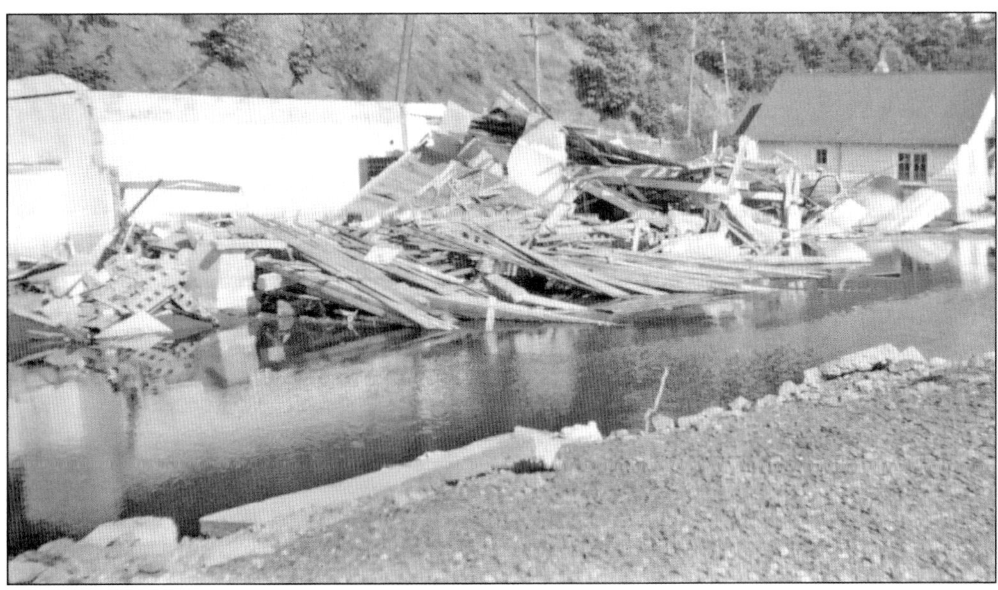

Very strong and destructive floodwaters caused structures to collapse. The damage to this building is evident as the waters recede.

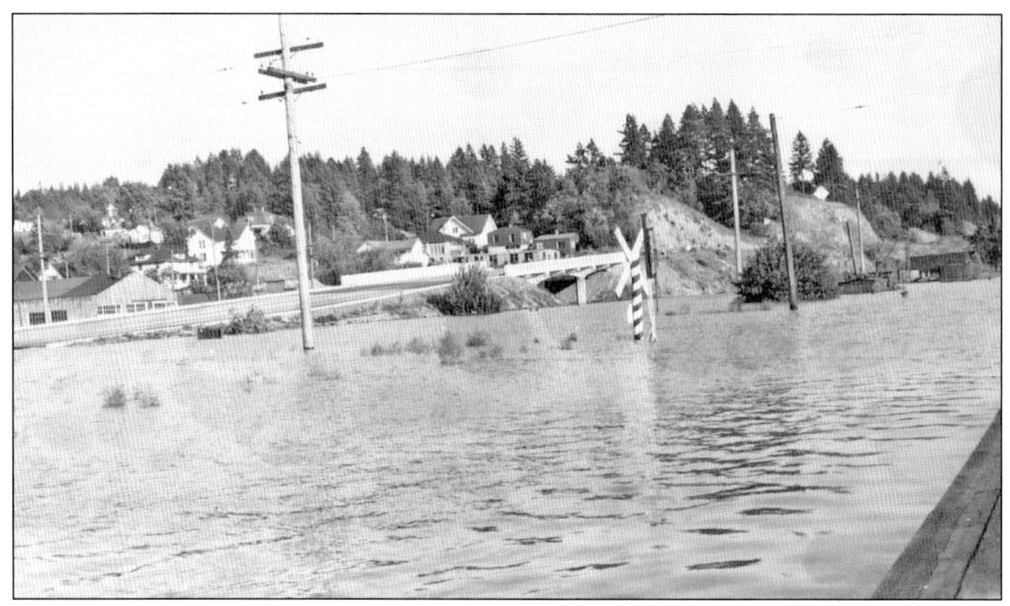

Pictured is the Old Pacific Highway. Floodwaters poured through and under the overpass into the city center. (Courtesy of John Norton.)

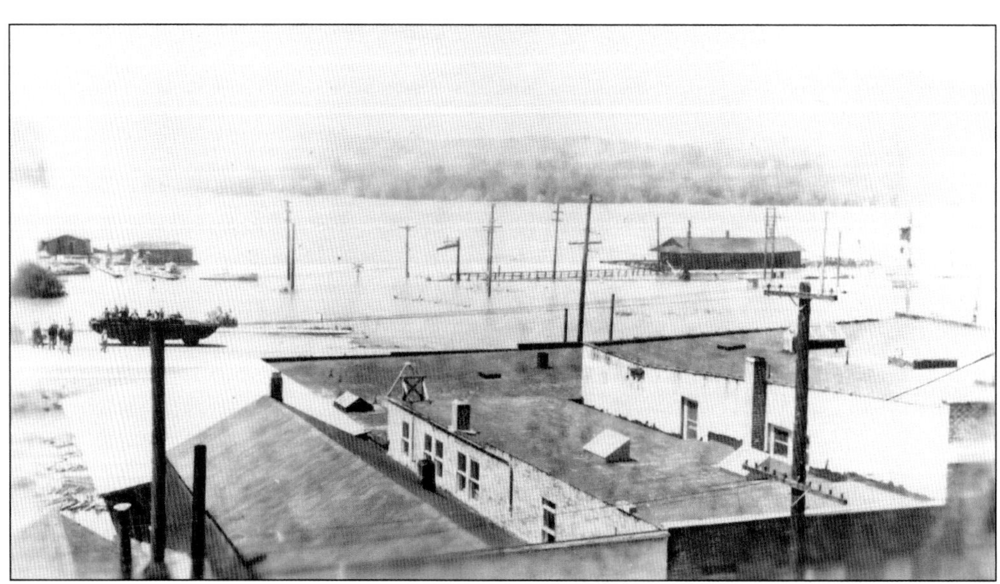

On the left side of the picture, an Army Duck is heading into the floodwaters. In the background to the right is the flooded Kalama train depot. (Courtesy of Art Godfrey.)

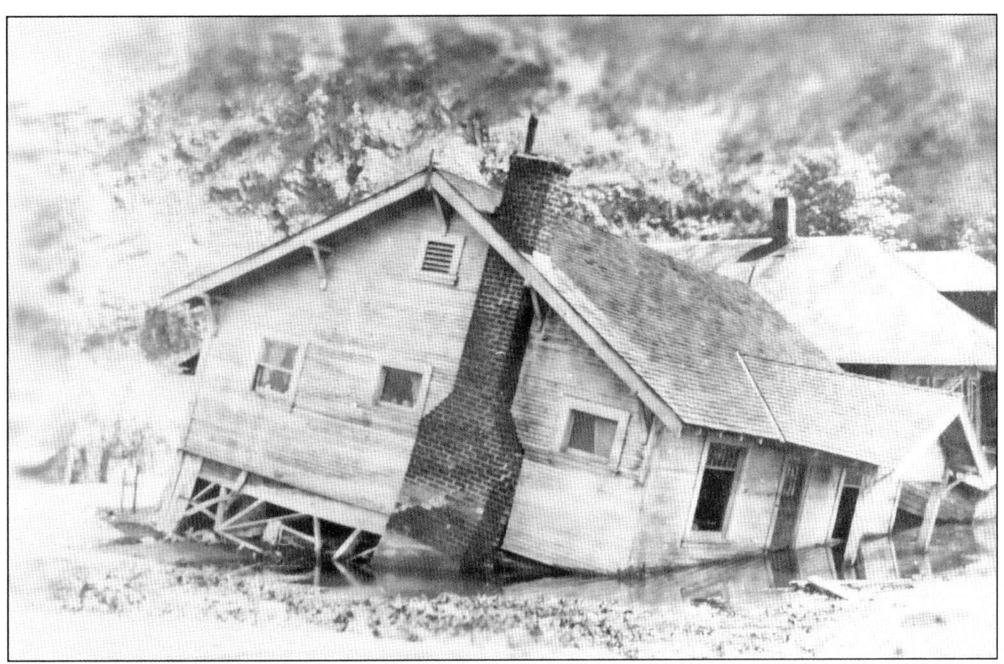

Tilting into the water, the house pictured has had its foundation destroyed. (Courtesy of Art Godfrey.)

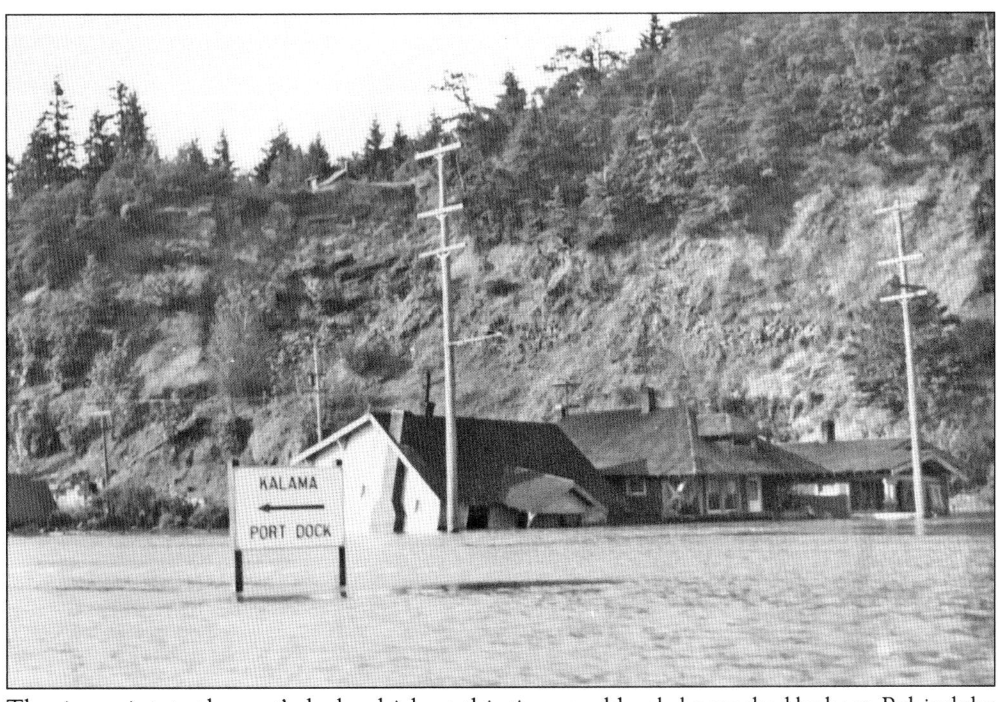

The sign points to the port's dock, which, at this time, could only be reached by boat. Behind the sign, residences are severely damaged by the floodwaters. (Courtesy of John Norton.)

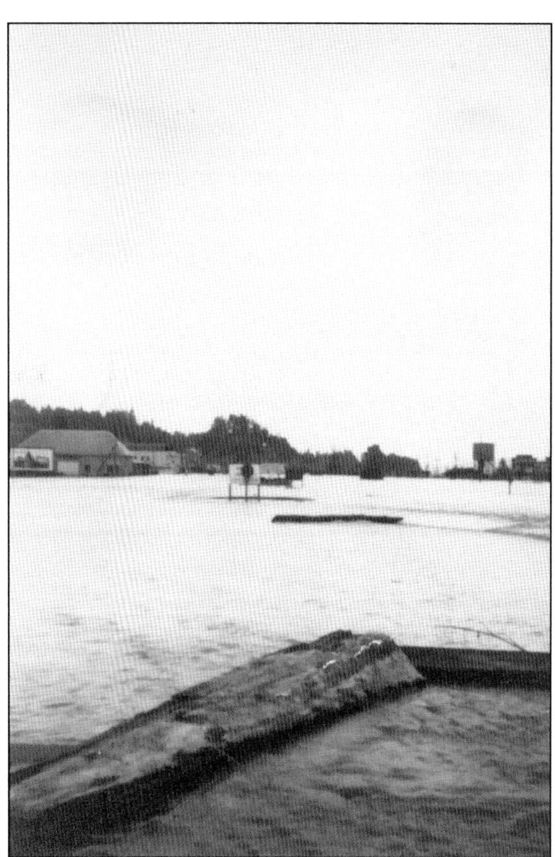

This photograph was taken by someone standing on Old Pacific Highway (Highway 99), which is present-day Interstate 5. It shows the vast amount of area in Kalama that was underwater during the flood of 1948. (Courtesy of Cleone Kockritz.)

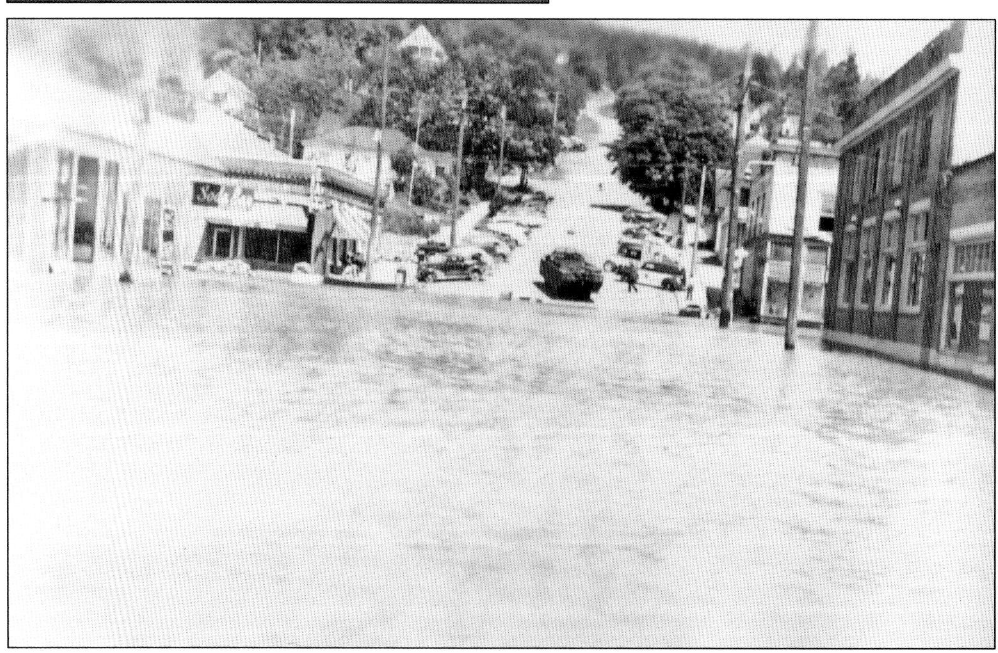

At the corner of First and Fir Streets, an Army Duck is about to enter the floodwaters. To the right is the bank building. (Courtesy of Art Godfrey.)

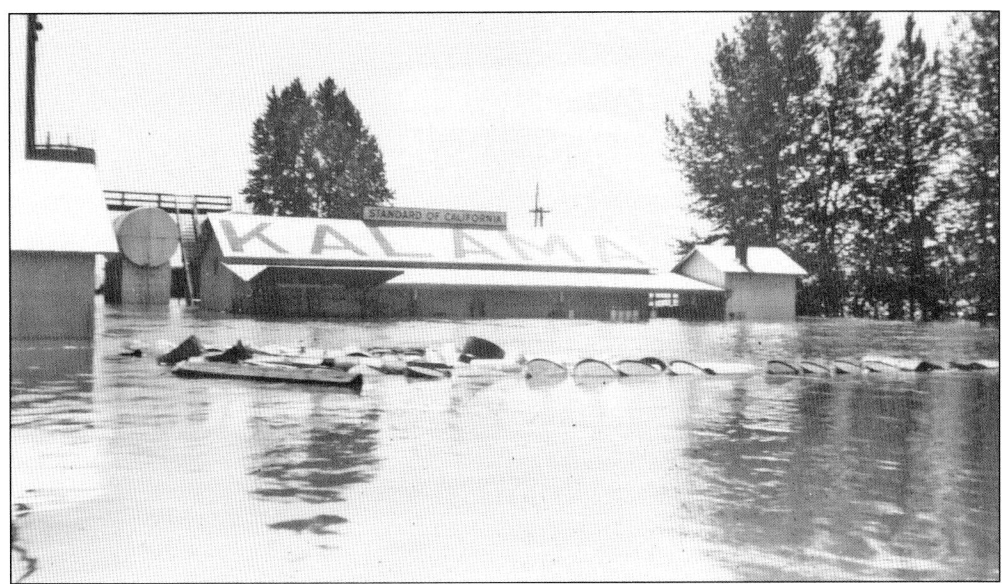

In the foreground, barrels, filled with petroleum products, are half submerged by the floodwaters and are floating in front of the inundated Kalama Chevron station.

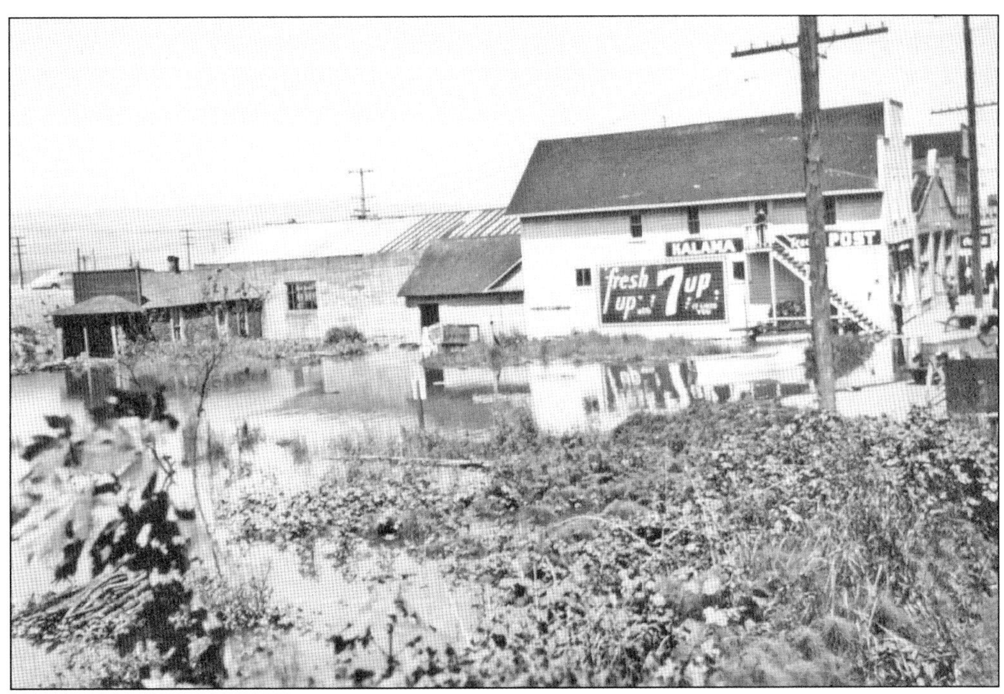

Here, the floodwaters have receded, and only pools of water remain. To the right, the sidewalks are no longer flooded and the cleanup has begun. The streets and sidewalks in the business district are once again usable.

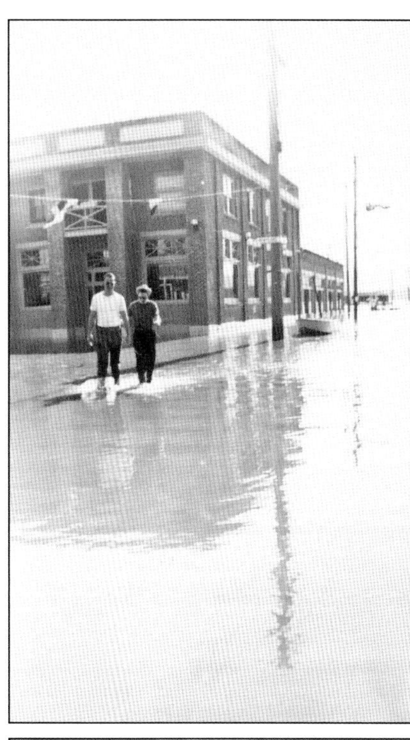

An unidentified couple wades in water in front of the bank building. In this photograph, the floodwaters are still deep enough to moor a boat in, but the Kalama citizens are no doubt ready to rebuild after the devastating flood. (Courtesy of Janice Whiteaker.)

This aerial view of Kalama shows its location adjacent to the Columbia River and how it is nestled in the foothills of the Cascade Mountains. A highway bisects the waterfront and the community. With its small-town charm, Kalama is truly where rail, road, and river meet.

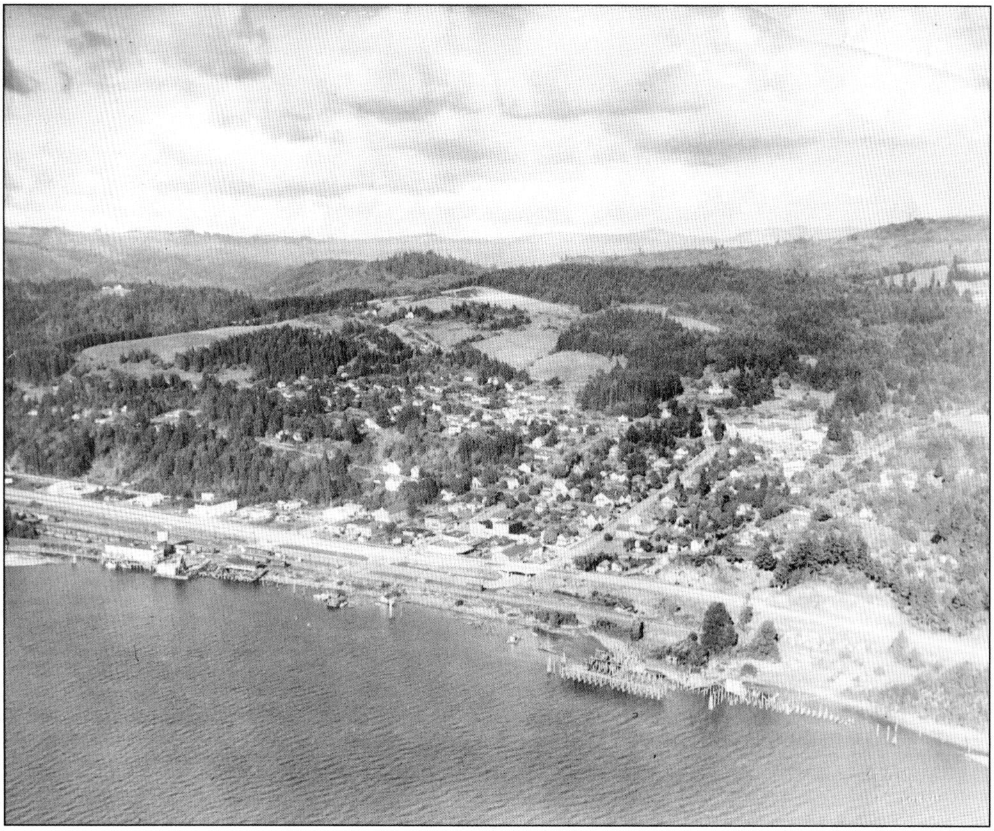

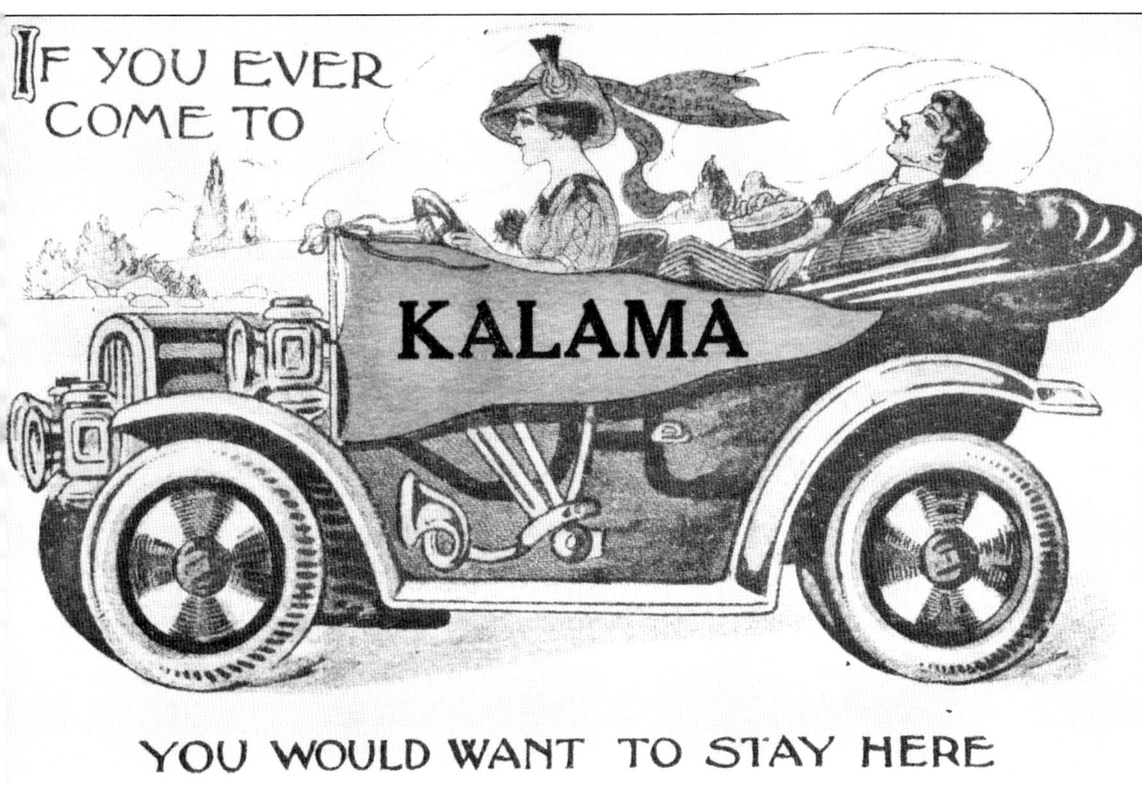

Kalama is a small community located beside Interstate 5 and the Columbia River. It retains its "Mayberry," small-town charm as it meets the challenges and promises of a new century. (Courtesy of John Norton.)

Consistent with our mission to preserve history on a local level, this book was printed in South Carolina on American-made paper and manufactured entirely in the United States. Products carrying the accredited Forest Stewardship Council (FSC) label are printed on 100 percent FSC-certified paper.

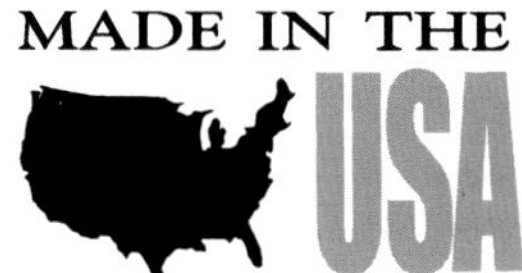